The Gothic History Of Jordanes

Charles Christopher Mierow

THE GOTHIC HISTORY

OF

JORDANES

IN ENGLISH VERSION

WITH AN INTRODUCTION AND A COMMENTARY

BY

CHARLES CHRISTOPHER MIEROW, Ph.D.

Instructor in Classics in Princeton University

PRINCETON UNIVERSITY PRESS
PRINCETON
LONDON: HUMPHREY MILFORD
OXFORD UNIVERSITY PRESS
1915

PREFACE

This edition of the *Getica* of Jordanes is based upon the authoritative text and critical apparatus of Mommsen as found in the *Monumenta Germaniae Historica, Auctores Antiquissimi* 5 (Berlin 1882), with other material added. I have adhered closely to his spelling of proper names, especially Gothic names, except in a few words which are of common use in another form. I have carefully reviewed all the existing evidence on controverted points, dissenting in several instances from the conclusions of Mommsen, particularly in regard to the supposedly Gothic writer *Ablabius,* the ecclesiastical status of Jordanes, and the place of composition of the *Getica.* For the Latinity of Jordanes the studies of E. Wölfflin (Arch. f. lat. Lex. 11, 361), J. Bergmüller (Augsburg 1903), and Fritz Werner (Halle 1908) have been consulted, and for ready convenience of illustration in historical matters frequent reference is made in the commentary to Hodgkin's "Italy and Her Invaders" (2nd. edition, Clarendon Press, 1892), Gibbon's "Decline and Fall of the Roman Empire" (edited by J. B. Bury, London 1896), Bury's "History of the Later Roman Empire" (MacMillan & Co., 1889), and "The Cambridge Medieval History" (The MacMillan Co., New York 1911).

The translation, already separately printed (Princeton University Press, 1908) and thus far the only existing English version, has been revised throughout, and a few slight changes have been made. As the Latin text of Mommsen is available elsewhere, it is not reprinted in this edition.

I desire to make especial acknowledgment of the many helpful criticisms received from Dean West and to express my gratitude for his constant and unfailing interest in this as in all my studies in the later Latin.

CHARLES CHRISTOPHER MIEROW.

Princeton University.

CONTENTS

CONTENTS

INTRODUCTION

I. JORDANES: HIS LIFE AND WORKS

Jordanes. The author of "The Origin and Deeds of the Goths" is not a model of literary excellence or originality. .He tells us himself[1] that he was an unlearned man before his conversion, and his writings fully bear out this statement. His book is mainly a compilation, not very carefully made; his style is irregular, rambling, uneven, and exhibits to a marked degree the traits of the decadent, crumbling later Latin. Yet he is important as the earliest Gothic historian — whose work has survived, and he gives much information in regard to the Goths that is nowhere else recorded. Across the scene he unfolds before us pass some of the greatest—and some of the most terrible—figures in history: Attila the Hun, "the scourge of God," the Visigoth Alaric who thrice sacked the Eternal City, Gaiseric the Vandal and the great Theodoric. So for the matter, if not for the style of his history of the Goths, Jordanes deserves careful consideration.

And there is too a certain irresistible charm in his naïve simplicity. He is so credulous, and tells in all sincerity such marvellous tales of the mighty achievements of his people, that the reader is drawn to him by his very loyalty and devotion to the defeated Gothic race in whose greatness he has so confident a belief. For despite the fact that he is following closely in another's footsteps and is giving at second hand practically all the matters of fact he relates, his own simple, trustful personality so pervades the whole work as to awaken sympathy for the writer and his great tale of the lost cause.

[1] *Getica* L 266.

The Author's Name. Of his life little is known apart
from the scant information contained in a few brief sentences of his own. The very spelling of his name was
long a matter of controversy, and Jacob Grimm[2] (followed later by Dietrich[3]) argued in favor of the form
Jornandes, which appears in the first printed editions of
his works. But the authority for this spelling is only
the second class of manuscripts, while the name Jordanes
is attested by the primary family of manuscripts and by
the only ancient author who mentiones him—the Geographer of Ravenna.

His Family. Jordanes was himself a Goth[4] and held
the office of secretary or notary (*notarius*) in a noble
family of the Gothic race. Here is his own brief but
tangled account of himself and his ancestors:[5]

*Scyri vero et Sadagarii et certi Alanorum cum duce
suo nomine Candac Scythiam minorem inferioremque
Moesiam acceperunt. cuius Candacis Alanoviiamuthis
patris mei genitor Paria, id est meus avus, notarius, quous-
que Candac ipse viveret, fuit, eiusque germanae filio Gunthicis, qui et Baza dicebatur, mag. mil., filio Andages fili
Andele de prosapia Amalorum descendente, ego item
quamvis agramatus Iordannis ante conversionem meam
notarius fui.*

From this passage it appears that at the time of Attila's
death (453 A.D.) Candac was leader of part of the Alani.
Candac's sister was the wife of the Ostrogoth Andag,
whom Jordanes mentions elsewhere[6] as the slayer of
Theodorid I in the Battle of the Catalaunian Plains. This

---

[2] Abhandlungen der Berliner Akademie 1846, pp. 1-59 = Kleine
Schriften III 171-235.
[3] Über die Aussprache des Gothischen (1862).
[4] *Getica* LX 316.
[5] L 266.
[6] XL 209.

Andag was the son of Andela who was descended from the family of the Amali. The son of Andag and Candac's sister was Gunthigis (or Baza), whose notary Jordanes was. Paria, the grandfather of Jordanes, had served Candac in the same capacity. It would appear from Mommsen's text that the name of Jordanes' father was *Alanoviiamuthis*. For this long and unwieldly word Erhardt[7] suggested the reading *Alanorum ducis*, to be taken in apposition with *Candacis*. The conjecture was reasonable enough; the serious objection to it is the unnatural omission of his father's name in a passage where Jordanes is avowedly giving an account of his ancestry. Grienberger[8] more plausibly explains the form as ALAN. D. UIIAMUThIS; that is, the abbreviation of *Alanorum ducis* (in apposition with the preceding *Candacis*) followed by the name of Jordanes' father, which would thus be *Uiiamuth* (Gothic *Veihamôths*).

His Nationality. This Gothic name accords also with the statement of the author himself as to his nationality,[9] and tends to overthrow Mommsen's theory that in reality he belonged to the tribe of the Alani, like the leader whom he served.[10] Not only is this an unnecessary assumption, but if Jordanes belonged to that tribe he might well be expected to mention the fact explicitly in the passage quoted above. It is difficult to find in the *Getica* any such prejudice in favor of the Alani as Mommsen mentions, and Jordanes has certainly not

[7] Göttingische gelehrte Anzeigen 17 (1886), pp. 669-708.
[8] Die Vorfahren des Jordanes, Germania 34 (1889), pp. 406-409.
[9] LX 316: *nec me quis in favorem gentis praedictae, quasi ex ipsa trahenti originem, aliqua addidisse credat.*
[10] Friedrich (Über die Kontroversen Fragen im Leben des gotischen Geschichtschreiber's Jordanes, Sb. d. philos.-philol. u. hist. Kl. d. K. B. Ak. d. W. 1907, III pp. 379-442) cites a number of instances of leaders of barbarian tribes whose secretaries were not of the same race as themselves.

availed himself of the opportunity here presented to
glorify Candac, as he could easily have done if he were
eager to bring this race into prominence. It seems more
reasonable therefore to take his words in their simplest
and most obvious meaning when he says that he traces
his descent from the race of the Goths.

His Position in Life.   The office of secretary in military life was a position of some distinction, and was
often conferred by leaders upon their equals ;[11] in this case
the fact that Paria, the grandfather of Jordanes, had held
a like office under Candac gives added distinction to the
secretaryship as an honor perhaps hereditary in this family.   The Gunthigis or Baza whom Jordanes served has
been identified with some plausibility by Friedrich[12] with
Godigisclus, a leader of the Goths mentioned by Procopius,[13] and further with the Batza of Marcellinus Comes,[14]
who was in 536 *dux* of the Euphrates *limes* and entrusted
with the defense of the empire's farthest frontier.   Friedrich argues that Jordanes must have resigned his office
before this year (since he shows no intimate knowledge
of Asia), acting as secretary for Gunthigis only during
the time that he was stationed in the European part of
the Eastern Empire, and accordingly that a considerable
space of time elapsed between the resignation of his office

[11] See for example Anonymus Valesianus 38: *Orestes Pan-
nonius eo tempore, quando Attila in Italiam venit, se illi iunxit et
eius notarius factus fuerat: unde profecit et usque ad patriciatus
dignitatem pervenit.*

[12] o. c.

[13] *Bell. Pers.* I 8 (on the years 502-505): Γοδίδισκλός τε καὶ Βέσσας
Γότθοι ἄνδρες. Compare with this the mention of *nostri temporis
Bessa patricius* by Jordanes in the same passage (L 265-266) with
Gunthicis . . . mag. mil.

[14] On the year 536: *limitem Euphratesiae ingressa, ubi Batzas
dux eosdem partim blanditiis partim districtione pacifica fovit et
inhiantes bellare repressit.*

and the writing of the *Getica*.[15]   At all events it is evident that Jordanes, writing in 551, was an elderly man when he composed his history: for his grandfather was almost contemporary with the Battle of the Catalaunian Plains in 451—just a century before—and he himself had served the son of a man who had taken part in the same conflict.[16]

His Ecclesiastical Condition.   The words *ante conversionem meam* in the passage quoted above have occasioned much difference of opinion with regard to the author's status during the latter part of his life.   The phrase has been variously interpreted as referring to conversion to Christianity,[17] conversion from Arianism to the Nicene belief,[18] entrance upon the monastic state,[19] or merely a withdrawal from everyday activities into a life of meditation and quiet.[20]   It is by no means necessary to infer from these words that Jordanes became a monk, as Mommsen sought to prove,[21] for the expression may just as well be understood to refer to entrance upon the life of an ecclesiastic,[22] and Jordanes is probably to

[15] In further support of which see the letter to Vigilius prefaced to the *Romana: me longo per tempore dormientem vestris tandem interrogationibus excitastis.*

[16] See Erhardt, *l.c.*

[17] Bergmüller, Einige Bemerkungen zur Latinität des Jordanes. Progr. Augsburg 1903.

[18] Ebert, Allgemeine Geschichte der Literatur des Mittelalters (Leipzig 1889), p. 557, n. 2.

[19] So Mommsen, following Muratori (*Scriptores rerum Italicarum* Vol. 1, 1723).   In support of his view he quotes the preface of the *de orthographia* of Cassiodorus (*gramm. Lat. ed.* Keil 7, 144): *post commenta psalterii, ubi . . . conversionis meae tempore primum studium laboris impendi.*

[20] Friedrich, *o.c.* pp. 395-402, feels convinced that he became a *religiosus.*

[21] Mommsen claimed further that he wrote in a Moesian, Thracian or Illyrian Monastery (Introduction to the *Getica* p. ix, and Mommsen's edition of Marcellinus Comes p. 53).

[22] See Simson, Neues Archiv 22, pp. 741-743; Pope Gelasius I

be identified with the Bishop Jordanes of Crotona who
was with Pope Vigilius in Constantinople in the
year 551.[23]

Mommsen opposed the theory that Jordanes was a
bishop, asserting that he became and remained a simple
monk. Yet the first class of manuscripts calls him *episcopus*[24] in the title of the *Romana,* while the third class,
in the title of the *Getica,* speaks of him as Bishop of
Ravenna. This he certainly was not, as Muratori
showed,[25] basing his proof on an extremely accurate list
of the archbishops of Ravenna by Rubens, Ughelli and
others. Moreover we find no trace of Jordanes in the
lives of these prelates by Agnellus, who wrote in the
ninth century under the Emperor Lothar I. It is hard
to believe that he could have escaped the investigations
of Agnellus, particularly as the church at Ravenna was
so celebrated and abundantly supplied with records.
Simson's attempt[26] to show that Jordanes was possibly a
bishop of Africa was not very successful, and has found
few supporters. But there was a Bishop of Crotona
named Jordanes who was in Constantinople with Pope
Vigilius in the year 551, and it seems reasonably certain that he is identical with the author of the *Getica.*[27]

We find mention of Bishop Jordanes in the document

(Thiel p. 370) : *sub religiosae conversionis obtentu vel ad monasteria
sese conferre, vel ad ecclesiasticum famulatum . . . indifferenter
admitti.*

[23] See below (p. 7-10). There was also a *Iordanes defensor ecclesiae Romanae* in 556 (mentioned by Pope Pelagius in his fifth
letter to the bishops of Tuscia, Mansi 9, 716).

[24] So also Sigebert of Gembloux, *de script. eccl.* 35: *Iordanus
episcopus Gothorum scripsit historiam.*

[25] Muratori, *Scriptores* 1, 189.

[26] N. A. 22, 741-747.

[27] Among the adherents to this theory are Bessell, Cassell, Erhardt, Grimm, von Gutschmid, Manitius, Martens, Schirren and
Wattenbach.

known as the *Damnatio Theodori*[28] in which the Pope
says: *nos . . . cum Dacio Mediolanensi . . . Paschasio
Aletrino atque Iordane Crotonensi fratribus et episcopis
nostris.* As Bishop of Crotona in Bruttium Jordanes
would have lived not far from the monastery (*monas-
terium Vivariense*) to which Cassiodorus had retired in
his old age. Here then is the one place where he might
easily have obtained the twelve books of the Gothic History of Cassiodorus,[29] and his inability to refer to them
later when he was actually writing his compilation[30]
would be explained by his absence in Constantinople.

It is furthermore probable that he wrote his work at
Constantinople because of his evident ignorance of the
later and contemporary events in Italy and his accurate
knowledge of the trend of affairs in the Eastern Empire.[31] His eulogy of the Emperor Justinian and his
general Belisarius is also just what might be expected
from one who wrote in the vicinity of the imperial court.
And finally it has been pointed out that his words to
Castalius in the introduction to the *Getica: si quid parum
dictum est et tu, ut vicinus genti, commemoras, adde,* are
peculiarly appropriate if we may suppose that his friend
was a fellow-townsman of his and lived at Crotona, which
was in close contact with the Goths but not actually in
their possession.

The fact that the *Romana* is dedicated to a Vigilius has
made this theory still more plausible, and it is hard to
avoid the conclusion that this Vigilius is the Pope of
that name. Mommsen follows Ebert[32] in denying even

[28] *Acta concil tom.* 5, p. 1314; Mansi 9, p. 60.
[29] See below (p. 10).
[30] *Getica*, preface 2.
[31] Friedrich (*o.c.* pp. 402-428) in support of his theory that Jordanes wrote in Thessalonica cites arguments which indicate an
eastern rather than a western origin of the work and which are
at least equally applicable to Constantinople.
[32] *Geschichte d. christlich lat. Lit.* I, pp. 556-562 (1889).

the possibility of this, and Friedrich still more scornfully rejects the hypothesis;[33] their arguments are based on both the form and the content of the letter to Vigilius which forms the introduction to the *Romana*. With regard to the salutation, *nobilissime frater,* and later *novilissime et magnifice frater,* while it is not, indeed, the way in which a simple monk would have addressed the pope, yet a bishop might perhaps use such expressions to one who was his friend. And, as Grimm has pointed out,[34] these words of greeting sound more respectful than the *frater Castali* and *frater carissime* in the opening sections of the *Getica*.[35]   Even so, *frater carissime* is the very salutation used by Cyprian, Bishop of Carthage, in a letter[36] to the Roman Pope Cornelius in the year 250-251, and again in 433 we find John, Bishop of Antioch, addressing Pope Xystus simply as "brother."[37]

It will be remembered too that Pope Vigilius held the office under trying circumstances which detracted from

[33] p. 433: So töricht spricht kein Bischof oder gar ein römischer *defensor ecclesiae* zu einem Papst. Others who agree with Mommsen on this point are Teuffel § 485 and Werner, Die Latinität der Getica des Jordanis, Halle 1908.

[34] Kleinere Schriften 3, pp. 171-235.

[35] Friedrich claims that no argument can be based upon a comparison of the salutations of these two letters because the introduction of the *Getica* is borrowed from Rufinus, asserting that even the words *frater Castali* merely correspond to the *frater Heracli* of that author! And since *magnificus* was a title of respect bestowed upon the holders of certain offices of importance, he would see in Jordanes, Castalius and Vigilius three men in secular life, perhaps veterans of the imperial army. Yet Friedrich elsewhere calls attention to the fact that Pope Vigilius was of distinguished ancestry, a Roman and the son of a consul, which might in itself account for such a title of respect, and further the use of the word *frater* in both letters is a significant fact; it surely savors more of ecclesiastical than military life.

[36] In *Epist. roman. pontif. ed.* Constant, Paris 1721, pp. 125, 131, 139.

[37] *Ibid.* p. 1242.

the dignity usual to the position. He was made Pope at Rome in 537 through the influence of Belisarius and at the request of the Empress Theodora, who hoped that he would be unorthodox. In 547 he was summoned to Constantinople because of his refusal to sign the Three Chapters issued by Justinian. It was not until 554 that he finally obtained permission to return to Italy, and during the seven years of his captivity—for he was virtually a prisoner in Constantinople—he was much persecuted by the imperial party, and was twice compelled to flee to a church for sanctuary.[88] It was in Constantinople and in 551, the very year when Jordanes was writing the *Romana* and *Getica*, that Vigilius issued the *Damnatio Theodori* from which we have quoted above a sentence containing the name Jordanes.[89]

Bearing these facts in mind, let us now glance at the dedication of the *Romana* to Vigilius, and see if its content is such as to preclude its having been written to the pope of that name. Jordanes says that he is sending the universal history which he has just completed *iungens ei aliud volumen de origine actusque Getice gentis, quam iam dudum communi amico Castalio ededissem, quatinus diversarum gentium calamitate conperta ab omni erumna liberum te fieri cupias et ad deum convertas, qui est vera libertas. legens ergo utrosque libellos, scito quod diligenti mundo semper necessitas imminet. tu vero ausculta Iohannem apostolum, qui ait: 'carissimi, nolite dilegere mundum neque ea que in mundo sunt. quia mundus transit et concupiscentia eius: qui autem fecerit voluntatem dei, manet in aeternum.' estoque toto corde diligens deum et proximum, ut adimpleas legem et ores pro me novilissime et magnifice frater.*

If this, as Mommsen would have us believe, is merely

---

[88] See Vigilius *Encyclica* p. 55 Migne.
[89] See above (p. 7).

an exhortation to a friend, bidding him to follow his own example, renounce the world, and become a monk, why should Jordanes already address him as "brother" and ask for his prayers? On the contrary, we can easily understand these words as an attempt on the part of Jordanes to console his distinguished friend in the midst of his trials—and we have seen that this pope had his share of cares and tribulations—by recalling to his mind the disasters that have overtaken men in all ages, and by exhorting him anew to find freedom from anxiety in trusting God's purposes, while he continues steadfast in doing what he feels is the divine will, and persists in that love of God and of his neighbor which is the fulfilling of the law.

His Literary Activity. There are two books that have come down under the name of Jordanes. One is a compendium of universal history, which he entitled *De summa temporum vel origine actibusque gentis Romanorum.* The other is the abbreviation of the Gothic History of Cassiodorus, a large work of twelve books which Jordanes reduced to the small pamphlet which alone has survived. This, like the original work of which it is an abridgment, is entitled *De origine actibusque Getarum.* The terms *Romana* and *Getica,* introduced by Mommsen, are most convenient for compendious reference to the two works.

As we learn from Jordanes himself in the introductory sections of the *Getica,* he was engaged in the work of "the abbreviation of the Chronicles," that is, he was writing the *Romana,* when his friend Castalius requested him to undertake the composition of the Gothic History. So laying aside for a time the work he had in hand (which was probably almost completed), he first wrote and published the *Getica* and then returned to the *Romana.* The

latter work was dedicated to Vigilius and sent to him
with the *Getica*.[40]

Where the books were written. Where Jordanes
was when he wrote these books is a matter of dispute.
Of course if the author can be identified with that Bishop
Jordanes who accompanied Pope Vigilius to Constantinople, this difficulty is at once cleared up; and we have
tried to show the reasonableness of this theory.

Mommsen believed that Jordanes makes his whole
narrative hinge upon the home of his ancestors, namely
the two Roman provinces of Scythia, with its capital at
Tomi, and Moesia Inferior, with its capital at Marcianople. He found too that there is an enormously dis-
proportionate number of Moesian names in the *Getica*
compared with those belonging to other provinces of the
empire. He believed he could discover a pushing forward of Moesia and Thrace and an intimate acquaintance
with these regions, from which he drew the conclusion
that Jordanes was himself a Moeso-Goth dwelling in this
part of the country, and that he wrote his book perhaps
at Tomi, Marcianople or Anchiali.[41]

And yet, as Erhardt[42] and Schirren[48] have shown, even
granting Mommsen's premises, the conclusions he draws
therefrom do not necessarily follow. For these regions
were in a sense the cradle of the race, and must naturally
have a central interest for all Goths, and the subject
itself makes it proper that they should be placed in the
foreground. Jordanes' personal knowledge of the country may be easily explained by his previous office as notary,
and it is not necessary to assume that he continued to

* See the letter to Vigilius § 4.
" Friedrich (pp. 402-428) adduces a number of arguments in
support of an eastern origin, and favors Thessalonica as the place
of writing.
" Gött. gel. Anzeigen 1886 N. 17 p. 669.
" Deutsche Literaturzeitung 1882 N. 40 p. 1420.

dwell in Moesia and wrote his books there just because he
shows an intimate acquaintance with these regions. In
fact, when Jordanes borrowed the work of Cassiodorus
from his steward (*dispensator*) for a three days' reading[44] he must naturally have lived—for the time at least—
in the neighborhood of where the book was, and we know
that Cassiodorus lived only in Bruttium.[45] Of course it
does not follow that Jordanes wrote in the place where
he read the book of Cassiodorus, for his own language
indicates a composition considerably later than the reading. The weight of evidence is still in favor of Constantinople rather than Moesia. The very fact that he calls
upon the absent Castalius to corroborate his statements
as "a neighbor to the race" seems to show that he wrote
from the non-Gothic Constantinople, and not from
Moesia, where remnants of the Gothic race were still
dwelling in their ancestral regions.

Date of Composition of the Romana, 551 A.D. There
can be little doubt with regard to the date of the completed
composition of the *Romana*, for Jordanes himself says in
his introduction[46] that he wrote it *in vicensimo quarto
anno Iustiniani imperatoris,* and again in the body of the
work[47] we find this sentence: *Iustinianus imperator regnat
iam iubante domino ann. XXIIII.* The twenty-fourth year
of the reign of Justinian is the year beginning April 1,
551. The content of the work is in agreement with these
statements of the author, for we find recorded the death
of Germanus[48] which occurred in the autumn of 550 and
the birth of his posthumous son. Mention is likewise
made of the "daily"[49] *instantia . . . Bulgarum, Antium*

[44] *Getica* preface 2.
[45] So W. A. in Lit. Centralblatt 1883 p. 1060.
[46] *Romana* § 4.
[47] *Romana* § 363.
[48] *Romana* § 383.
[49] *Romana* § 388.

et Sclavinorum (that is, their expedition into Thrace in 550), and finally[50] of the victory of the Lombards over the Gepidae in 551. On the other hand, there is no mention of later events.

Of the Getica, 551 A.D. If then Jordanes wrote the *Getica* after he had begun the *Romana,* and published it first, we may conclude that it too was written in 551. In this work also we find the death of Germanus mentioned, while there is no record of events later than those recounted in the *Romana.* Furthermore, he speaks of the plague[51] *quod nos ante hos novem annos experti sumus.* Now this is probably the pestilence which arose in Egypt[52] in 541, reached Byzantium in October 542, and there caused great desolation for four months, and finally in 543 devastated Italy. So this too serves to support the opinion that the *Getica* was written in 551. Jordanes says, to be sure, in the preface to the *Romana* that he has published the *Getica* "*iam dudum,*" but this expression may readily indicate as short an interval as several months.

Nature of the Work. Now as already seen, Jordanes himself admits that the *Getica* is merely an abridgment of the history of Cassiodorus. Furthermore he claims that in writing it he was obliged to rely largely upon his memory, as he did not have the original work before him at the time.[53] He says of the twelve books of the Gothic History:[54] "The words I recall not, but the sense and the deeds related I think I retain entire. To this I have added fitting matters from some Greek and Latin histories. I

[50] *Romana* §§ 386, 387; Procopius *bell. Goth.* 4, 25 p. 638.
[51] *Getica* xix 104.
[52] See Clinton's Fasti for 542.
[53] Friedrich (p. 438) flatly refuses to believe this statement: "Er hatte sie ja in Wirklichkeit vor sich."
[54] *Getica* preface 2, 3.

have also put in an introduction and a conclusion, and have inserted many things of my own authorship."

His Originality.   These are statements hard to believe. His introduction, as we shall see,[55] is taken almost word for word from Rufinus.   At the end of the work, in relating events not found in the work of Cassiodorus, he makes use of Marcellinus Comes as an authority without once mentioning him—though to be sure we must credit him here with first-hand quotation.   Most of the sixteen authors from whom he quotes as if from personal knowledge were perhaps not known to him at all except at second hand, for in the *Romana,* written but a short time before, he apparently knows nothing of these sources, even when relating the same events on which he cites them as authorities in the *Getica.*   The inference is that he has taken over quotations and references to sources directly from the work of Cassiodorus.   As to the "many things of my own authorship" which Jordanes claims to have inserted, it is difficult indeed to locate many of these.   Mommsen goes so far as to believe that almost his sole original contribution consists in quotations from Orosius at first hand![56]   The unfairness of Mommsen's view lies in the fact that he overlooks the personal tone of the style of Jordanes, which colors the entire work, and that he minimizes the evident joining and fitting that have to be done to connect the parts of the narrative. Perhaps Jordanes does little more than bow in and bow out his authors as they appear and disappear; but this at least he does.   Moreover we must not underestimate our indebtedness to this ecclesiastic whose compiled book has become practically the sole authority for much of our information about the Goths, and notably for the Battle

---

[55] Literary Sources (p. 36).
[56] See Literary Sources (p. 26).

of the Catalaunian Plains (451 A.D.) and Attila's memorable defeat, so far-reaching in its consequences.

Cassiodorus Senator. Cassiodorus Senator, the great statesman and man of letters, who was secretary both to Theodoric the Great and to Athalaric, his grandson and successor, wrote his history at the personal bidding of Theodoric.[57] In it (as Cassiodorus himself says in a speech[58] written for the young King Athalaric) "he carried his researches up to the very cradle of the Gothic race, gathering from the stores of his learning what even hoar antiquity scarce remembered. He drew forth the kings of the Goths from the dim lurking-place of ages, restoring to the Amal line the splendor that truly belonged to it, and clearly proving that for seventeen generations Athalaric's ancestors had been kings. Thus did he assign a Roman origin to Gothic history, weaving as it were into one chaplet the flowers which he had culled from the pages of widely scattered authors."

"Consider therefore," Athalaric continues in his address to the Roman senate, "what love he showed to you in praising us, by his proof that the nation of your sovereign has been from antiquity a marvellous people; so that ye who from the days of your forefathers have ever been deemed noble, are still ruled by the ancient progeny of kings."

The Aim of Cassiodorus. His intention then was to reconcile the Romans to the rule of those whom they regarded as barbarians by glorifying the Gothic race in general, tracing its history back into the dim past and bringing it into close contact with the great classical nations of antiquity, and to exalt in particular the House of

[57] Usener's *Anecdoton Holderi* p. 4; and see the Literary Sources (p. 24). On the spelling *Cassidor(i)us*, see Manitius, Geschichte der Lateinischen Literatur des Mittelalters, I page 39.
[58] Cassiodorus *Var.* 9, 25, Hodgkin's version. This is a eulogy of Cassiodorus upon his appointment as Praetorian Prefect in 533 A.D.

the Amali, a line of kings from whom Theodoric traced his descent. In order to win for his race a place in the remote past, he identified the Goths with the Getae and with the Scythians—a very vague term which covered practically all the tribes who had their homes east of the Vistula and Danube and north of the Black Sea. And the Amazons, according to his account, were Gothic women. Though he may have done this in good faith, these are mistaken identifications, and accordingly we must reject as evidence for true history the chapters that deal with these peoples.[59]

The Aim of Jordanes. When Jordanes wrote his abridgment of this great work, he rested his hope for the future of the Gothic race as much upon the Romans as upon his own people. It is the union of the two races that he feels sure will bring peace and prosperity to both in the days to come. So he refers frequently[60] to the marriage of Mathesuentha the Goth to Germanus the Roman, and of their young son Germanus he says:[61] "This union of the race of the Anicii with the stock of the Amali gives hopeful promise, by the Lord's favor, to both peoples."

So it is evident that the *Getica*, though primarily a historical work, naturally concludes somewhat in the manner of a political pamphlet, portraying the reconcilement of Goth and Roman under the beneficent rule of Justinian.

Language and Style.[61a] To the student of classical Latin only, the text of Jordanes as exhibited in Momm-

---

[59] Hodgkin omits entirely chapters V-XIII of the *Getica* in using Jordanes as a source.

[60] XIV 81, XLVIII 251, LX 314.

[61] LX 314.

[61a] The Latinity of Jordanes has been investigated by Wölfflin (Arch. f. l. Lex. 11, 361), Bergmüller (Augsburg 1903), and most recently and exhaustively by Fritz Werner (Halle 1908), whose satisfactory exposition I have followed.

sen's edition appears uncouth and almost barbarous.
Interchange of vowel sounds gives rise to such forms as
*paenitus, Grecia, efoebi, distinavit, helaritatem, prumtis-
simum, Eoropam.* Consonantal changes are fully as frequent, resulting in such spellings as *lacrimaviliter, Atri-
atici, storicus, habundans, Cauchasum.* In consequence
of the omission of final *m* the accusative is often identical
in form with the ablative, as *manu moverit, confidentia
addebat,* and sometimes *-um* is represented by *-o*, as in
Danubio transmeantes.

As regards inflection, there are fourth declension
words now changed to the second (*laco, grados*), and
conversely (*inmensu*); third declension adjectives
changed to the second declension (*acri ingenii*) and second to third (*magnanimis*). There are ablatives of *i*
stems in *e* (*mare*), datives in *e* (*tali hoste*), and nouns
ordinarily inflected now changed to indeclinables (*a corpus, foedus inito*). There are also many changes in
gender, as may be seen from such phrases as *laetus vulgus, iugus antefatus, quod dolus reminiscens.* In matters
of conjugation, we find deponents that have become active
(*remorasse*) and the reverse (*diuque certati*), and
frequent interchange of conjugations (*inquiret,* 3rd.
sing. pres. indic., *cognoscent,* 3rd. plu. pres. indic.,
accersientes).

In syntax the changes are no less marked. Preposi-
tions occur in combination with unexpected cases (*inter
Danubium Margumque fluminibus; a Pannonios fines
. . . distabat; cum multas opes; sine ipsos*). Among
other peculiarities in the use of cases the following ex-
amples may be cited: *omnem . . . phylosphiam eos in-
struxit; equo insidens; ipsius urbis ferre subsidium; vix
biennio . . . perseverantes; Orestem interfectum* (accusative absolute). Verb constructions are marked by
many changes of voice, mood and tense: there are pres-

ent participles used like perfects (*egressi . . . et transeuntes*), unusual infinitive combinations (*quis . . . cedere faciebat armatos?*), and indicatives in indirect questions (*doceamus, quomodo . . . explevit*). The use of conjunctions is likewise distinguished by many peculiarities, such as the use of *quia* and the indicative in indirect discourse, a confusion of *dum* and *cum, mox* equivalent to *simul atque,* and a great variety in conditional usage.   Moreover the periodic structure has in large measure disappeared.   Clauses and phrases whether of principal or subordinate character are loosely swung along in careless and sometimes clumsy succession, not infrequently tangling the sense and at times making close translation impossible.

Finally, there are many changes in the meanings of words, and substitutions of new words for the familiar expressions of classical Latin, as: *amplus, grandis* and *immensus* for *magnus; proprius* for *suus; germanus* for *frater; solacium* for *auxilium; civitas* for *urbs.* We find also *patria* synonymous with *terra, pelagus* usurping the place of *mare,* and *pars* and *plaga* used as equivalents for *regio.* There is a frequent use of abstracts, and some specifically Christian phrases of course appear in the work of this ecclesiastic.   Jordanes is fond of circumlocutions and sententious utterances, and his style is at times almost hopelessly confusing.   In seeking a cause for these many and exasperating peculiarities of form and expression, we must take account not only of the changing language itself, with its many alterations similar in nature to the changes in Western Latin, glimmerings which preceded the dawn of the Romance languages, but also of the candid confession of this Gothic secretary to whom Latin was at best an imperfectly mastered foreign tongue: *ego . . . agramatus Iordannis ante conversionem meam . . . fui.*

2. THE LITERARY SOURCES USED IN THE *GETICA*

In the preface to his *Getica,* after stating that the book is an epitome of the larger Gothic History of Cassiodorus Senator, Jordanes says:[62] "To this I have added fitting matters from some Greek and Latin histories," and in the chapters that follow sixteen ancient writers are cited as authorities. Besides those whom he mentions, some seven or eight others have evidently been used.

The question of the literary sources of Jordanes was investigated by Sybel,[63] and again by Mommsen in his edition. The following consideration of the sources is largely an abridgment of Mommsen's thorough treatment of the subject, although in several important points (notably his opinion of the value of the unknown writer Ablabius and his low estimate of the personal element in Jordanes' work) his views cannot be accepted without question. The authorities mentioned by Jordanes are here taken up in alphabetical order; his indebtedness to each can be more clearly traced by comparing the text of the *Getica* with the passages cited in Mommsen's footnotes and here given in the commentary.

Ablabius. This otherwise unknown *descriptor Gothorum gentis egregius* is mentioned three times by Jordanes: once his *verissima historia*[64] is cited as authority, and in two other passages he is referred to as *Ablabius . . . storicus.*[65] He can not be identified with any writer

[62] Preface 3.
[63] *De fontibus libri Iordanis de origine actuque Getarum,* Berlin 1838.
[64] IV 28.
[65] XIV 82, XXIII 117.

19

known to have borne this name (which is not an uncommon one), and it is not even clear whether he was a Greek, a Roman or a Goth.[66] Upon this meagre foundation of fact Mommsen has built up an elaborate theory, ascribing to Ablabius all the material in the *Getica* which comes ultimately from narratives of the Goths. According to his view Cassiodorus could hardly have collected from the lips of the people such legends and traditions, as he was busied his life long with affairs of state, and perhaps not even skilled in the Gothic tongue, as he was a Bruttian by birth. In fact he undertakes to prove that Cassiodorus condemned oral tradition as a source in saying:[67] *nec eorum fabulas alicubi repperimus scriptas, qui eos* (the Goths) *dicunt in Brittania . . . in servitute redactos et in unius caballi praetio a quodam ereptos,* adding further: *nos potius lectioni credimus quam fabulis anilibus consentimus.* Concluding therefore that he used literary sources entirely, Mommsen decides that of all the authors mentioned by Jordanes the only one to whom such legends can be attributed is Ablabius. He regards this unknown writer as the author of a book on Gothic History (rather than of a Roman History merely containing references to the Goths), and believes that his work concerned itself largely with the origins of that race. And since the third passage[68] quoted as from Ablabius seems really to be from Dexippus, Mommsen makes the further inference that Greek too was beyond the attainments of Cassiodorus, and that most of the references to Greek authors (and notably those to Priscus) are really quoted through Ablabius.[69] Mommsen believed, therefore, that Cassiodorus

---

[66] The passage about the Heruli (XXIII 117) might just as well be derived from a Greek as from a Roman writer.

[67] V 38.

[68] See XXIII 117, and commentary.

[69] To support this theory Mommsen points out that what is said of Vidigoia (V 43, XXXIV 178) is undoubtedly derived from the same author as the Gothic legends.

was indebted to this Ablabius for the greatest and most valuable part of his Gothic History, including the first part of the work that deals with the three abodes of the Goths,[70] and among the passages derived from Ablabius he would include XI 72, XI 69, III, XIV, XVII, XXIII 116.

Schirren[71] presented some strong objections to this highly complicated theory of the importance of Ablabius. He justly observes that Mommsen goes too far in assigning to this Ablabius practically everything in Jordanes that goes back to old Gothic tradition, in spite of the fact that no definite statements can be made about the man or his work. Indeed there is no real proof of any specific Gothic tradition that can be attributed to him, and in the passages that can be assigned with certainty to Ablabius as a source his knowledge is only such as a Greek writer might have had. In his rebuttal of Mommsen's view Schirren makes three main points:

(1) Mommsen states: *omnes* (referring to the passages in which this author is mentioned) *ostendunt Ablabium egisse de Gothorum originibus.* On the contrary, in one of the three instances we must read this meaning into the passage, and in the other two we cannot even do that much.

(2) Mommsen claims that Ablabius deserves high place as an author because Jordanes speaks of him as *descriptor Gothorum gentis egregius.* We might with equal right have judged Jordanes himself, had his works been lost, by the reference in the anonymous Geographer of Ravenna (4, 14) : *Iordanis Cosmographus subtilius exposuit.*

(3) As to the various passages cited as probably ascribable to Ablabius, some are thus assigned arbitrarily (for

---

[70] V 38-42. Mommsen held that this was practically attributed to Ablabius by the statement in XIV 82.

[71] Deutsche Literaturzeitung 1882, N. 40, pp. 1420-1424.

example, XI 69 and XI 72), and some can even be definitely referred to another writer. So the *stemma Amalorum* in XIV is almost certainly to be attributed to
Cassiodorus, who emphatically claims it as his own.

So that whereas Mommsen laments the lost Herodotus
of the Goths, and would even favor changing the reading
Favius in XXIX 151 to *Ablabius,* despite all the manuscripts, we find that everything that may be clearly assigned to Ablabius corresponds with Dexippus, and the
other passages are attributed to Ablabius on very doubtful grounds. Now regarding Mommsen's argument from
the sentences found in V 38: *nec eorum fabulas . . .
consentimus.* He holds, as has been seen, that this is a
remark made by Cassiodorus, and that Cassiodorus could
not have used any oral Gothic tradition but was indebted
to reading (*lectioni*) for everything. As to the story
about the horse, which has called forth the author's disap-
proval, Mommsen believes Cassiodorus undoubtedly
found it mentioned in some author. But the speaker
expressly states that he nowhere found the story in
written form. So it must have come to him orally, and
moreover as a generally known tale (as is seen from the
use of the plural *eorum*). Consequently Cassiodorus
did have some knowledge of Gothic tradition, and Mommsen's theory, based on the opposite assumption, falls to
the ground. Schirren suggests that it is perhaps more
plausible to ascribe this passage directly to Jordanes himself, a view made more probable by the use of the first
person *repperimus.* Then the word *lectioni* would refer to
Cassiodorus, whom Jordanes followed. As to the fable
itself, it may have been a story not known to Cassiodorus
at all—perhaps a good joke told at Constantinople at
the expense of the Goths.

Cassiodorus.[72] Flavius Magnus Aurelius Cassiodorus Senator (about 487—about 583) of Bruttii was one of the most eminent men of his time and came of distinguished ancestors; his grandfather had been tribune and *notarius* under Valentinian III, who died in 455; his father filled the highest offices under Odoacer and Theodoric, and was made patrician by the latter. He himself was *quaestor sacri palatii* shortly after 500, afterwards patrician, and then in the year 514 *consul ordinarius* and finally *magister officiorum*. This office he seems to have held for many years; at any rate, he held it in 526 when Theodoric died and his grandson Athalaric succeeded to the throne, but he resigned it when appointed *praefectus praetorio* in 533-534. In the year 534, when Athalaric died, Cassiodorus delivered a public eulogy of his successor Theodahad, and both under him and under Vitiges (who became king in 536) he held the office of *quaestor*. When the Goths were overcome he forsook secular life and became a monk. In the monastery he founded Cassiodorus wrote a number of theological, historical and educational works, and sought to impress upon his monks the value of the ancient literature. Even after his ninety-third year he wrote a book on orthography, and died probably as late as his ninety-fifth year.

Of his work on Gothic history we learn solely from Jordanes and from Cassiodorus himself. The earliest mention he makes of it is in a letter written in 533 to the senate of Rome.[73] He writes in Athalaric's name of himself: *tetendit se . . . in antiquam prosapiam nostram lectione discens quod vix maiorum notitia cana retinebat. iste reges Gothorum longa oblivione celatos latibulo vetustatis eduxit. iste Amalos cum generis sui claritate resti-*

[72] For his life see Mommsen's Introduction (from which this account is taken) and Hermann Usener: Festschrift zur Philologenversammlung in Wiesbaden 1877, p. 66 onward.

[73] *Var.* 9, 25.

*tuit, evidenter ostendens in decimam septimam progeniem
stirpem nos habere regalem. originem Gothicam historiam fecit esse Romanam colligens quasi in unam coronam
germen floridum quod per librorum campos passim fuerat
ante dispersum. perpendite quantum vos in nostra laude
dilexerit, qui vestri principis nationem docuit ab antiquitate mirabilem, ut, sicut fuistis a maioribus semper nobiles
aestimati, ita vos regum antiqua progenies imperaret.*

When made *praefectus praetorio* and entering upon his
office he wrote a letter to the senate[74] in which he makes
mention of the line of Amal kings, which is taken from
this work, and again[75] he refers to a passage in his history which Jordanes has epitomized.[76]   Finally, in the
preface to his *Variae*, apparently written in 538, his
friends address him thus: *duodecim libris Gothorum historiam defloratis prosperitatibus condidisti: cum tibi in
illis fuerit secundus eventus, quid ambigis et haec publico
dare, qui iam cognosceris dicendi tirocinia posuisse?*

Moreover in the *Codex Caroliruhensis* edited by Usener[77] we have preserved the *ordo generis Cassiodoriorum
eorumque qui scriptores extiterint ex eorum progenie vel
qui eruditi,* and from it we learn the following: *Cassiodorus Senator vir eruditissimus et multis dignitatibus
pollens iuvenis adeo dum patris Cassiodori patricii et praefecti praetorii consiliarius fieret et laudes Theodorichi
regis Gothorum facundissime recitasset, ab eo quaestor
est factus, patricius et consul ordinarius, postmodum dehinc magister officiorum et praefuisset formulas dictionum,
quas in XII libris ordinavit, et variarum titulum superposuit. scripsit praecipiente Theodoricho rege historiam
Gothicam originem et loca mores in* (moresque XII is
Usener's emendation) *libris annuntians.*   Usener be-

---

[74] *Var.* II, I.
[75] *Var.* 12. 20.
[76] See *Getica* XXX 156 and note.
[77] *Ancedoton Holderi;* for full title see p. 23, note 72.

lieved that the book from which these excerpts are made
had been written by Cassiodorus in 522,[78] and that therefore the History of the Goths must have been published
before that date. But Mommsen points out that this
very passage mentions his *praefectura praetorii*, which he
obtained in 534, and the publication of the *Variae*, which
is to be dated about 538. Furthermore, in the very beginning Cassiodorus is called *monachus servus dei*. So
this fragment is evidently from a book published after
Cassiodorus became a monk, or else (as is possibly the
case) it has been added to by others. But it is unrea-
sonable to say that the part relating to the *Variae* is an
interpolation and then to make use of this fragment as
evidence to define the date of the appearance of the
Gothic History. It seems entirely probable that the history was begun at Theodoric's suggestion, and all indica-
tions point toward its publication between 526, the year
of Theodoric's death, and 533, when it is mentioned in
the letter cited above.[79] Mommsen calls attention to the
fact that Cassiodorus (who was not sparing of self-
praise) mentions this work only in the last years of his
office. Furthermore the statement, apparently taken from
the history itself, that Athalaric, the successor of Theodoric, is reigning as the seventeenth in the succession,
makes it clear that Cassiodorus could not have finished his
Gothic History in Theodoric's lifetime.

The title of the Gothic History of Cassiodorus was in
all likelihood the same as that given by Jordanes to his
abridgment, *De origine actibusque Getarum*;[80] it was divided into twelve books, like most of the other works of

[78] Mainly because it gives the lives of Symmachus and Boethius
without making any mention of their trial and death.

[79] Page 15.

[80] See the passage from the *Variae* quoted on page 24 with its
mention of *originem Gothicam*, and the preface to the *Getica* I.
When Cassiodorus speaks of the work as *historiam* he is referring
to its content rather than its title.

Cassiodorus, and starting from the beginnings of the Gothic race carried on the account to his own day, *per generationes regesque,* as Jordanes states in his own preface. Aside from making an epitome, the author of the *Getica* claims that he has added to the work: *ad quos et ex nonnullis historiis Grecis ac Latinis addedi convenientia initium finemque et plura in medio mea dictione permiscens.* As regards the latter part of the book this statement must, of course, be true, for Cassiodorus closed his account with the year 526. But Mommsen is loath to give any further credit for originality. He wholly discredits the statement that Jordanes has himself added *convenientia* from various Greek and Latin authors, assigning rather to Cassiodorus all that comes from Priscus, both Dios, Strabo and Ptolemaeus, and ultimately referring even this back to Ablabius and Ammianus Marcellinus. He concedes to Jordanes as a possible personal contribution at the beginning of the work quotations from Orosius at first hand (regarding this author as an authority whom Cassiodorus did not hold in especially high regard),[81] and even goes so far as to admit that perhaps all the passages from Orosius throughout the *Getica* are quoted by Jordanes and make up the *plura in medio.*[82] Mommsen expresses small confidence in the truth of any of the author's claims, however, remarking that Jordanes was not ashamed to appropriate for his *Getica* an introduction from Rufinus and to pretend to give a quotation from Iamblichus at the beginning of the *Romana,* that he might adorn his book by that distinguished name.

[81] In support of this he quotes from *Inst. div. litt.* 17: *Orosius quoque Christianorum temporum paganorumque collator praesto vobis est, si eum volueritis legere.*

[82] But Mommsen is in error, as Erhardt first pointed out, when he says that Orosius is the only author referred to in the *Getica* with the addition of the number of the book; references to books are found also in III 16 (Ptolomaeus) and XV 83 (Symmachus).

Of course what Jordanes says of himself and his own people[83] cannot be referred back to Cassiodorus, nor can so sharp a denunciation of Arianism[84] have been found in the larger work, for Theodoric's *magister officiorum* though orthodox himself was mindful of the Arian convictions of his king. In general, to discover what·passages are the actual work of Jordanes one must start from the *Romana,* and after observing what authorities are there employed note whether in the *Getica* the quotations from these same writers are also made by Jordanes himself.[85] Schirren,[86] in his careful investigation, found in many passages an ornate style (whether peculiar to Cassiodorus or to his age) which is very different from the meagreness of Jordanes as he reveals himself in the *Romana* and in those sections of the *Getica* which treat of events later than 526.

According to Mommsen's theory, Jordanes was a Moeso-Goth and a subject of the Eastern Empire (whereas Cassiodorus was a Gotho-Roman attached to Theodoric's court), and in his epitome the account of the *Foederatio* of Gothic mercenaries and the history of the provinces on the Danube has taken the place held in the work of Cassiodorus by the account of the kingdom of Theodoric the Great; in short, he held that as Cassiodorus made the Gothic History Roman, so Jordanes made it Moesian.

It will be noted, however, that Mommsen himself

---

[*] L-LI.

[*] XXV 131-132; XXVI 138.

[*] So Mommsen points out that the death of Valens is described in the *Romana* 314 in the words of Victor's epitome, whereas in the *Getica* he has fused with this the account taken from Ammianus Marcellinus which he found in Cassiodorus.

[*] *De ratione quae inter Iordanem et Cassiodorium intercedat commentatio,* Dorpat 1858. See Gutschmid's review of this, Kleine Schriften 5, 293-336.

admits[87] that these very Moeso-Thracian references to
which he calls so much attention appeared also in Cassiodorus, and, as Schirten first observed, there is need of a
more convincing proof than Mommsen has given to
establish the fact that in Cassiodorus the Gotho-Moesian
history stood in a noticeably different proportion to the
Gotho-Italian than is the case in Jordanes. For after all,
the Gotho-Italian history begins with Theodoric, and
what precedes must necessarily have occupied a considerable space in Cassiodorus as it does in the abridgment of
his work.[88]   Mommsen is unfair in his charges of plagiarism, for in his borrowed preface Jordanes indicates,
in some measure at least, his indebtedness to Rufinus by
the words *ut quidam ait;* moreover the author of the
Getica should be judged by the standards of his own age,
in which such customary open incorporation of another's
writings was not viewed as plagiarism.   The accusation
that Jordanes has at the beginning of his *Romana* used the
name of Iamblichus to add lustre to his own work, in
pretending to quote from him while in reality putting forward his own ideas, is likewise too severe a criticism.
Friedrich[89] makes clear that Jordanes is accrediting Iamblichus merely with the phrase *armis et legibus exer-
centes,* which may well have been circulated under his
name, as it is quite in accord with a passage from his
work.

Erhardt,[90] while agreeing in the main with Mommsen's
views on the literary sources and pointing out that these
conclusions are strengthened by a comparison of the
Romana with the *Getica,* inasmuch as the former work
contains few citations because Florus[90a] seldom refers to

[87] Introduction XIII.
[88] See also the introduction to this book, p. 15.
[89] Pp. 379-442.
[90] Gött. gel. Anz. 1886, p. 669.
[90a] Jordanes follows Florus in the *Romana.*

his authorities, while the latter bristles with them since Cassiodorus loves to make a show of learned quotations, would still not go so far as to say that Jordanes added nothing of his own. He thinks that the quotations from Symmachus regarding Maximin and perhaps some of the geographical digressions have been added by Jordanes to the account as found in Cassiodorus.

Claudius Ptolemaeus. The geographer of Alexandria, *orbis terrae discriptor egregius,* a contemporary of Marcus Aurelius, is quoted on Scandza in III 16-19.

Dexippus. This author, who wrote in Greek in the period before Diocletian, is cited[91] in regard to the march of the Vandals from the ocean to the Roman frontier. Moreover the passage about the Heruli,[92] which is credited to Ablabius, comes from Dexippus. Mommsen believed that in both instances Dexippus was quoted through Ablabius.[93]

Dio. In his description of Britain, Jordanes once cites[93a] and elsewhere makes use of *Dio . . . celeberrimus scriptor annalium,* and later refers to him as an authority on Ravenna[94] and on the siege of Odessus.[95] He also praises him[96] as: *Dio storicus et antiquitatum diligentissimus inquisitor, qui operi suo Getica titulum dedit,* and again[97] as *Dio, qui historias* (of the Goths) *annalesque Greco stilo composuit.* But both Cassiodorus and Suidas[98] have erred in assigning to Dio Cassius the

[91] XXII 113.
[92] XXIII 117.
[93] See above, p. 20.
[93a] II 14.
[94] XXIX 151.
[95] X 65.
[96] IX 58.
[97] V 40.
[98] Δίων ὁ Κάσσιος · · · ἔγραψε ῾Ρωμαικὴν . . . Περσικά, Γετικὰ ἐνόδια.

work on the Getae, contrary to the testimony of Philos-
tratus.[99]   It is Dio Chrysostom (b. 40 A.D.) who wrote
the Γετικά.

Fabius. It seems impossible to identify this author,
from whom part of the description of Ravenna[100] is
taken. Mommsen's view is that Jordanes may have written Fabius where Cassiodorus had named Ablabius.

Josephus. The historian of the Jewish War (b. 37
A.D.), *annalium relator verissimus,* as he is called in
the *Getica,* is referred to in IV 29. Cassiodorus[101] regarded him as *paene secundus Livius.*

Livy. As Sybel pointed out,[102] the apparent quotation from Livy in II 10 rests in reality upon a passage
in the Agricola of Tacitus where Livy's name is
mentioned.

Lucan. Lucan (39-65 A.D.) *plus storico quam poeta,*
as Jordanes says, accepting the judgment of former
critics, is cited once, in V 43.

Pompeius Trogus. This contemporary of Livy is
now known chiefly through the epitome of his *Historiae
Philippicae* by Justinus. According to Gutschmïd[103]
Jordanes or his authority Cassiodorus used, not the epitome, but the original work of Trogus. He is cited in
VI 48 and X 61 and used also in VII 50 and in VIII
(see commentary).

Pomponius Mela. Pomponius Mela, of Tingentera
in Spain, wrote under Caligula or Claudius three books

---

[99] *Vit. soph.* I, 7 p. 487.
[100] XXIX 151.
[101] *Inst. div. litt.* 17.
[102] *De fontibus libri Iordanis,* p. 13.
[103] Jahn's Jahrbücher für classische Philologie, suppl. 1856/7 pp.
193-202.

De Chorographia, the oldest extant Latin treatise on geography. He is cited in III 16 and is used also with no mention of his name throughout the whole of II and in V 44-45, XII 75. Manitius (Neues Archiv 1888, p. 213) calls attention to the verbal resemblance between V 37 and Mela 3, 34.

Priscus. In the year 448 Priscus, a Thracian from the town of Panium, accompanied Maximin, the general of Theodosius II, on his celebrated embassy to Attila, and to his account of this trip we owe our detailed knowledge of the great Hun.[104] Priscus is cited in XXIV 123, XXXIV 178, XXXV 183, XLII 222, XLIX 254-255, and Mommsen argues from the agreement of fragments of Priscus elsewhere preserved with the account of Jordanes that the following passages also come from his work: XXIV 126, XXXVI 184, XLII 223, XLIII 225, and probably III 21. He would also refer to the same source what Jordanes says of the sons of Attila (L 266, LIII 272, and compare LII 268), remarking that in the *Getica* all the passages derived from Priscus deal with Attila, and that conversely there is no account of Attila which does not come from Priscus. Among the excerpts from this author, three passages appear to have been added to from other sources:

(1) In XL 209, where credit for the victory at the Catalaunian Plains is wrongfully given to the Goths (as also in the chronicle of Cassiodorus).

(2) In XLII 223, where the account of Pope Leo's embassy to Attila is increased by material from Prosper's chronicle.

(3) In XXXV 181, concerning the murder of Bleda, where the sententious statement at the close, *librante iustitia detestabili remedio crescens deformes exitus suae*

[104] He wrote in Greek a ἱστορίαν βυζαντιακὴν καὶ τὰ κατὰ τὸν Ἀττήλαν, in eight books.

crudelitatis invenit, is not in accord with the simple and dignified manner of Priscus.

Mommsen calls particular attention to the difference in style between the general clumsiness and difficulty of the *Getica* and the smoothness and charm of those passages which are based upon Priscus.[105] In these are found accurate descriptions of the distinguishing traits of various peoples,[106] a life-like and truthful portrayal of men,[107] a keen and careful analysis of the causes and meanings of various events,[108] and the use of apt figures of speech and comparisons.[109] Mommsen believed that Jordanes was impressed by the beauty of the narrative of Priscus (evident even in the version of Cassiodorus) and copied out these passages rather than condensed them.

Strabo. The geographer, *Grecorum nobilis scriptor* (b. 64 B.C.) is cited in II 12 concerning Britain, and is elsewhere used as an authority on the same subject.

Symmachus. Jordanes speaks of the life of the Emperor Maximin recorded by a certain Symmachus *in quinto suae historiae libro,*[110] and there seems to have been a *consul ordinarius* of that name in 485 who wrote a Roman history in seven books. The passages preserved by Jordanes correspond almost word for word with the life of Maximin given in the *Scriptores historiae Augustae* under the name of Julius Capitolinus; so it seems that Symmachus borrowed his account from that work.

Tacitus. *Cornelius annalium scriptor* is cited in II 13 and used elsewhere on the same subject, namely Britain.

[105] See XXXVI 187, XXXIX 202, XLIX 257.
[106] L 261.
[107] XXXV 182, XXXVIII 200, XLIX 254.
[108] See the passages on the number of Attila's soldiers, XXXV 182; the funeral pyre, XL 213; Honoria, XLII 224.
[109] XXXVIII 200; XL 212.
[110] XV 83, and see 88.

Manitius (Neues Archiv 1888, p. 213) sees a resemblance between X 62 and the Germania 36; also between XXXIV 176 and Annals 12, 49.

Vergil. "The Mantuan," as Jordanes calls him, is quoted in I 9, V 40 and VII 50. A paraphrase of a verse of the Aeneid is found in XXVI 134. In XXXV 182 is the expression *huc atque illuc circumferens oculos,* reminiscent of Aeneid 4, 363. To these Manitius (Neues Archiv 1888, p. 214) would add the following resemblances between the two authors: XX 108 and Aeneid 9, 450; XXIX 150 and Georgics 1, 482; XLIX 254 and Aeneid 6, 520; LVI 288 and Aeneid 1, 249.

This completes the list of authorities actually named by Jordanes as sources. Aside from these there are several whom he almost certainly made use of without acknowledging his indebtedness. It is worth while to consider these also.

Dictys. Lucius Septimius wrote in the second half of the fourth century what purported to be a Latin version of a Greek story of the Trojan War by a certain Dictys of Crete. Mommsen's opinion, that the story of Telephus in the *Getica* rests not on the Latin version of Dictys but upon the lost original, is rendered more plausible by the discovery of part of the Greek original in Egypt.[111]

Marcellinus. Ammianus Marcellinus of Antioch (about 330-400) wrote at Rome a continuation of Tacitus. He himself says that his work covered the period from Nerva to the death of Valens (that is, 96-378 A.D.),

[111] See Grenfell, Hunt and Goodspeed, Tebtunis Papyri vol. II N. 268, London 1907. Also Dares and Dictys, N. E. Griffin, Baltimore 1907; Ihm, Der Griechische und Lateinische Dictys, Hermes 1909, 1-22; The Greek Dictys, Griffin, American Journal of Philology 29, 329.

but only books XIV-XXXI are extant, beginning with the
last years of Constantius II (353-378). Jordanes records
some events of Roman history of this period in XXIV
126, 127, 128. In XXV and XXVI he also uses Ammianus; not much, to be sure, for after the victories of
Claudius and Aurelian almost to the time of Valens the
Goths *per longa saecula siluerunt immobiles*,[112] and accordingly Jordanes passes directly from Constantine to
Valens. Schirren conjectured that such passages as XVI
89-93, XVIII 101, XX 109, and XXI 111, 112, pertain-
ing to the emperors from Philip to Constantine I are
taken from the lost parts of the work of Ammianus.[113]
The story of the war between the Goths and the
Gepidae,[114] and the account given of Geberich and of
Hermanaric[115] does not seem to be taken from Ammianus, for he says[116] that Hermanaric committed suicide through fear of the Huns, while Jordanes tells of
his murder by the brothers Sarus and Ammius. Mommsen
believed that the passages in the *Getica* based on extant
portions of Ammianus Marcellinus reveal how Jordanes
(or Cassiodorus) perverts the records in his zeal for the
Goths, pointing out as a notable instance of this the account of Fritigern's escape in XXVI 136-137 (see
commentary).

A Continuator of Marcellinus. In Mommsen's opinion some continuator has been made use of between the
excerpts from Ammianus, which end in XXVI 138, and
those from Priscus, which begin in XXXIV 178.[117]

---

[112] Ammianus Marcellinus 31, 5, 17.
[113] See also notes on XVI 93, XVIII 101, 103, XX 108.
[114] XVII.
[115] XXII, XXIII and XXIV.
[116] In 31, 3, 2.
[117] Koepke (Anfänge d. Königthums bei den Gothen p. 81) suggests Eunapius.

Marcellinus Comes. As this author's work[118] was not published until 534, Cassiodorus, writing between 526 and 533, could not have used it, but Jordanes evidently availed himself of this chronicle, probably in fuller form than the version we now possess, in writing the latter part of both his works.[119]

Mommsen believed that there are traces of *consularia* also in those part of the *Getica* which can be referred with reasonable assurance to Cassiodorus himself,[120] and that this chronicle began either from the end of Prosper or perhaps from the end of Hieronymus. Cassiodorus could not make use of his own annals (published in 519) on account of their brevity, but we find that such passages as he there changed (in abbreviating Prosper) because of his Gothic tendencies are similarly treated in the *Getica*, so that the germs of the greater work may be said to appear in the smaller.[121] In narrating the events of Theodoric's time, Cassiodorus availed himself of the so-called Ravenna Annals.

Prosper. Prosper of Aquitaine (b. about 400 A.D.) wrote a continuation of the chronicle of Hieronymus, covering the years 379-455. Cassiodorus used Prosper in writing his chronicle of the world (to the year 519), and also commended the work to his monks.[122] In

---

[118] A chronicle by Count Marcellinus, an Illyrian, exclusively on events in the eastern empire. It falls into three parts: (1) the chronicle proper, 379-518; (2) a continuation to 534; (3) a further continuation to 548.

[119] See what is said in *Romana* 388 of the *annales consulumque seriem.*

[120] In XLV and XLVI (on the years 455-477), and perhaps also in XXXII 165-166 (on the years 411-427).

[121] See the commentary on: XVIII 103 (Decius); XXVIII 144 (Athanaric); XXX 154 (Pollentia); XXX 156 (Capture of Rome); XXXII 166 ("Flight" of the Vandals into Spain); XL 209 (Battle of the Catalaunian Plains); XLII 221 (Siege of Aquileia).

[122] *Inst. div. litt.* 17.

XXXIV 177 the story of Litorius is taken over from Prosper, consuls and all,[128] and in XLII 223 the account of Pope Leo's embassy to Attila is from the same source. These passages must go back to Cassiodorus, for in the *Romana* there is no trace of Prosper.

Rufinus. Rufinus of Aquileia (about 345-410) devoted himself almost exclusively to the production of Latin versions of the works of the Greek patristic writers, and it is from one of these that Jordanes borrowed his preface to the *Getica.*[124]

Solinus. C. Iulius Solinus, the grammarian, who lived probably in the time before Diocletian, composed a *Collectanea rerum memorabilium,* based mainly on Pliny's Natural History, and containing a selection of the curiosities therein mentioned, arranged from a geographical point of view. While Cassiodorus probably did not make use of this writer directly, yet certain passages in the *Getica* (V 46, VII 53-55) so closely resemble the *Collectanea* as to suggest the inference that both writers drew from a common source.

A Geographical Map. Finally, it is Mommsen's belief that such geographical passages as the descriptions of Scythia,[125] Pannonia,[126] the Danube,[127] Scandza,[128] the mouths of the Vistula, and the river Vagus,[129] in which places are portrayed as they would appear on a map, are based upon an actual map. Even the list of the islands of the Indian Ocean[130] is given in exactly the same order

---

[128] See commentary on Litorius, XXXIV 177.
[124] See commentary on the preface to the *Getica.*
[125] V 30.
[126] L 264.
[127] XII 75.
[128] III 16.
[129] III 17.
[130] I 6.

as in the work of Julius Honorius who wrote from a map. Mommsen would ascribe to a like source five passages in which countries or tribes are located with reference to the points of the compass.[181] Now the provinces there mentioned are of the time before Diocletian, and the descriptions do not hold good for the time of Cassiodorus or Jordanes, but for about the second century, whereas the other names of localities and races found in the *Getica* accord properly with fifth century conditions. It would be difficult, however, to decide whether Cassiodorus actually made use of a map of the world as it was in the second century or merely of an epitome from such a map, like the extant books of Julius Honorius[182] and the Geographer of Ravenna.[183] As Cassiodorus[184] speaks highly of this very *Cosmographia* of Honorius, it not unlikely that he used it, perhaps in fuller form than it is now known.

To these Manitius (Neues Archiv 1888, pp. 213-214) would add the following as possible sources: Sallust, Jugurtha 60, 1 and 7 for XVII 99 and 100; Caesar, B. G. 8, 27 for XXXI 161; Martianus Capella 6, 628 for XLIV 230. But there is no evidence that Jordanes read or used these writers.

[181] Galicia XLIV 230, Pannonia L 264, the Vandals XXII 114, Dacia XII 74, Scythia V 31 (compare 33).
[182] This work, although dating from the 5th century, contains the names taken from a map constructed about 360 A.D.
[183] End of the 7th century.
[184] *Inst. div. litt.* 25.

3. CHRONOLOGICAL TABLE

(Following Gutschmid)

Jordanes says (LX 313), probably following the figures of Cassiodorus and adding in on his own account the fourteen years from the death of Theodoric in 526 to the capture of Vitiges in 540, that the Kingdom of the Goths endured 2030 years. This statement assigns the beginning of the Gothic Kingdom to the year 1490 B.C. Gutschmid (in Mommsen's preface, XX-XXI) sought to explain the chronology as follows:

Five generations of the first kings of the
Goths, from Berig to Filimer son of
Gadaric (IV 25, XXIV 121), about
167 years.   B.C. 1490^{1}–1324

Tanausis,[2] shortly before the Amazons
(VI 47, VII 49), about 33 years.   1323–1290

Three generations of Amazons (Lampeto and Marpesia, Menalippe and Hippolyte, Penthesilea), about 100 years
VII 52).   1289–1190

From the Trojan War, or the death of
Penthesilea (VIII 57), or the death of

---

[1] This year rests on the testimony of Herodotus, 4, 7: ἔτεα σφίσι (the Scythians) ἐπείτε γεγόνασι τὰ σύμπαντα λέγουσι εἶναι ἀπὸ τοῦ πρώτου βασιλέος Ταργιτάου ἐς τὴν Δαρείου διάβασιν τὴν ἐπὶ σφέας χιλίων οὐ πλέω ἀλλὰ τοσαῦτα. Hieronymus assigns the battle of Marathon to the year of Abraham 1525 = B.C. 492.

[2] Tanausis, a contemporary of Vesosis or Sesostris, reigned according to Eusebius from 1374-1319 B.C. Cassiodorus has assigned him a more reasonable date.

Eurypylus (IX 60), to the reign of Cyrus,[3] almost 630 years (X 61), actually
631.   1190–559

From Cyrus to Sulla   558–91

Buruista, king in Sulla's time (XI 67)   90–57

King Comosicus (XI 73)   56–23

The forty-year reign of Coryllus (XII 73)
   the time of Tiberius (XI 68)?   B.C. 22–18 A.D.

Interval of one generation (XIII 76)   19–50

Amali	*Balthae*	
Gapt[4]	King Dorpaneus time of Domitian (XIII 76)	51–83
Hulmul		84–117
Augis		118–150
Amal		151–183
Hisarnis		184–217
Ostrogotha	Nidada	218–250
Hunuil	Ovida (King Cniva? XVIII 101)	251–283
Athal	Hilderith	284–317
Achiulf	Geberich[5] (XXII 113)	318–350

[3] This is the year Jordanes meant, although he has indicated the last year of his reign.

[4] Accordingly both King Dorpaneus and the first of the Amali, whom Jordanes mentions together (XIII 78), lived in the reign of Domitian.

[5] Constantine, who established the Vandals in Pannonia (XXII 115) died in 337; if the Vandals lived there for 70 years (so Gutschmid would emend, in place of LX) they went off into Gaul in 406. Thus the victory of Geberich over the Vandals occurred in 336, approximately.

Hermanaric	351–376
Vinitharius	. . . .
Hunimund	. . . .
Thorismud	. . .404?
40-year interregnum (XLVIII 251)	405?–444?
Valamir	445?–. . .
Thiudimer	. . . .
Theodoric	475–526
Athalaric	526–534
Theodahad	534–536
Vitiges	536–540

Years of the reign of the Goths amount to 1490 + 540 = 2030 (LX 313).

KINGS OF THE VISIGOTHS

Alaric I	395–410
Athavulf	410–415
Segeric	415
Valia	415–419
Theodorid I	419–451
Thorismud	451–453
Theodorid II	453–466
Eurich	466–485

Friderich ⎫
Retemer ⎬ Brothers of the three preceding
Himnerith ⎭

Alaric II	485–507
Amalaric	507–531
Thiudis	531–548
Thiudigisclus	548–549
Agil	549–554
Athanagild	554–567

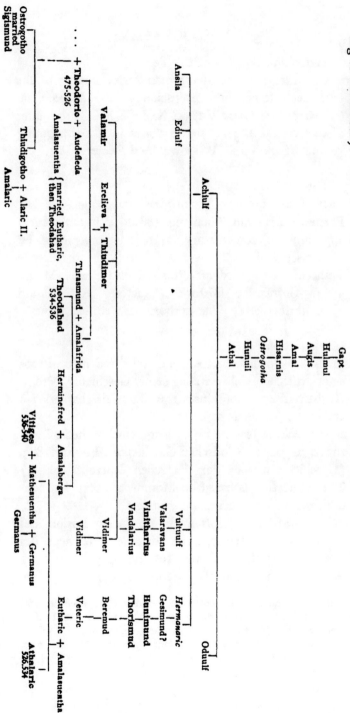

5. BIBLIOGRAPHY[1]

1. Manuscript Sources of the Text.

For a detailed account of the manuscript sources of the text, see Mommsen's discussion in the *Monumenta Germaniae Historica* V 1, pp. XLIV-LXX. For a later discussion see the article *Iordanes* in a forthcoming volume of the Pauly-Wissowa *Real Encyclopädie*.

2. Editions.[2]

Holder, A.: Iordanis, De origine actibusque Getarum. Freiburg I.B. und Tübingen 1882. Without critical apparatus or commentary, and fully superseded by Mommsen's edition.

Mommsen, Th.: Iordanis Romana et Getica. Monumenta Germaniae Historica, Auctores Antiquissimi V 1, Berlin 1882. The authoritative edition.

3. Translations.

Jordan, J.: Jordanes Leben und Schriften nebst Probe einer deutschen Uebersetzung seiner Geschichte. Progr. Ansbach 1843. Contains a translation of chapters 1-4 and 24-27, made as samples.

Martens, W.: Jordanes Gothengeschichte nebst Auszügen aus seiner Römischen Geschichte. Leipzig 1883. (Geschichtschreiber der deutschen Vorzeit Vol. 5.) The translation is based on Mommsen's text, but contains many inaccuracies and mistakes.

Savagner, M. A.: Jornandès de la succession des royaumes et des temps, et de l'origine et des actes des Goths. Paris 1842. A faithful rendering of an older text, in the main that of Muratori (1723).

[1] This bibliography does not give references to such general works as the histories of literature by Ebert, Manitius and Teuffel, Wattenbach's Geschichtsquellen, or similar general source books.

[2] Mommsen records nineteen editions that preceded his own, all now of little value.

4. Special Monographs, Journal Articles, and Reviews.

Arndt, W.: Review of Mommsen, in Literarisches Centralblatt 1883 N. 31 pp. 1060-1063.

Arndt, W.: Review of Holder, in Literarisches Centralblatt 1883 N. 36 p. 1263.

Bachmann, A: Zu Iordanis, in Neues Archiv der Gesellschaft für ältere deutsche Geschichtskunde 1898 (23) pp. 175-176.

Bergmüller, L.: Einige Bemerkungen zur Latinität des Jordanes. Progr. Augsburg 1903.

Cipolla, C.: Considerazioni sulle "Getica" di Jordanes e sulle loro relazioni colla Historia Getarum di Cassiodorio Senatore. Torino 1892. (Mem. della R. Accad. di Torino ser. II tom. 43, 116.)

Erhardt, L.: Review of Mommsen, Holder and Martens, in Historische Zeitschrift 1886 (56, or Neue Folge 20) N. 6 pp. 513-519.

Erhardt, L.: Review of Mommsen, in Göttingische gelehrte Anzeigen 1886 N. 17 pp. 669-708.

Frick, C.: Review of Cipolla, in Berliner philologische Wochenschrift 1894 N. 44 pp. 1387-1392.

Friedrich, J.: Ueber die kontroversen Fragen im Leben des Gotischen Geschichtschreibers Jordanes, in Sitzungsberichte der philosophisch-philologischen und der historischen Klasse der K.B. Akademie der Wissenschaften zu München 1907 pp. 379-442.

Grienberger, Th. v.: Die Vorfahren des Jordanes, in Germania 1889 pp. 406-409.

Grimm, Jac.: Ueber Iornandes und die Geten, Kleinere Schriften III pp. 171-235. Berlin 1866.

Gutschmid, A. v.: Review of Schirren, in Jahn's Jahrbücher für classische Philologie 1862 pp. 124-151. (Kleine Schriften V pp. 288-336, Leipzig 1894.)

Jordan, J.: see above, under Translations.

Köpke, R.: Die Anfänge des Königthums bei den Gothen pp. 44-77. Berlin 1859.

Manitius, M.: Zu Ekkehard und Jordanes, in Neues Archiv der Gesellschaft für ältere deutsche Geschichtskunde 1888 (13) pp. 213-214.

Manitius, M.: Geschichtliches aus mittelalterlichen Bibliothekskatalogen: Iordanis, in Neues Archiv 1907 (32) pp. 651-652.

Manitius, M.: Review of Bergmüller, in Wochenschrift für Klassische Philologie 1903 N. 44 pp. 1204-1207.

Manitius, M.: Review of Bergmüller, in Blätter für das Gymnasial-Schulwesen herausgegeben vom bayer. Gymnasialschulwesen 1904 I/II pp. 94-95.

Martens, W.: Review of Mommsen and Holder, in Literaturblatt für germanische und romanische Philologie 1883 N. 3 pp. 85-87.

Schirren, C.: de ratione quae inter Iordanem et Cassiodorium intercedat commentatio. Dorpat 1858.

Schirren, C.: Review of Mommsen and Holder, in Deutsche Literaturzeitung 1882 N. 40 pp. 1420-1424.

Simson, B. v.: Zu Jordanis, in Neues Archiv 1897 (22) pp. 741-747.

Sybel, H. v.: de fontibus libri Iordanis De origine actuque Getarum. Berlin 1838.

Sybel, H. v.: Review of Köpke and Schirren, in Historische Zeitschrift 1859 N. 2 pp. 511-516.

Usener, H.: Anecdoton Holderi, Festschrift zur Philologenversammlung in Wiesbaden 1877.

Weise, O.: Review of Bergmüller, in Neue Philologische Rundschau 1904 N. 23 pp. 539-540.

Werner, F.: Die Latinität der Getica des Jordanis. Halle 1908.

Wölfflin E.: Zur Latinität des Jordanes, in Archiv für Lateinische Lexicographie und Grammatik XI pp. 361-368. Leipzig 1900.

THE GOTHIC HISTORY
OF JORDANES

6. LITERARY ANALYSIS OF THE *GETICA*

[The Arabic numbers, printed in the Literary Analysis below and in the margin of the English version, correspond to the Arabic numbers which mark the sections in Mommsen's text.]

Preface 1-3

time of Constantine I. King Geberich conquers the Vandals. 111-115
King Hermanaric conquers the Heruli, Venethi and Aesti 116-120
[Origin and history of the Huns 121-128]
Battle of Hermanaric with the Huns. His death. The Goths separate into Visigoths and Ostrogoths. 129-130.

III The Divided Goths 131-314
1. The Visigoths 131-245
Fritigern with the Visigoths enters Thrace and the two Moesias 131-137
They defeat and slay the Emperor Valens 138
King Athanaric makes peace with Gratian and Theodosius I. Dies at Constantinople 139-144
The Visigoths, serving under Theodosius, conquer the usurper Eugenius 145
Deeds of Alaric I in the time of Arcadius and Honorius. His death 146-158
[Description of Ravenna 148-151]
Deeds and death of King Athavulf 159-163
King Segeric 163
Deeds of King Valia 164-175
[Digression: The Kingdom of the Vandals 166-173]
[Digression: Migration of the Amali to the Visigoths 174-175]
First breach between King Theodorid I and the Romans 176-177
[Character of Attila the Hun 178-183]
League of the Visigoths and Romans against Attila 184-191

THE ORIGIN AND DEEDS OF THE GOTHS

Preface

1   Though it had been my wish to glide in my little boat by the edge of the peaceful shore and, as a certain writer says, to catch little fishes from the pools of the ancients, you, brother Castalius, bid me set my sails toward the deep. You urge me to leave the little work I have in hand, that is, the abbreviation of the Chronicles, and to condense in my own style in this small book the twelve volumes of Senator on the origin and deeds of the Getae from olden time to the present day, descending

2 through the generations of the kings. Truly a hard command, and imposed by one who seems unwilling to realize the burden of the task. Nor do you note this, that my utterance is too slight to fill so magnificent a trumpet of speech as his. But worse than every other burden is the fact that I have no access to his books that I may follow his thought. Still—and let me lie not—I have in times past read the books a second time by his steward's loan for a three days' reading. The words I recall not, but the sense and the deeds related I think I retain entire. To

3 this I have added fitting matters from some Greek and Latin histories. I have also put in an introduction and a conclusion, and have inserted many things of my own authorship. Wherefore reproach me not, but receive and read with gladness what you have asked me to write. If aught be insufficiently spoken and you remember it, do you as a neighbor to our race add to it, praying for me, dearest brother. The Lord be with you. Amen.

Geographical Introduction

I Our ancestors, as Orosius relates, were of opinion   4
that the circle of the whole world was surrounded
by the girdle of Ocean on three sides. Its three parts
they called Asia, Europe and Africa. Concerning this
threefold division of the earth's extent there are almost
innumerable writers, who not only explain the situations
of cities and places, but also measure out the number of
miles and paces to give more clearness. Moreover they
locate the islands interspersed amid the waves, both the
greater and also the lesser islands, called the Cyclades or
Sporades, as situated in the vast flood of the Great Sea.
But the impassable farther bounds of Ocean not only has
no one attempted to describe, but no man has been allowed to reach; for by reason of obstructing seaweed and
the failing of the winds it is plainly inaccessible and is
unknown to any save to Him who made it. But the
nearer border of this sea, which we call the circle of the
world, surrounds its coasts like a wreath. This has
become clearly known to men of inquiring mind, even
to such as desired to write about it. For not only is the
coast itself inhabited, but certain islands off in the sea
are habitable. Thus there are to the East in the Indian
Ocean, Hippodes, Iamnesia, Solis Perusta (which though
not habitable, is yet of great length and breadth), besides
Taprobane, a fair island wherein there are towns or
estates and ten strongly fortified cities. But there is yet
another, the lovely Silefantina, and Theros also. These,
though not clearly described by any writer, are nevertheless well filled with inhabitants. This same Ocean has
in its western region certain islands known to almost
everyone by reason of the great number of those that
journey to and fro. And there are two not far from the
neighborhood of the Strait of Gades, one the Blessed
Isle and another called the Fortunate. Although some

OCEAN
AND ITS
LESSER ISLES

reckon as islands of Ocean the twin promontories of Galicia and Lusitania, where are still to be seen the Temple of Hercules on one and Scipio's Monument on the other, yet since they are joined to the extremity of the Galician country, they belong rather to the continent

8 of Europe than to the islands of Ocean. However, it has other islands deeper within its own tides, which are called the Baleares; and yet another, Mevania, besides the Orcades, thirty-three in number, though not all in-

9 habited. And at the farthest bound of its western expanse it has another island named Thule, of which the Mantuan bard makes mention:

"And Farthest Thule shall serve thee."

The same mighty sea has also in its arctic region, that is, in the north, a great island named Scandza, from which my tale (by God's grace) shall take its beginning. For the race whose origin you ask to know burst forth like a swarm of bees from the midst of this island and came into the land of Europe. But how or in what wise we shall explain hereafter, if it be the Lord's will.

10 II But now let me speak briefly as I can concerning the island of Britain, which is situated in the bosom of Ocean between Spain, Gaul and Germany. Although Livy tells us that no one in former days sailed around it, because of its great size, yet many writers have held various opinions about it. It was long unapproached by Roman arms, until Julius Caesar disclosed it by battles. fought for mere glory. In the busy age which followed it became accessible to many through trade and by other means. Thus it revealed more clearly its position, which I shall here explain as I have found it in Greek and Latin

11 authors. Most of them say it is like a triangle pointing between the north and west. Its widest angle faces the mouths of the Rhine. Then the island shrinks in breadth and recedes until it ends in two other angles. Its two

BRITAIN

Caesar's two
invasions
of Britain
B.C. 55-54

long sides face Gaul and Germany. Its greatest breadth
is said to be over two thousand three hundred and ten
stadia, and its length not more than seven thousand
one hundred and thirty-two stadia. In some parts   1.
it is moorland, in others there are wooded plains, and
sometimes it rises into mountain peaks. The island is
surrounded by a sluggish sea, which neither gives readily
to the stroke of the oar nor runs high under the blasts
of the wind. I suppose this is because other lands are
so far removed from it as to cause no disturbance of the
sea, which indeed is of greater width here than anywhere
else. Moreover Strabo, a famous writer of the Greeks,
relates that the island exhales such mists from its soil,
soaked by the frequent inroads of Ocean, that the sun is
covered throughout the whole of their disagreeable sort
of day that passes as fair, and so is hidden from sight.

Cornelius also, the author of the Annals, says that in   13
the farthest part of Britain the night gets brighter and
is very short. He also says that the island abounds in
metals, is well supplied with grass and is more productive in all those things which feed beasts rather than men.
Moreover many large rivers flow through it, and the
tides are borne back into them, rolling along precious
stones and pearls. The Silures have swarthy features
and are usually born with curly black hair, but the inhabitants of Caledonia have reddish hair and large loose-
jointed bodies. They are like the Gauls or the Spaniards,
according as they are opposite either nation. Hence some   14
have supposed that from these lands the island received
its inhabitants, alluring them by its nearness. All the
people and their kings are alike wild. Yet Dio, a most
celebrated writer of annals, assures us of the fact that
they have been combined under the name of Caledo-
nians and Maeatae. They live in wattled huts, a shelter
used in common with their flocks, and often the woods
are their home. They paint their bodies with iron-red,

whether by way of adornment or perhaps for some other
15   reason. They often wage war with one another, either
because they desire power or to increase their possessions.
They fight not only on horseback or on foot, but even
with scythed two-horse chariots, which they commonly
call *essedae*. Let it suffice to have said thus much on the
shape of the island of Britain.

16   III Let us now return to the site of the island of   SCANDZA
Scandza, which we left above. Claudius Ptolemaeus, an
excellent describer of the world, has made mention of it
in the second book of his work, saying: "There is a
great island situated in the surge of the northern Ocean,
Scandza by name, in the shape of a juniper leaf with
bulging sides which taper to a point at a long end."
Pomponius Mela also makes mention of it as situated in
the Codan Gulf of the sea, with Ocean lapping its shores.

17   This island lies in front of the river Vistula, which rises
in the Sarmatian mountains and flows through its triple
mouth into the northern Ocean in sight of Scandza, separating Germany and Scythia. The island has in its
eastern part a vast lake in the bosom of the earth, whence
the Vagus river springs from the bowels of the earth and
flows surging into the Ocean. And on the west it is surrounded by an immense sea. On the north it is bounded
by the same vast unnavigable Ocean, from which by
means of a sort of projecting arm of land a bay is cut off

18   and forms the German Sea. Here also there are said to
be many small islands scattered round about. If wolves
cross over to these islands when the sea is frozen by
reason of the great cold, they are said to lose their sight.
Thus the land is not only inhospitable to men but cruel
even to wild beasts.

19   Now in the island of Scandza, whereof I speak, there
dwell many and divers nations, though Ptolemaeus mentions the names of but seven of them. There the honey-
making swarms of bees are nowhere to be found on

account of the exceeding great cold. In the northern part
of the island the race of the Adogit live, who are said
to have continual light in midsummer for forty days and
nights, and who likewise have no clear light in the winter
season for the same number of days and nights. By   20
reason of this alternation of sorrow and joy they are like
no other race in their sufferings and blessings. And why?
Because during the longer days they see the sun returning
to the east along the rim of the horizon, but on the shorter
days it is not thus seen. The sun shows itself differently
because it is passing through the southern signs, and
whereas to us the sun is seen to rise from below, it is said
to go around them along the edge of the earth. There
also are other peoples. There are the Screrefennae, who   21
do not seek grain for food but live on the flesh of wild
beasts and birds' eggs; for there are such multitudes of
young game in the swamps as to provide for the natural
increase of their kind and to afford satisfaction to the
needs of the people. But still another race dwells there,
the Suehans, who, like the Thuringians, have splendid
horses. Here also are those who send through innumerable other tribes the sapphire colored skins to trade for
Roman use. They are a people famed for the dark beauty
of their furs and, though living in poverty, are most richly
clothed. Then comes a throng of various nations, Theu-   2
stes, Vagoth, Bergio, Hallin, Liothida. All their habita-
tions are in one level and fertile region. Wherefore they
are disturbed there by the attacks of other tribes. Behind
these are the Ahelmil, Finnaithae, Fervir and Gauthigoth,
a race of men bold and quick to fight. Then come the
Mixi, Evagre, and Otingis. All these live like wild animals in rocks hewn out like castles. And there are be-   2
yond these the Ostrogoths, Raumarici, Aeragnaricii, and
the most gentle Finns, milder than all the inhabitants of
Scandza. Like them are the Vinovilith also. The Suetidi
are of this stock and excell the rest in stature. However,

the Dani, who trace their origin to the same stock, drove
from their homes the Heruli, who lay claim to preëmi-
nence among all the nations of Scandza for their tallness.

24 Furthermore there are in the same neighborhood the
Grannii, Augandzi, Eunixi, Taetel, Rugi, Arochi and
Ranii, over whom Roduulf was king not many years ago.
But he despised his own kingdom and fled to the embrace
of Theodoric, king of the Goths, finding there what he
desired. All these nations surpassed the Germans in size
and spirit, and fought with the cruelty of wild beasts.

The United Goths

25 IV Now from this island of Scandza, as from a hive
of races or a womb of nations, the Goths are said to have
come forth long ago under their king, Berig by name.
As soon as they disembarked from their ships and set
foot on the land, they straightway gave their name to the
place. And even to-day it is said to be called Gothi-
26 scandza. (Soon they moved from here to the abodes of
the Ulmerugi, who then dwelt on the shores of Ocean,
where they pitched camp, joined battle with them and
drove them from their homes. Then they subdued their
neighbors, the Vandals, and thus added to their victories.
But when the number of the people increased greatly and
Filimer, son of Gadaric, reigned as king—about the fifth
since Berig—he decided that the army of the Goths with
27 their families should move from that region. In search
of suitable homes and pleasant places they came to the
land of Scythia, called *Oium* in that tongue. Here they
were delighted with the great richness of the country,
and it is said that when half the army had been brought
over, the bridge whereby they had crossed the river fell
in utter ruin, nor could anyone thereafter pass to or fro.
For the place is said to be surrounded by quaking bogs
and an encircling abyss, so that by this double obstacle
nature has made it inaccessible. And even to-day one

HOW THE
GOTHS CAME
TO SCYTHIA

may hear in that neighborhood the lowing of cattle and may find traces of men, if we are to believe the stories of travellers, although we must grant that they hear these things from afar.

This part of the Goths, which is said to have crossed the river and entered with Filimer into the country of Oium, came into possession of the desired land, and there they soon came upon the race of the Spali, joined battle with them and won the victory. Thence the victors hastened to the farthest part of Scythia, which is near the sea of Pontus; for so the story is generally told in their early songs, in almost historic fashion. Ablabius also, a famous chronicler of the Gothic race, confirms this in his most trustworthy account. Some of the ancient writers also agree with the tale. Among these we may mention Josephus, a most reliable relator of annals, who everywhere follows the rule of truth and unravels from the beginning the origin of things;—but why he has omitted the beginnings of the race of the Goths, of which I have spoken, I do not know. He barely mentions Magog of that stock, and says they were Scythians by race and were called so by name.

Before we enter on our history, we must describe the boundaries of this land, as it lies.

SCYTHIA

V Now Scythia borders on the land of Germany as far as the source of the river Ister and the expanse of the Morsian Swamp. It reaches even to the rivers Tyra, Danaster and Vagosola, and the great Danaper, extending to the Taurus range—not the mountains in Asia but our own, that is, the Scythian Taurus—all the way to Lake Maeotis. Beyond Lake Maeotis it spreads on the other side of the straits of Bosphorus to the Caucasus Mountains and the river Araxes. Then it bends back to the left behind the Caspian Sea, which comes from the northeastern ocean in the most distant parts of Asia, and so is formed like a mushroom, at first narrow and then

broad and round in shape. It extends as far as the Huns,
31 Albani and Seres. This land, I say—namely, Scythia,
stretching far and spreading wide—has on the east the
Seres, a race that dwelt at the very beginning of their
history on the shore of the Caspian Sea. On the west are
the Germans and the river Vistula; on the arctic side,
namely the north, it is surrounded by Ocean; on the south
by Persis, Albania, Hiberia, Pontus and the farthest
channel of the Ister, which is called the Danube all the
32 way from mouth to source. But in that region where
Scythia touches the Pontic coast it is dotted with towns
of no mean fame:—Borysthenis, Olbia, Callipolis, Cherson, Theodosia, Careon, Myrmicion and Trapezus. These
towns the wild Scythian tribes allowed the Greeks to build
to afford them means of trade. In the midst of Scythia is
the place that separates Asia and Europe, I mean the
Rhipaeian mountains, from which the mighty Tanais
flows. This river enters Maeotis, a marsh having a circuit of one hundred and four miles and never sub-
siding to a depth of less than eight cubits.
33 In the land of Scythia to the westward dwells, first of
all, the race of the Gepidae, surrounded by great and
famous rivers. For the Tisia flows through it on the
north and northwest, and on the southwest is the great
Danube. On the east it is cut by the Flutausis, a swiftly
eddying stream that sweeps whirling into the Ister's
34 waters. Within these rivers lies Dacia, encircled by the
lofty Alps as by a crown. Near their left ridge, which
inclines toward the north, and beginning at the source of
the Vistula, the populous race of the Venethi dwell, occupying a great expanse of land. Though their names are
now dispersed amid various clans and places, yet they are
35 chiefly called Sclaveni and Antes. The abode of the
Sclaveni extends from the city of Noviodunum and the
lake called Mursianus to the Danaster, and northward as
far as the Vistula. They have swamps and forests for

their cities. The Antes, who are the bravest of these
peoples dwelling in the curve of the sea of Pontus, spread
from the Danaster to the Danaper, rivers that are many
days' journey apart. But on the shore of Ocean, where   36
the floods of the river Vistula empty from three mouths,
the Vidivarii dwell, a people gathered out of various
tribes. Beyond them the Aesti, a subject race, likewise
hold the shore of Ocean. To the south dwell the Acatziri
a very brave tribe ignorant of agriculture, who subsist
on their flocks and by hunting. Farther away and above   37
the Sea of Pontus are the abodes of the Bulgares, well
known from the disasters our neglect has brought
upon us. From this region the Huns, like a fruitful
root of bravest races, sprouted into two hordes of people.
Some of these are called Altziagiri, others Sabiri; and
they have different dwelling places. The Altziagiri are
near Cherson, where the avaricious traders bring in the
goods of Asia. In summer they range the plains, their
broad domains, wherever the pasturage for their cattle
invites them, and betake themselves in winter beyond the
sea of Pontus. Now the Hunuguri are known to us from
the fact that they trade in marten skins. But they have
been cowed by their bolder neighbors.

THE
THREE ABODES
OF THE GOTHS

We read that in their first abode the Goths dwelt   38
in the land of Scythia near Lake Maeotis; in their
second in Moesia, Thrace and Dacia, and in their
third they dwelt again in Scythia, above the sea of
Pontus. Nor do we find anywhere in their written
records legends which tell of their subjection to
slavery in Britain or in some other island, or of their
redemption by a certain man at the cost of a single horse.
Of course if anyone in our city says that the Goths had an
origin different from that I have related, let him object.
For myself, I prefer to believe what I have read, rather
than put trust in old wives' tales.

39   To return, then, to my subject. The aforesaid race of which I speak is known to have had Filimer as king while they remained in their first home in Scythia near Maeotis. In their second home, that is, in the countries of Dacia, Thrace and Moesia, Zalmoxes reigned, whom many writers of annals mention as a man of remarkable learning in philosophy. Yet even before this they had a learned man Zeuta, and after him Dicineus; and the third was Zalmoxes of whom I have made mention above. Nor did

40 they lack teachers of wisdom. Wherefore the Goths have ever been wiser than other barbarians and were nearly like the Greeks, as Dio relates, who wrote their history and annals with a Greek pen. He says that those of noble birth among them, from whom their kings and priests were appointed, were called first Tarabostesei and then Pilleati. Moreover so highly were the Getae praised that Mars, whom the fables of poets call the god of war, was reputed to have been born among them. Hence Vergil says:

41   "Father Gradivus rules the Getic fields."

Now Mars has always been worshipped by the Goths with cruel rites, and captives were slain as his victims. They thought that he who is lord of war ought to be appeased by the shedding of human blood. To him they devoted the first share of the spoil, and in his honor arms stripped from the foe were suspended from trees. And they had more than all other races a deep spirit of religion, since the worship of this god seemed to be really bestowed upon their ancestor.

42   In their third dwelling place, which was above the Sea of Pontus, they had now become more civilized and, as I have said before, were more learned. Then the people were divided under ruling families. The Visigoths served the family of the Balthi and the Ostrogoths served the

43 renowned Amali. They were the first race of men to string the bow with cords, as Lucan, who is more of a historian than a poet, affirms:

"They string Armenian bows with Getic cords."

In earliest times they sang of the deeds of their ancestors in strains of song accompanied by the cithara; chanting of Eterpamara, Hanala, Fritigern, Vidigoia and others whose fame among them is great; such heroes as admiring antiquity scarce proclaims its own to be. Then, as the story goes, Vesosis waged a war disastrous to himself against the Scythians, whom ancient tradition asserts to have been the husbands of the Amazons. Concerning these female warriors Orosius speaks in convincing language. Thus we can clearly prove that Vesosis then fought with the Goths, since we know surely that he waged war with the husbands of the Amazons. They dwelt at that time along a bend of Lake Maeotis, from the river Borysthenes, which the natives call the Danaper, to the stream of the Tanais. By the Tanais I mean the river which flows down from the Rhipaeian mountains and rushes with so swift a current that when the neighboring streams or Lake Maeotis and the Bosphorus are frozen fast, it is the only river that is kept warm by the rugged mountains and is never solidified by the Scythian cold. It is also famous as the boundary of Asia and Europe. For the other Tanais is the one which rises in the mountains of the Chrinni and flows into the Caspian Sea. The Danaper begins in a great marsh and issues from it as from its mother. It is sweet and fit to drink as far as half-way down its course. It also produces fish of a fine flavor and without bones, having only cartilage as the frame-work of their bodies. But as it approaches the Pontus it receives a little stream called Exampaeus, so very bitter that although the river is navigable for the length of a forty days' voyage, it is so altered by the water of this scanty stream as to become tainted and unlike itself, and flows thus tainted into the sea between the Greek towns of Callipidae and Hypanis. At its mouth there is an island named Achilles. Between these two

THE RIVER DON

THE DNIEPER

rivers is a vast land filled with forests and treacherous
swamps.

47   VI   This was the region where the Goths dwelt when
Vesosis, king of the Egyptians, made war upon them.
Their king at that time was Tanausis. In a battle at the
river Phasis (whence come the birds called pheasants,
which are found in abundance at the banquets of the great
all over the world) Tanausis, king of the Goths, met
Vesosis, king of the Egyptians, and there inflicted a
severe defeat upon him, pursuing him even to Egypt.
Had he not been restrained by the waters of the impassable Nile and the fortifications which Vesosis had long
ago ordered to be made against the raids of the Ethio-
pians, he would have slain him in his own land. But
finding he had no power to injure him there, he returned
and conquered almost all Asia and made it subject and
tributary to Sornus, king of the Medes, who was then his
dear friend. At that time some of his victorious army,
seeing that the subdued provinces were rich and fruitful, deserted their companies and of their own accord
remained in various parts of Asia.

48   From their name or race Pompeius Trogus says the
stock of the Parthians had its origin. Hence even to-day
in the Scythian tongue they are called Parthi, that is,
Deserters. And in consequence of their descent they are
archers—almost alone among all the nations of Asia—
and are very valiant warriors. Now in regard to the
name, though I have said they were called Parthi because
they were deserters, some have traced the derivation of
the word otherwise, saying that they were called Parthi
because they fled from their kinsmen. Now when this
Tanausis, king of the Goths, was dead, his people worshipped him as one of their gods.

49   VII   After his death, while the army under his successors was engaged in an expedition in other parts, a
neighboring tribe attempted to carry off women of the

DEFEAT OF
VESOSIS
(SESOSTRIS)

Goths as booty. But they made a brave resistance, as they had been taught to do by their husbands, and routed in disgrace the enemy who had come upon them. When they had won this victory, they were inspired with greater daring. Mutually encouraging each other, they took up arms and chose two of the bolder, Lampeto and Marpesia, to act as their leaders. While they were in command, they cast lots both for the defense of their own country and the devastation of other lands. So Lampeto remained to guard their native land and Marpesia took a company of women and led this novel army into Asia. After conquering various tribes in war and making others their allies by treaties, she came to the Caucasus. There she remained for some time and gave the place the name Rock of Marpesia, of which also Vergil makes mention:

"Like to hard flint or the Marpesian Cliff."

It was here Alexander the Great afterwards built gates and named them the Caspian Gates, which now the tribe of the Lazi guard as a Roman outpost. Here, then, the Amazons remained for some time and were much strengthened. Then they departed and crossed the river Halys, which flows near the city of Gangra, and with equal success subdued Armenia, Syria, Cilicia, Galatia, Pisidia and all the places of Asia. Then they turned to Ionia and Aeolia, and made provinces of them after their surrender. Here they ruled for some time and even founded cities and camps bearing their name. At Ephesus also they built a very costly and beautiful temple for Diana, because of her delight in archery and the chase— arts to which they were themselves devoted. Then these Scythian-born women, who had by such a chance gained control over the kingdoms of Asia, held them for almost a hundred years, and at last came back to their own kinsfolk in the Marpesian rocks I have mentioned above, namely the Caucasus mountains.

Inasmuch as I have twice mentioned this mountain-range, I think it not out of place to describe its extent and situation, for, as is well known, it encompasses a great

53 part of the earth with its continuous chain. Beginning at the Indian Ocean, where it faces the south it is warm, giving off vapor in the sun; where it lies open to the north it is exposed to chill winds and frost. Then bending back into Syria with a curving turn, it not only sends forth many other streams, but pours from its plenteous breasts into the Vasianensian region the Euphrates and the Tigris, navigable rivers famed for their unfailing springs. These rivers surround the land of the Syrians and cause it to be called Mesopotamia, as it truly is. Their

54 waters empty into the bosom of the Red Sea. Then turning back to the north, the range I have spoken of passes with great bends through the Scythian lands. There it sends forth very famous rivers into the Caspian Sea—the Araxes, the Cyrus and the Cambyses. It goes on in continuous range even to the Rhipaeian mountains. Thence it descends from the north toward the Pontic Sea, furnishing a boundary to the Scythian tribes by its ridge, and even touches the waters of the Ister with its clustered hills. Being cut by this river, it divides, and in Scythia

55 is named Taurus also. Such then is the great range, almost the mightiest of mountain chains, rearing aloft its summits and by its natural conformation supplying men with impregnable strongholds. Here and there it divides where the ridge breaks apart and leaves a deep gap, thus forming now the Caspian Gates, and again the Armenian or the Cilician, or of whatever name the place may be. Yet they are barely passable for a wagon, for both sides are sharp and steep as well as very high. The range has different names among various peoples. The Indian calls it Imaus and in another part Paropamisus. The Parthian calls it first Choatras and afterward Niphates; the Syrian and Armenian call it Taurus; the Scythian names it Cau-

casus and Rhipaeus, and at its end calls it Taurus. Many other tribes have given names to the range. Now that we have devoted a few words to describing its extent, let us return to the subject of the Amazons from which we have digressed.

THE
AMAZONS

VIII   Fearing their race would fail, they sought marriage with neighboring tribes. They appointed a day for meeting once in every year, so that when they should return to the same place on that day in the following year each mother might give over to the father whatever male child she had borne, but should herself keep and train for warfare whatever children of the female sex were born. Or else, as some maintain, they exposed the males, destroying the life of the ill-fated child with a hate like that of a stepmother. Among them childbearing was detested, though everywhere else it is desired. The terror of their cruelty was increased by common rumor; for what hope, pray, would there be for a captive, when it was considered wrong to spare even a son?. Hercules, they say fought against them and overcame Menalippe, yet more by guile than by valor. Theseus, moreover, took Hippolyte captive, and of her he begat Hippolytus. And in later times the Amazons had a queen named Penthesilea, famed in the tales of the Trojan war. These women are said to have kept their power even to the time of Alexander the Great.

REIGN
OF TELEFUS
AND
EURYPYLUS

IX   But say not "Why does a story which deals with the men of the Goths have so much to say of their women?" Hear, then, the tale of the famous and glorious valor of the men. Now Dio, the historian and diligent investigator of ancient times, who gave to his work the title "Getica" (and the Getae we have proved in a previous passage to be Goths, on the testimony of Orosius Paulus)—this Dio, I say, makes mention of a later king of theirs named Telefus. Let no one say that this name is quite foreign to the Gothic tongue, and let no one who is ignorant cavil at the fact that the tribes of men make

use of many names, even as the Romans borrow from the
Macedonians, the Greeks from the Romans, the Sarmatians from the Germans, and the Goths frequently from
the Huns. [This Telefus, then, a son of Hercules by
Auge, and the husband of a sister of Priam, was of
towering stature and terrible strength.] He matched his
father's valor by virtues of his own and also recalled the
traits of Hercules by his likeness in appearance. Our
ancestors called his kingdom Moesia. This province has
on the east the mouths of the Danube, on the south
Macedonia, on the west Histria and on the north the
Danube. Now this king we have mentioned carried on
wars with the Greeks, and in their course he slew in battle
Thesander, the leader of Greece. But while he was making a hostile attack upon Ajax and was pursuing Ulysses,
his horse became entangled in some vines and fell. He
himself was thrown and wounded in the thigh by a javelin
of Achilles, so that for a long time he could not be healed.
Yet, despite his wound, he drove the Greeks from his
land. Now when Telefus died, his son Eurypylus succeeded to the throne, being a son of the sister of Priam,
king of the Phrygians. For love of Cassandra he sought
to take part in the Trojan war, that he might come to the
help of her parents and his own father-in-law; but soon
after his arrival he was killed.

X   Then Cyrus, king of the Persians, after a long
interval of almost exactly six hundred and thirty years
(as Pompeius Trogus relates), waged an unsuccessful
war against Tomyris, queen of the Getae. Elated by his
victories in Asia, he strove to conquer the Getae, whose
queen, as I have said, was Tomyris. Though she could
have stopped the approach of Cyrus at the river Araxes,
yet she permitted him to cross, preferring to overcome
him in battle rather than to thwart him by advantage of
position. And so she did. As Cyrus approached, fortune
at first so favored the Parthians that they slew the son

Cyrus the
Great
B.C. 559-529

QUEEN
TOMYRIS AND
CYRUS
B.C. 529

of Tomyris and most of the army. But when the battle
was renewed, the Getae and their queen defeated, conquered and overwhelmed the Parthians and took rich
plunder from them. There for the first time the race of
the Goths saw silken tents. After achieving this victory
and winning so much booty from her enemies, Queen
Tomyris crossed over into that part of Moesia which is
now called Lesser Scythia—a name borrowed from great
Scythia—and built on the Moesian shore of Pontus the
city of Tomi, named after herself.

Darius
B.C. 521-485

Afterwards Darius, king of the Persians, the son of
Hystaspes, demanded in marriage the daughter of Antyrus, king of the Goths, asking for her hand and at the
same time making threats in case they did not fulfil his
wish. The Goths spurned this alliance and brought his

DARIUS
REPELLED

embassy to naught. Inflamed with anger because his
offer had been rejected, he led an army of seven hundred
thousand armed men against them and sought to avenge
his wounded feelings by inflicting a public injury. Crossing on boats covered with boards and joined like a bridge
almost the whole way from Chalcedon to Byzantium, he
started for Thrace and Moesia. Later he built a bridge
over the Danube in like manner, but he was wearied by
two brief months of effort and lost eight thousand armed
men at Tapae. Then, fearing the bridge over the Danube
would be seized by his foes, he marched back to Thrace
in swift retreat, believing the land of Moesia would not
be safe for even a short sojourn there.

Xerxes
B.C. 485-465

After his death, his son Xerxes planned to avenge his
father's wrongs and so proceeded to undertake a war
against the Goths with seven hundred thousand of his
own men and three hundred thousand armed auxiliaries,
twelve hundred ships of war and three thousand trans-
ports. But he did not venture to try them in battle, being
overawed by their unyielding courage. So he returned
with his force just as he had come, and without fighting
a single battle.

65   Then Philip, the father of Alexander the Great, made alliance with the Goths and took to wife Medopa, the daughter of King Gudila, so that he might render the kingdom of Macedon more secure by the help of this marriage. It was at this time, as the historian Dio relates, that Philip, suffering from need of money, determined to lead out his forces and sack Odessus, a city of Moesia, which was then subject to the Goths by reason of the neighboring city of Tomi. Thereupon those priests of the Goths that are called the Holy Men suddenly opened the gates of Odessus and came forth to meet them. They bore harps and were clad in snowy robes, and chanted in suppliant strains to the gods of their fathers that they might be propitious and repel the Macedonians. When the Macedonians saw them coming with such confidence to meet them, they were astonished and, so to speak, the armed were terrified by the unarmed. Straightway they broke the line they had formed for battle and not only refrained from destroying the city, but even gave back those whom they had captured outside by right of war. Then they made a truce and returned to their own country.

66   After a long time Sitalces, a famous leader of the Goths, remembering this treacherous attempt, gathered a hundred and fifty thousand men and made war upon the Athenians, fighting against Perdiccas, King of Macedon. This Perdiccas had been left by Alexander as his successor to rule Athens by hereditary right, when he drank his destruction at Babylon through the treachery of an attendant. The Goths engaged in a great battle with him and proved themselves to be the stronger. Thus in return for the wrong which the Macedonians had long before committed in Moesia, the Goths overran Greece and laid waste the whole of Macedonia.

67   XI Then when Buruista was king of the Goths, Dicineus came to Gothia at the time when Sulla ruled the

Philip of Macedon B.C. 359-336

SIEGE OF ODESSUS

Sulla's Dictatorship B.C. 82-79

Romans. Buruista received Dicineus and gave him almost royal power. It was by his advice the Goths ravaged
the lands of the Germans, which the Franks now possess.

THE WISE
RULE OF
DICINEUS

Then came Caesar, the first of all the Romans to assume
imperial power and to subdue almost the whole world,
who conquered all kingdoms and even seized islands lying
beyond our world, reposing in the bosom of Ocean. He

Caesar's
Dictatorship
B.C. 49-44

made tributary to the Romans those that knew not the
Roman name even by hearsay, and yet was unable to prevail against the Goths, despite his frequent attempts.

Tiberius
A.D. 14-37

Soon Gaius Tiberius reigned as third emperor of the
Romans, and yet the Goths continued in their kingdom
unharmed. Their safety, their advantage, their one hope
lay in this, that whatever their counsellor Dicineus advised should by all means be done; and they judged it
expedient that they should labor for its accomplishment.
And when he saw that their minds were obedient to him
in all things and that they had natural ability, he taught
them almost the whole of philosophy, for he was a skilled
master of this subject. Thus by teaching them ethics he
restrained their barbarous customs; by imparting a knowledge of physics he made them live naturally under laws
of their own, which they possess in written form to this
day and call *belagines*. He taught them logic and made
them skilled in reasoning beyond all other races; he
showed them practical knowledge and so persuaded them
to abound in good works. By demonstrating theoretical
knowledge he urged them to contemplate the courses of
the twelve signs and of the planets passing through them,
and the whole of astronomy. He told them how the disc
of the moon gains increase or suffers loss, and showed
them how much the fiery globe of the sun exceeds in size
our earthly planet. He explained the names of the three
hundred and forty-six stars and told through what signs
in the arching vault of the heavens they glide swiftly from
their rising to their setting. Think, I pray you, what

pleasure it was for these brave men, when for a little space they had leisure from warfare, to be instructed in the teachings of philosophy! You might have seen one scanning the position of the heavens and another investigating the nature of plants and bushes. Here stood one who studied the waxing and waning of the moon, while still another regarded the labors of the sun and observed how those bodies which were hastening to go toward the east are whirled around and borne back to the west by the rotation of the heavens. When they had learned the

71 reason, they were at rest. These and various other matters Dicineus taught the Goths in his wisdom and gained marvellous repute among them, so that he ruled not only the common men but their kings. He chose from among them those that were at that time of noblest birth and superior wisdom and taught them theology, bidding them worship certain divinities and holy places. He gave the name of Pilleati to the priests he ordained, I suppose because they offered sacrifice having their heads covered

72 with tiaras, which we otherwise call *pillei*. But he bade them call the rest of their race Capillati. This name the Goths accepted and prized highly, and they retain it to this day in their songs.

73 After the death of Dicineus, they held Comosicus in almost equal honor, because he was not inferior in knowledge. By reason of his wisdom he was accounted their priest and king, and he judged the people with the greatest uprightness.

XII When he too had departed from human affairs, Coryllus ascended the throne as king of the Goths and for forty years ruled his people in Dacia. I mean ancient

74 Dacia, which the race of the Gepidae now possesses. This country lies across the Danube within sight of Moesia, and is surrounded by a crown of mountains. It has only two ways of access, one by way of Boutae and the other by Tapae. This Gothia, which our ancestors

DACIA

called Dacia and now, as I have said, is called Gepidia, was then bounded on the east by the Roxolani, on the west by the Iazyges, on the north by the Sarmatians and Basternae and on the south by the river Danube. The Iazyges are separated from the Roxolani by the Aluta river only.

THE
DANUBE

And since mention has been made of the Danube, I   75 think it not out of place to make brief notice of so excellent a stream. Rising in the fields of the Alamanni, it receives sixty streams which flow into it here and there in the twelve hundred miles from its source to its mouths in the Pontus, resembling a spine inwoven with ribs like a basket. It is indeed a most vast river. In the language of the Bessi it is called the Hister, and it has profound waters in its channel to a depth of quite two hundred feet. This stream surpasses in size all other rivers, except the Nile. Let this much suffice for the Danube. But let us now with the Lord's help return to the subject from which we have digressed.

Domitian
A.D. 81-96

XIII Now after a long time, in the reign of the   76 Emperor Domitian, the Goths, through fear of his avarice, broke the truce they had long observed under other emperors. They laid waste the bank of the Danube, so

WAR WITH
DOMITIAN

long held by the Roman Empire, and slew the soldiers and their generals. Oppius Sabinus was then governor of that province, after Agrippa, while Dorpaneus held command over the Goths. Thereupon the Goths made war and conquered the Romans, cut off the head of Oppius Sabinus and invaded and boldly plundered many castles and cities belonging to the Emperor. In this plight   77 of his countrymen Domitian hastened with all his might to Illyricum, bringing with him the troops of almost the entire empire. He sent Fuscus before him as his general with picked soldiers. Then joining boats together like a bridge, he made his soldiers cross the river Danube above the army of Dorpaneus. But the Goths   78 were on the alert. They took up arms and presently over-

whelmed the Romans in the first encounter. They slew
Fuscus, the commander, and plundered the soldiers' camp
of its treasure. And because of the great victory they
had won in this region, they thereafter called their leaders, by whose good fortune they seemed to have conquered, not mere men, but demigods, that is *Ansis.* Their
genealogy I shall run through briefly, telling the lineage
of each and the beginning and the end of this line. And
do thou, O reader, hear me without repining; for I speak
truly.

79   XIV Now the first of these heroes, as they themselves relate in their legends, was Gapt, who begat
Hulmul. And Hulmul begat Augis; and Augis begat
him who was called Amal, from whom the name of the
Amali comes. This Amal begat Hisarnis. Hisarnis
moreover begat Ostrogotha, and Ostrogotha begat Hunuil, and Hunuil likewise begat Athal. Athal begat
Achiulf and Oduulf. Now Achiulf begat Ansila and
Ediulf, Vultuulf and Hermanaric. And Vultuulf begat
Valaravans and Valaravans begat Vinitharius. Vinitha-
80 rius moreover begat Vandalarius; Vandalarius begat
Thiudimer and Valamir and Vidimer; and Thiudimer
begat Theodoric. Theodoric begat Amalasuentha; Amalasuentha bore Athalaric and Mathesuentha to her husband Eutharic, whose race was thus joined to hers in
81 kinship. For the aforesaid Hermanaric, the son of
Achiulf, begat Hunimund, and Hunimund begat Thorismud. Now Thorismud begat Beremud, Beremud begat
Veteric, and Veteric likewise begat Eutharic, who married Amalasuentha and begat Athalaric and Mathesuentha. Athalaric died in the years of his childhood, and
Mathesuentha married Vitiges, to whom she bore no
child. Both of them were taken together by Belisarius to
Constantinople. When Vitiges passed from human affairs, Germanus the patrician, a nephew of the Emperor
Justinian, took Mathesuentha in marriage and made her

GENEALOGY OF THE ANSIS OR AMALI

a Patrician Ordinary. And of her he begat a son, also called Germanus. But upon the death of Germanus, she determined to remain a widow. Now how and in what wise the kingdom of the Amali was overthrown we shall keep to tell in its proper place, if the Lord help us.

But let us now return to the point whence we made our digression and tell how the stock of this people of whom I speak reached the end of its course. Now Ablabius the historian relates that in Scythia, where we have said that they were dwelling above an arm of the Pontic Sea, part of them who held the eastern region and whose king was Ostrogotha, were call Ostrogoths, that is, eastern Goths, either from his name or from the place. But the rest were called Visigoths, that is, the Goths of the western country.

XV   As already said, they crossed the Danube and dwelt a little while in Moesia and Thrace. From the remnant of these came Maximin, the Emperor succeeding Alexander the son of Mamaea. For Symmachus relates it thus in the fifth book of his history, saying that upon the death of Caesar Alexander, Maximin was made Emperor by the army; a man born in Thrace of most humble parentage, his father being a Goth named Micca, and his mother a woman of the Alani called Ababa. He reigned three years and lost alike his empire and his life while making war on the Christians. Now after his first years spent in rustic life, he had come from his flocks to military service in the reign of the Emperor Severus and at the time when the latter was celebrating his son's birthday. It happened that the Emperor was giving military games. When Maximin saw this, although he was a semi-barbarian youth, he besought the Emperor in his native tongue to give him permission to wrestle with the trained soldiers for the prizes offered. Severus marvelling much at his great size—for his stature, it is said, was more than eight feet—bade him contend in wrestling

MAXIMIN,
THE GOTH
WHO BECAME
A ROMAN
EMPEROR

Septimius
Severus
A.D. 193-211

with the camp followers, in order that no injury might
befall his soldiers at the hands of this wild fellow. Thereupon Maximin threw sixteen attendants with so great
ease that he conquered them one by one without taking
any rest by pausing between the bouts. So then, when
he had won the prizes he was ordered into the army
and served his first campaign with the cavalry. On
the third day after this, when the Emperor went out
to the field, he saw him coursing about in barbarian
fashion and bade a tribune restrain him and teach
him Roman discipline. But when he understood that
the Emperor was speaking about him, he came for-
86 ward and began to run ahead of him as he rode. Then
the Emperor spurred on his horse to a slow trot and
wheeled in many a circle hither and thither with various
turns, until he was weary. And then he said to him "Are
you willing to wrestle now after your running, my little
Thracian?" "As much as you like, O Emperor," he
answered. So Severus leaped from his horse and ordered
the freshest soldiers to wrestle with him. But he threw
to the ground seven very powerful youths, even as before,
taking no breathing space between the bouts. So he alone
was given prizes of silver and a golden necklace by Caesar. Then he was bidden to serve in the body guard of
87 the Emperor. After this he was an officer under Antoninus Caracalla, often increasing his fame by his deeds,
and rose to many military grades and finally to the cen-
turionship as a reward of his active service. Yet afterwards, when Macrinus became Emperor, he refused military service for almost three years, and though he held
the office of tribune, he never came into the presence of
Macrinus, thinking his rule shameful because he had won
88 it by committing a crime. Then he returned to Heliogabalus, believing him to be the son of Antoninus, and
entered upon his tribuneship. After his reign, he fought
with marvellous success against the Parthians, under

Antoninus
Caracalla
A.D. 198-217

Macrinus
A.D. 217-218

Antoninus
Elagabalus
A.D. 218-222

Alexander the son of Mamaea. When he was slain in an uprising of the soldiers at Mogontiacum, Maximin himself was made Emperor by a vote of the army, without a decree of the senate. But he marred all his good deeds by persecuting the Christians in accordance with an evil vow and, being slain by Pupienus at Aquileia, left the kingdom to Philip. These matters we have borrowed from the history of Symmachus for this our little book, in order to show that the race of which we speak attained to the very highest station in the Roman Empire. But our subject requires us to return in due order to the point whence we digressed.

XVI Now the Gothic race gained great fame in the region where they· were then dwelling, that is, in the Scythian land on the shore of Pontus, holding undisputed sway over great stretches of country, many arms of the sea and many river courses. By their strong right arm the Vandals were often laid low; the Marcomanni held their footing by paying tribute and the princes of the Quadi were reduced to slavery. Now when the aforesaid Philip—who, with his son Philip, was the only Christian emperor before Constantine—ruled over the Romans, in the second year of his reign Rome completed its one thousandth year. He withheld from the Goths the tribute due them; whereupon they were naturally enraged and instead of friends became his foes. For though they dwelt apart under their own kings, yet they had been allied to the Roman state and received annual gifts. And what more? Ostrogotha and his men soon crossed the Danube and ravaged Moesia and Thrace. Philip sent the senator Decius against him. And since he could do nothing against the Getae, he released his soldiers from military service and sent them back to private life, as though it had been by their neglect that the Goths had crossed the Danube. When, as he supposed, he had thus taken vengeance on his soldiers, he returned to Philip. But when

89

90

the soldiers found themselves expelled from the army after so many hardships, in their anger they had recourse

91 to the protection of Ostrogotha, king of the Goths. He received them, was aroused by their words and presently led out three hundred thousand armed men, having as allies for this war some of the Taifali and Astringi and also three thousand of the Carpi, a race of men very ready to make war and frequently hostile to the Romans. But in later times when Diocletian and Maximian were Emperors, the Caesar Galerius Maximianus conquered them and made them tributary to the Roman Empire. Besides these tribes, Ostrogotha had Goths and Peucini from the island of Peucē, which lies in the mouths of the Danube where they empty into the Sea of Pontus. He placed in command Argaith and Guntheric, the noblest leaders

92 of his race. They speedily crossed the Danube, devastated Moesia a second time and approached Marcianople, the famed metropolis of that land. Yet after a long siege they departed, upon receiving money from the inhabitants.

93 Now since we have mentioned Marcianople, we may briefly relate a few matters in connection with its founding. They say that the Emperor Trajan built this city for the following reason. While his sister's daughter Marcia was bathing in the stream called Potamus—a   MARCIANOPLE
river of great clearness and purity that rises in the midst of the city—she wished to draw some water from it and by chance dropped into its depths the golden pitcher she was carrying. Yet though very heavy from its weight of metal, it emerged from the waves a long time afterwards. It surely is not a usual thing for an empty vessel to sink; much less that, when once swallowed up, it should be cast up by the waves and float again. Trajan marvelled at hearing this and believed there was some divinity in the stream. So he built a city and called it Marcianople after the name of his sister.

94 XVII From this city, then, as we were saying, the

Getae returned after a long siege to their own land, enriched by the ransom they had received. Now the race
of the Gepidae was moved with envy when they saw them
laden with booty and so suddenly victorious everywhere,
and made war on their kinsmen. Should you ask how
the Getae and Gepidae are kinsmen,. I can tell you in a
few words. You surely remember that in the beginning
I said the Goths went forth from the bosom of the island
of Scandza with Berig, their king, sailing in only three
ships toward the hither shore of Ocean, namely to
Gothiscandza. One of these three ships proved to be   95
slower than the others, as is usually the case, and thus is
said to have given the tribe their name, for in their
language *gepanta* means slow. Hence it came to pass
that gradually and by corruption the name Gepidae was
coined for them by way of reproach. For undoubtedly
they too trace their origin from the stock of the Goths,
but because, as I have said, *gepanta* means something
slow and stolid, the word Gepidae arose as a gratuitous
name of reproach. I do not believe this is very far
wrong, for they are slow of thought and too sluggish for
quick movement of their bodies.

These Gepidae were then smitten by envy while they   9(
dwelt in the province of Spesis on an island surrounded
by the shallow waters of the Vistula. This island they
called, in the speech of their fathers, Gepedoios; but it is
now inhabited by the race of the Vividarii, since the
Gepidae themselves have moved to better lands. The
Vividarii are gathered from various races into this one
asylum, if I may call it so, and thus they form a nation.
So then, as we were saying, Fastida, king of the Gepidae,   9
stirred up his quiet people to enlarge their boundaries by
war. He overwhelmed the Burgundians, almost annihi-
lating them, and conquered a number of other races also.
He unjustly provoked the Goths, being the first to break
the bonds of kinship by unseemly strife. He was greatly

puffed up with vain glory, but in seeking to acquire new
lands for his growing nation, he only reduced the num-
98 bers of his own countrymen. For he sent ambassadors
to Ostrogotha, to whose rule Ostrogoths and Visigoths
alike, that is, the two peoples of the same tribe, were still
subject. Complaining that he was hemmed in by rugged
mountains and dense forests, he demanded one of two
things, that Ostrogotha should either prepare for war
99 or give up part of his lands to them. Then Ostrogotha,
king of the Goths, who was a man of firm mind, answered the ambassadors that he did indeed dread such a
war and that it would be a grievous and infamous thing
to join battle with their kin—but he would not give up
his lands. And why say more? The Gepidae hastened
to take arms and Ostrogotha likewise moved his forces
against them, lest he should seem a coward. They met
at the town of Galtis, near which the river Auha flows,
and there both sides fought with great valor; indeed the
similarity of their arms and of their manner of fighting
turned them against their own men. But the better cause
00 and their natural alertness aided the Goths. Finally night
put an end to the battle as a part of the Gepidae were
giving way. Then Fastida, king of the Gepidae, left the
field of slaughter and hastened to his own land, as much
humiliated with shame and disgrace as formerly he had
been elated with pride. The Goths returned victorious,
content with the retreat of the Gepidae, and dwelt in
peace and happiness in their own land so long as Ostrogotha was their leader.

01   XVIII   After his death, Cniva divided the army into
two parts and sent some to waste Moesia, knowing that it
was undefended through the neglect of the emperors.
He himself with seventy thousand men hastened to
Euscia, that is, Novae. When driven from this place by
the general Gallus, he approached Nicopolis, a very famous town situated near the Iatrus river. This city

KING CNIVA
AT WAR WITH
DECIUS

Decius
A.D. 249-251

Trajan built when he conquered the Sarmatians and named it the City of Victory. When the Emperor Decius drew near, Cniva at last withdrew to the regions of Haemus, which were not far distant. Thence he hastened to Philippopolis, with his forces in good array. When the Emperor Decius learned of his departure, he was eager to bring relief to his own city and, crossing Mount Haemus, came to Beroa. While he was resting his horses and his weary army in that place, all at once Cniva and his Goths fell upon him like a thunderbolt. He cut the Roman army to pieces and drove the Emperor, with a few who had succeeded in escaping, across the Alps again to Euscia in Moesia, where Gallus was then stationed with a large force of soldiers as guardian of the frontier. Collecting an army from this region as well as from Oescus, he prepared for the conflict of the coming war.

Capture of
Philippopolis
A.D. 250

But Cniva took Philippopolis after a long siege and then, laden with spoil, allied himself to Priscus, the commander in the city, to fight against Decius. In the battle that followed they quickly pierced the son of Decius with an arrow and cruelly slew him. His father saw it, and although he is said to have exclaimed, to cheer the hearts of his soldiers: "Let no one mourn; the death of one soldier is not a great loss to the republic," he was yet unable to endure it, because of his love for his son. So he rode against the foe, demanding either death or vengeance, and when he came to Abrittus, a city of Moesia, he was himself cut off by the Goths and slain, thus making an end of his dominion and of his life. This place is to-day called the Altar of Decius, because he there offered strange sacrifices to idols before the battle.

Death of
Decius at
Abrittus
A.D. 251

Gallus
A.D. 251-253

XIX Then upon the death of Decius, Gallus and Volusianus succeeded to the Roman Empire. At this time a destructive plague, almost like death itself, such as we suffered nine years ago, blighted the face of the whole earth and especially devastated Alexandria and all

Volusianus
A.D. 252-253

the land of Egypt. The historian Dionysius gives a
mournful account of it and Cyprian, our own bishop and
venerable martyr in Christ, also describes it in his book
entitled "On Mortality." At this time the Goths frequently ravaged Moesia, through the neglect of the Em-
05 perors. When a certain Aemilianus saw that they were
free to do this, and that they could not be dislodged by
anyone without great cost to the republic, he thought that
he too might be able to achieve fame and fortune. So he
seized the rule in Moesia and, taking all the soldiers he
could gather, began to plunder cities and people. In the
next few months, while an armed host was being gathered against him, he wrought no small harm to the state.
Yet he died almost at the beginning of his evil attempt,
thus losing at once his life and the power he coveted.
06 Now though Gallus and Volusianus, the Emperors we
have mentioned, departed this life after remaining in
power for barely two years, yet during this space of two
years which they spent on earth they reigned amid universal peace and favor. Only one thing was laid to their
charge, namely the great plague. But this was an accusation made by ignorant slanderers, whose custom it is
to wound the lives of others with their malicious bite.
Soon after they came to power they made a treaty with
the race of the Goths. When both rulers were dead, it
was no long time before Gallienus usurped the throne.
07   XX While he was given over to luxurious living of
every sort, Respa, Veduc and Thuruar, leaders of the
Goths, took ship and sailed across the strait of the Hellespont to Asia. There they laid waste many populous
cities and set fire to the renowned temple of Diana at
Ephesus, which, as we said before, the Amazons built.
Being driven from the neighborhood of Bithynia, they
destroyed Chalcedon, which Cornelius Avitus afterwards
restored to some extent. Yet even to-day, though it is
happily situated near the royal city, it still shows some

THE GOTHS IN
THE TIME OF
GALLUS,
VOLUSIANUS AND
AEMILIANUS

Aemilianus
A.D. 253

The Plague
A.D. 252-267

Gallienus
A.D. 253-268

THE GOTHS
PLUNDER
ASIA MINOR
A.D. 262 or 263

traces of its ruin as a witness to posterity. After their 10
success, the Goths recrossed the strait of the Hellespont,
laden with booty and spoil, and returned along the same
route by which they had entered Asia, sacking Troy
and Ilium on the way. These cities, which had scarce re- ˅.
covered a little from the famous war with Agamemnon,
were thus destroyed anew by the hostile sword. After
the Goths had thus devastated Asia, Thrace next felt
their ferocity. For they went thither and presently
attacked Anchiali, a city at the foot of Haemus and not
far from the sea. Sardanapalus, king of the Parthians,
had built this city long ago between an inlet of the sea
and the base of Haemus. There they are said to have IC
stayed for many days, enjoying the baths of the hot
springs which are situated about twelve miles from the
city of Anchiali. There they gush from the depths of
their fiery source, and among the innumerable hot springs
of the world they are particularly famous and efficacious
to heal the sick.

XXI After these events, the Goths had already re- I ˙
turned home when they were summoned at the request
of the Emperor Maximian to aid the Romans against the
Parthians. They fought for him faithfully, serving as

auxiliaries. But after Caesar Maximian by their aid had
routed Narseus, king of the Persians, the grandson of
Sapor the Great, taking as spoil all his possessions, together with his wives and his sons, and when Diocletian
had conquered Achilles in Alexandria and Maximianus
Herculius had broken the Quinquegentiani in Africa, thus
winning peace for the empire, they began rather to neg-
-lect the Goths.

[Now it had long been a hard matter for the Roman I
army to fight against any nations whatsoever without
them.˙ This is evident from the way in which the Goths

were so frequently called upon. Thus they were summoned by Constantine to bear arms against his kinsman

Licinius.   Later, when he was vanquished and shut up
in Thessalonica and deprived of his power, they slew him
112 with the sword of Constantine the victor.   In like manner
it was the aid of the Goths that enabled him to build the
famous city that is named after him, the rival of Rome,
inasmuch as they entered into a truce with the Emperor
and furnished him forty thousand men to aid him against
various peoples.   This body of men, namely, the Allies,
and the service they rendered in war are still spoken of in
the land to this day.   Now at that time they prospered
under the rule of their kings Ariaric and Aoric.   Upon
their death Geberich appeared as successor to the throne,
a man renowned for his valor and noble birth.

113   XXII   For he was the son of Hilderith, who was the
son of Ovida, who was the son of Nidada; and by his
illustrious deeds he, equalled the glory of his race.   Soon
he sought to enlarge his country's narrow bounds at the
expense of the race of the Vandals and Visimar, their
king.   This Visimar was of the stock of the Asdingi,
which is eminent among them and indicates a most warlike descent, as Dexippus the historian relates.   He states
furthermore that by reason of the great extent of their
country they could scarcely come from Ocean to our frontier in a year's time.   At that time they dwelt in the land
where the Gepidae now live, near the rivers Marisia,
Miliare, Gilpil and the Grisia, which exceeds in size all
114 previously mentioned.   They then had on the east the
Goths, on the west the Marcomanni, on the north the
Hermunduli and on the south the Hister, which is also
called the Danube.   At the time when the Vandals were
dwelling in this region, war was begun against them by
Geberich, king of the Goths, on the shore of the river
Marisia which I have mentioned.   Here the battle raged
for a little while on equal terms.   But soon Visimar himself, the king of the Vandals, was overthrown, together
115 with the greater part of his people.   When Geberich, the

GEBERICH
CONQUERS
THE VANDALS
336

famous leader of the Goths, had conquered and spoiled the Vandals, he returned to his own place whence he had come. Then the remnant of the Vandals who had escaped, collecting a band of their unwarlike folk, left their ill-fated country and asked the Emperor Constantine for Pannonia. Here they made their home for about sixty years and obeyed the commands of the emperors like subjects. A long time afterward they were summoned thence by Stilicho, Master of the Soldiery, Ex-Consul and Patrician, and took possession of Gaul. Here they plundered their neighbors and had no settled place of abode.

XXIII   Soon Geberich, king of the Goths, departed   11◄ from human affairs and Hermanaric, noblest of the Amali, succeeded to the throne. He subdued many warlike peoples of the north and made them obey his laws, and some of our ancestors have justly compared him to Alexander the Great. Among the tribes he conquered were the Golthescytha, Thiudos, Inaunxis, Vasinabroncae, Merens, Mordens. Imniscaris, Rogas, Tadzans, Athaul, Navego, Bubegenae and Coldae. But though famous   11 for his conquest of so many races, he gave himself no rest until he had slain some in battle and then reduced to his sway the remainder of the tribe of the Heruli, whose chief was Alaric. Now the aforesaid race, as the historian Ablabius tells us, dwelt near Lake Maeotis in swampy places which the Greeks call *helē;* hence they were named Heluri. They were a people swift of foot, and on that account were the more swollen with pride, for there was   1▸ at that time no race that did not choose from them its light-armed troops for battle. But though their quickness often saved them from others who made war upon them, yet they were overthrown by the slowness and steadiness of the Goths; and the lot of fortune brought it to pass that they, as well as the other tribes, had to serve Hermanaric, king of the Getae. After the slaughter of the   1 Heruli, Hermanaric also took arms against the Venethi.

CONQUEST OF THE HERULI, VENETHI AND AESTI

This people, though despised in war, was strong in numbers and tried to resist him. But a multitude of cowards
is of no avail, particularly when God permits an armed
multitude to attack them. These people, as we started
to say at the beginning of our account or catalogue of
nations, though off-shoots from one stock, have now
three names, that is, Venethi, Antes and Sclaveni. Though
they now rage in war far and wide, in consequence of
our neglect, yet at that time they were all obedient to Her-
120 manaric's commands. This ruler also subdued by his
wisdom and might the race of the Aesti, who dwell on
the farthest shore of the German Ocean, and ruled all the
nations of Scythia and Germany by his own prowess
alone.

121   XXIV But after a short space of time, as Orosius
relates, the race of the Huns, fiercer than ferocity itself,
flamed forth against the Goths. We learn from old traditions that their origin was as follows: Filimer, king of
the Goths, son of Gadaric the Great, who was the fifth in
succession to hold the rule of the Getae after their departure from the island of Scandza—and who, as we have
said, entered the land of Scythia with his tribe—found
among his people certain witches, whom he called in his
native tongue *Haliurunnae*. Suspecting these women, he
expelled them from the midst of his race and compelled
them to wander in solitary exile afar from his army.
122 There the unclean spirits, who beheld them as they wandered through the wilderness, bestowed their embraces
upon them and begat this savage race, which dwelt at
first in the swamps, a stunted, foul and puny tribe,
scarcely human and having no language save one which
bore but slight resemblance to human speech. Such was
the descent of the Huns who came to the country of the
Goths.

123   This cruel tribe, as Priscus the historian relates, settled on the farther bank of the Maeotic swamp. They

ORIGIN
AND HISTORY
OF THE HUNS

were fond of hunting and had no skill in any other art. After they had grown to a nation, they disturbed the peace of neighboring races by theft and rapine. At one time, while hunters of their tribe were as usual seeking for game on the farthest edge of Maeotis, they saw a doe unexpectedly appear to their sight and enter the swamp, acting as guide of the way; now advancing and again standing still. The hunters followed and 124 crossed on foot the Maeotic swamp, which they had supposed was impassable as the sea. Presently the unknown land of Scythia disclosed itself and the doe disappeared. Now in my opinion the evil spirits, from whom the Huns are descended, did this from envy of the Scythians. And the Huns, who had been wholly ignorant 125 that there was another world beyond Maeotis, were now filled with admiration for the Scythian land. As they were quick of mind, they believed that this path, utterly unknown to any age of the past, had been divinely revealed to them. They returned to their tribe, told them what had happened, praised Scythia and persuaded the people to hasten thither along the way they had found by the guidance of the doe. As many as they captured, when they thus entered Scythia for the first time, they sacrificed to Victory. The remainder they conquered and made subject to themselves. Like a whirlwind of 12 nations they swept across the great swamp and at once fell upon the Alpidzuri, Alcildzuri, Itimari, Tuncarsi and Boisci, who bordered on that part of Scythia. The Alani also, who were their equals in battle, but unlike them in civilization, manners and appearance, they exhausted by their incessant attacks and subdued. For by the terror 12 of their features they inspired great fear in those whom perhaps they did not really surpass in war. They made their foes flee in horror because their swarthy aspect was fearful, and they had, if I may call it so, a sort of shapeless lump, not a head, with pin-holes rather than eyes.

Their hardihood is evident in their wild appearance, and
they are beings who are cruel to their children on the
very day they are born. For they cut the cheeks of the
males with a sword, so that before they receive the nour-
ishment of milk they must learn to endure wounds.
128 Hence they grow old beardless and their young men are
without comeliness, because a face furrowed by the sword
spoils by its scars the natural beauty of a beard. They
are short in stature, quick in bodily movement, alert
horsemen, broad shouldered, ready in the use of bow and
arrow, and have firm-set necks which are ever erect in
pride. Though they live in the form of men, they have
the cruelty of wild beasts.

129   When the Getae beheld this active race that had invaded many nations, they took fright and consulted with
their king how they might escape from such a foe. Now
although Hermanaric, king of the Goths, was the conqueror of many tribes, as we have said above, yet while
he was deliberating on this invasion of the Huns, the
treacherous tribe of the Rosomoni, who at that time were
among those who owed him their homage, took this
chance to catch him unawares. For when the king had
given orders that a certain woman of the tribe I have
mentioned, Sunilda by name, should be bound to wild
horses and torn apart by driving them at full speed in
opposite directions (for he was roused to fury by her
husband's treachery to him), her brothers Sarus and
Ammius came to avenge their sister's death and plunged
a sword into Hermanaric's side. Enfeebled by this blow,
he dragged out a miserable existence in bodily weakness.
130 Balamber, king of the Huns, took advantage of his ill
health to move an army into the country of the Ostrogoths, from whom the Visigoths had already separated
because of some dispute. Meanwhile Hermanaric, who
was unable to endure either the pain of his wound or the
inroads of the Huns, died full of days at the great age of

FIRST
IRRUPTION OF
THE HUNS
as early as
375

one hundred and ten years. The fact of his death enabled the Huns to prevail over those Goths who, as we have said, dwelt in the east and were called Ostrogoths.

The Divided Goths: Visigoths

Valentinian I
364-375

THE
VISIGOTHS
SETTLE IN
THRACE AND
MOESIA
376

Valens
364-378

FAMINE
376-377

XXV   The Visigoths, who were their other allies and 131 inhabitants of the western country, were terrified as their kinsmen had been, and knew not how to plan for safety against the race of the Huns.   After long deliberation by common consent they finally sent ambassadors into Romania to the Emperor Valens, brother of Valentinian, the elder Emperor, to say that if he would give them part of Thrace or Moesia to keep, they would submit themselves to his laws and commands.   That he might have greater confidence in them, they promised to become Christians, if he would give them teachers who spoke their language.   When Valens learned this, he gladly and 132 promptly granted what he had himself intended to ask. He received the Getae into the region of Moesia and placed them there as a wall of defense for his kingdom against other tribes.   And since at that time the Emperor Valens, who was infected with the Arian perfidy, had closed all the churches of our party, he sent as preachers to them those who favored his sect.   They came and straightway filled a rude and ignorant people with the poison of their heresy.   Thus the Emperor Valens made the Visigoths Arians rather than Christians.   Moreover, 13: from the love they bore them, they preached the gospel both to the Ostrogoths and to their kinsmen the Gepidae, teaching them to reverence this heresy, and they invited all people of their speech everywhere to attach themselves to this sect.   They themselves, as we have said, crossed the Danube and settled Dacia Ripensis, Moesia and Thrace by permission of the Emperor.

XXVI   Soon famine and want came upon them, as 13. often happens to a people not yet well settled in a country. Their princes and the leaders who ruled them in place of kings, that is Fritigern, Alatheus and Safrac, began to lament the plight of their army and begged Lupicinus and Maximus, the Roman commanders, to open a market. But to what will not the "cursed lust for gold" compel men to assent? The generals, swayed by avarice, sold them at a high price not only the flesh of sheep and oxen, but even the carcasses of dogs and unclean animals, so that a slave would be bartered for a loaf

135 of bread or ten pounds of meat. When their goods and chattels failed, the greedy trader demanded their sons in return for the necessities of life. And the parents consented even to this, in order to provide for the safety of their children, arguing that it was better to lose liberty than life; and indeed it is better than one be sold, if he will be mercifully fed, than that he should be kept free only to die.

Now it came to pass in that troublous time that Lupicinus, the Roman general, invited Fritigern, a chieftain of the Goths, to a feast and, as the event revealed,

136 devised a plot against him. But Fritigern, thinking no evil, came to the feast with a few followers. While he was dining in the praetorium he heard the dying cries of his ill-fated men, for, by order of the general, the soldiers were slaying his companions who were shut up in another part of the house. The loud cries of the dying fell upon ears already suspicious, and Fritigern at once perceived the treacherous trick. He drew his sword and with great courage dashed quickly from the banqueting-hall, rescued his men from their threatening doom

137 and incited them to slay the Romans. Thus these valiant men gained the chance they had longed for—to be free to die in battle rather than to perish of hunger—and immediately took arms to kill the generals Lupicinus and Maximus. Thus that day put an end to the famine of the Goths and the safety of the Romans, for the Goths no

TREACHERY
OF THE
ROMANS

longer as strangers and pilgrims, but as citizens and lords, began to rule the inhabitants and to hold in their own right all the northern country as far as the Danube.

When the Emperor Valens heard of this at Antioch,   138
he made ready an army at once and set out for the country of Thrace. Here a grievous battle took place and the Goths prevailed. ' The Emperor himself was wounded and fled to a farm near Hadrianople. The Goths, not knowing that an emperor lay hidden in so poor a hut, set fire to it (as is customary in dealing with a cruel foe), and thus he was cremated in royal splendor. Plainly it was a direct judgment of God that he should be burned with fire by the very men whom he had perfidiously led astray when they sought the true faith, turning them aside from the flame of love into the fire of hell. From this time the Visigoths, in consequence of their glorious victory, possessed Thrace and Dacia Ripensis as if it were their native land.

Gratian
367-383

HOSTILE
RELATIONS
WITH ROME
ENDED BY
A TRUCE

Theodosius
379-395

XXVII Now in the place of Valens, his uncle, the   139
Emperor Gratian established Theodosius the Spaniard in the Eastern Empire. Military discipline was soon restored to a high level, and the Goth, perceiving that the cowardice and sloth of former princes was ended, became afraid. For the Emperor was famed alike for his acuteness and discretion. By stern commands and by generosity and kindness he encouraged a demoralized army to deeds of daring. But when the soldiers, who had ob-   140
tained a better leader by the change, gained new confidence, they sought to attack the Goths and drive them from the borders of Thrace. But as the Emperor Theodosius fell so sick at this time that his life was almost despaired of, the Goths were again inspired with courage. Dividing the Gothic army, Fritigern set out to plunder Thessaly, Epirus and Achaia, while Alatheus and Safrac with the rest of the troops made for Pannonia. Now the   141
Emperor Gratian had at this time retreated from Rome to

Gaul because of the invasions of the Vandals. When he learned that the Goths were acting with greater boldness because Theodosius was in despair of his life, he quickly gathered an army and came against them. Yet he put no trust in arms, but sought to conquer them by kindness and gifts. So he entered on a truce with them and made peace, giving them provisions.

142 XXVIII When the Emperor Theodosius afterwards recovered and learned that the Emperor Gratian had made a compact between the Goths and the Romans, as he had himself desired, he was very well pleased and gave his assent. He gave gifts to King Athanaric, who had succeeded Fritigern, made an alliance with him and in the most gracious manner invited him to visit him in 143 Constantinople. Athanaric very gladly consented and as he entered the royal city exclaimed in wonder, "Lo, now I see what I have often heard of with unbelieving ears," meaning the great and famous city. Turning his eyes hither and thither, he marvelled as he beheld the situation of the city, the coming and going of the ships, the splendid walls, and the people of divers nations gathered like a flood of waters streaming from different reregions into one basin. So too, when he saw the army in array, he said "Truly the Emperor is a god on earth, and whoso raises a hand against him is guilty of his own 144 blood." In the midst of his admiration and the enjoyment of even greater honors at the hand of the Emperor, he departed this life after the space of a few months. The Emperor had such affection for him that he honored Athanaric even more when he was dead than during his lifetime, for he not only gave him a worthy burial, but 145 himself walked before the bier at the funeral. Now when Athanaric was dead, his whole army continued in the service of the Emperor Theodosius and submitted to the Roman rule, forming as it were one body with the imperial soldiery. The former service of the Allies under the

PEACE CONFIRMED BY THEODOSIUS 380

DEATH OF KING ATHANARIC AT CONSTANTINOPLE 381

Emperor Constantine was now renewed and they were again called Allies. And since the Emperor knew that they were faithful to him and his friends, he took from their number more than twenty thousand warriors to serve against the tyrant Eugenius who had slain Gratian and seized Gaul. After winning the victory over this usurper, he wreaked his vengeance upon him.

XXIX But after Theodosius, the lover of peace and of the Gothic race, had passed from human cares, his sons began to ruin both empires by their luxurious living and to deprive their Allies, that is to say the Goths, of the customary gifts. The contempt of the Goths for the Romans soon increased, and for fear their valor would be destroyed by long peace, they appointed Alaric king over them. He was of famous stock, and his nobility was second only to that of the Amali, for he came from the family of the Balthi, who because of their daring valor had long ago received among their race the name *Baltha*, that is, The Bold. Now when this Alaric was made king, he took counsel with his men and persuaded them to seek a kingdom by their own exertions rather than serve others in idleness. In the consulship of Stilicho and Aurelian he raised an army and entered Italy, which seemed to be bare of defenders, and came through Pannonia and Sirmium along the right side. Without meeting any resistance, he reached the bridge of the river Candidianus at the third milestone from the royal city of Ravenna.

This city lies amid the streams of the Po between swamps and the sea, and is accessible only on one side. Its ancient inhabitants, as our ancestors relate, were called αἰνετοί, that is, "Laudable." Situated in a corner of the Roman Empire above the Ionian Sea, it is hemmed in like an island by a flood of rushing waters. On the east it has the sea, and one who sails straight to it from the region of Corcyra and those parts of Hellas sweeps with his oars along the right hand coast, first touching

Margin notes: ALARIC I KING OF THE GOTHS 395-410 · Stilicho and Aurelian Consuls in 400 · DESCRIPTION OF RAVENNA

Epirus, then Dalmatia, Liburnia and Histria and at last
the Venetian Isles. But on the west it has swamps
through which a sort of door has been left by a very
narrow entrance. To the north is an arm of the Po,
150 called the Fossa Asconis. On the south likewise is the
Po itself, which they call the King of the rivers of Italy;
and it has also the name Eridanus. This river was turned
aside by the Emperor Augustus into a very broad canal
which flows through the midst of the city with a seventh
part of its stream, affording a pleasant harbor at its
mouth. Men believed in ancient times, as Dio relates,
that it would hold a fleet of two hundred and fifty vessels
151 in its safe anchorage. Fabius says that this, which was
once a harbor, now displays itself like a spacious garden
full of trees; but from them hang not sails but apples.
The city itself boasts of three names and is happily placed
in its threefold location. I mean to say the first is called
Ravenna and the most distant part Classis; while midway
between the city and the sea is Caesarea, full of luxury.
The sand of the beach is fine and suited for riding.

152   XXX   But as I was saying, when the army of the
Visigoths had come into the neighborhood of this city,
they sent an embassy to the Emperor Honorius, who
dwelt within. They said that if he would permit the
Goths to settle peaceably in Italy, they would so live with
the Roman people that men might believe them both to
be of one race; but if not, whoever prevailed in war
should drive out the other, and the victor should hence-
forth rule unmolested. But the Emperor Honorius feared
to make either promise. So he took counsel with his
senate and considered how he might drive them from the
153 Italian borders. He finally decided that Alaric and his
race, if they were able to do so, should be allowed to
seize for their own home the provinces farthest away,
namely Gaul and Spain. For at this time he had almost
lost them, and moreover they had been devasted by the

Honorius
393-423

Honorius
grants the
Goths lands
in Gaul and
Spain

invasion of Gaiseric, king of the Vandals. The grant was confirmed by an imperial rescript, and the Goths, consenting to the arrangement, set out for the country given them.

When they had gone away without doing any harm in Italy, Stilicho, the Patrician and father-in-law of the Emperor Honorius—for the Emperor had married both his daughters, Maria and Thermantia, in succession, but God called both from this world in their virgin purity—this Stilicho, I say, treacherously hurried to Pollentia, a city in the Cottian Alps. There he fell upon the unsuspecting Goths in battle, to the ruin of all Italy and his own disgrace. When the Goths suddenly beheld him, at first they were terrified. Soon regaining their courage and arousing each other by brave shouting, as is their custom, they turned to flight the entire army of Stilicho and almost exterminated it. Then forsaking the journey they had undertaken, the Goths with hearts full of rage returned again to Liguria whence they had set out. When they had plundered and spoiled it, they also laid waste Aemilia, and then hastened toward the city of Rome along the Flaminian Way, which runs between Picenum and Tuscia, taking as booty whatever they found on either hand. When they finally entered Rome, by Alaric's express command they merely sacked it and did not set the city on fire, as wild peoples usually do, nor did they permit serious damage to be done to the holy places. Thence they departed to bring like ruin upon Campania and Lucania, and then came to Bruttii. Here they remained a long time and planned to go to Sicily and thence to the countries of Africa.

Now the land of the Bruttii is at the extreme southern bound of Italy , and a corner of it marks the beginning of the Apennine mountains. It stretches out like a tongue into the Adriatic Sea and separates it from the Tyrrhenian waters. It chanced to receive its name in ancient times

STILICHO'S
TREACHEROUS
ATTACK
402

ALARIC I
SACKS ROME
A.D. 410

154

155

156

157 from a Queen Bruttia. To this place came Alaric, king of the Visigoths, with the wealth of all Italy which he had taken as spoil, and from there, as we have said, he intended to cross over by way of Sicily to the quiet land of Africa. But since man is not free to do anything he wishes without the will of God, that dread strait sunk several of his ships and threw all into confusion. Alaric was cast down by his reverse and, while deliberating what he should do, was suddenly overtaken by an untimely death 158 and departed from human cares. His people mourned for him with the utmost affection. Then turning from its course the river Busentus near the city of Consentia—for this stream flows with its wholesome waters from the foot of a mountain near that city—they led a band of captives into the midst of its bed to dig out a place for his grave. In the depths of this pit they buried Alaric, together with many treasures, and then turned the waters back into their channel. And that none might ever know the place, they put to death all the diggers. They bestowed the kingdom of the Visigoths on Athavulf his kinsman, a a man of imposing beauty and great spirit; for though not tall of stature, he was distinguished for beauty. of face and form.

159 XXXI When Athavulf became king, he. returned again to Rome, and whatever had escaped the first sack his Goths stripped bare like locusts, not merely despoiling Italy of its private wealth, but even of its public resources. The Emperor Honorius was powerless to resist even when his sister Placidia, the daughter of the Emperor Theodosius by his second wife, was led away 60 captive from the city. But Athavulf was attracted by her nobility, beauty and chaste purity, and so he took her to wife in lawful marriage at Forum Julii, a city of Aemilia. When the barbarians learned of this alliance, they were the more effectually terrified, since the Empire and the Goths now seemed to be made one. Then Athavulf set

DEATH
OF
ALARIC I
A.D. 410

Athavulf
410-415

DEEDS OF
KING ATHAVULF

Marries
Galla Placidia
414

out for Gaul, leaving Honorius Augustus stripped of his
wealth, to be sure, yet pleased at heart because he was
now a sort of kinsman of his. Upon his arrival the   161
neighboring tribes who had long made cruel raids into
Gaul—Franks and Burgundians alike—were terrified and
began to keep within their own borders. Now the
Vandals and the Alani, as we have said before, had been
dwelling in both Pannonias by permission of the Roman
Emperors. Yet fearing they would not be safe even here
if the Goths should return, they crossed over into Gaul.
But no long time after they had taken possession of Gaul   162
they fled thence and shut themselves up in Spain, for they
still remembered from the tales of their forefathers what
ruin Geberich, king of the Goths, had long ago brought
on their race, and how by his valor he had driven them
from their native land. And thus it happened that Gaul
lay open to Athavulf when he came. Now when the   163
Goth had established his kingdom in Gaul, he began to
grieve for the plight of the Spaniards and planned to
save them from the attacks of the Vandals. So Athavulf
left with a few faithful men at Barcelona his treasures and
those who were unfit for war, and entered the interior of
Spain. Here he fought frequently with the Vandals and,
in the third year after he had subdued Gaul and Spain, fell
pierced through the groin by the sword of Euervulf, a
man whose short stature he had been wont to mock. After

KING
SEGERIC
415

his death Segeric was appointed king, but he too was slain
by the treachery of his own men and lost both his kingdom
and his life even more quickly than Athavulf.

XXXII Then Valia, the fourth from Alaric, was   164
KING VALIA
415-419
made king, and he was an exceeding stern and prudent
man. The Emperor Honorius sent an army against him
under Constantius, who was famed for his achievements
in war and distinguished in many battles, for he feared

that Valia would break the treaty long ago made with Athavulf and that, after driving out the neighboring tribes, he would again plot evil against the Empire. Moreover Honorius was eager to free his sister Placidia from the disgrace of servitude, and made an agreement with Constantius that if by peace or war or any means soever he could bring her back to the kingdom, he should

165 have her in marriage. Pleased with this promise, Constantius set out for Spain with an armed force and in almost royal splendor. Valia, king of the Goths, met him at a pass in the Pyrenees with as great a force. Hereupon embassies were sent by both sides and it was decided to make peace on the following terms, namely that Valia should give up Placidia, the Emperor's sister, and should not refuse to aid the Roman Empire when occasion demanded.

Now at that time a certain Constantine usurped imperial power in Gaul and appointed as Caesar his son Constans, who was formerly a monk. But when he had held for a short time the Empire he had seized, he was himself slain at Arelate and his son at Vienne. Jovinus and Sebastian succeeded them with equal presumption and thought they might seize the imperial power; but they perished by a like fate.

66   Now in the twelfth year of Valia's reign the Huns were driven out of Pannonia by the Romans and Goths, almost fifty years after they had taken possession of it. Then Valia found that the Vandals had come forth with bold audacity from the interior of Galicia, whither Athavulf had long ago driven them, and were devastating and plundering everywhere in his own territories, namely in the land of Spain. So he made no delay but moved his army against them at once, at about the time when Hierius and Ardabures had become consuls.

67   XXXIII   But Gaiseric, king of the Vandals, had already been invited into Africa by Boniface, who had

Constantine III
407-411
Constans
407-411

Jovinus
411-413

Sebastian
412

VALIA
MOVES AGAINST
THE
VANDALS
427

fallen into a dispute with the Emperor Valentinian and
was able to obtain revenge only by injuring the Empire.
So he invited them urgently and brought them across the
narrow strait known as the Strait of Gades, scarcely seven
miles wide, which divides Africa from Spain and unites
the mouth of the Tyrrhenian Sea with the waters of
Ocean. Gaiseric, still famous in the City for the disaster
of the Romans, was a man of moderate height and lame
in consequence of a fall from his horse. He was a man
of deep thought and few words, holding luxury in disdain, furious in his anger, greedy for gain, shrewd in
winning over the barbarians and skilled in sowing the
seeds of dissension to arouse enmity. Such was he who,
as we have said, came at the solicitous invitation of Boniface to the country of Africa. There he reigned for a
long time, receiving authority, as they say, from God
Himself. Before his death he summoned the band of his
sons and ordained that there should be no strife among
them because of desire for the kingdom, but that each
should reign in his own rank and order as he survived
the others; that is, the next younger should succeed his
elder brother, and he in turn should be followed by his
junior. By giving heed to this command they ruled their
kingdom in happiness for the space of many years and
were not disgraced by civil war, as is usual among other
nations; one after the other receiving the kingdom and
ruling the people in peace.

The six kings
of the Vandals
427-534

Now this is their order of succession: first, Gaiseric
who was the father and lord, next Huneric, the third
Gunthamund, the fourth Thrasamund, and the fifth
Ilderich. He was driven from his throne and slain
by Gelimer, who destroyed his race by disregarding
his ancestor's advice and setting up a tyranny. But
what he had done did not remain unpunished, for soon
the vengeance of the Emperor Justinian was mani-
fested against him. With his whole family and that

wealth over which he gloated like a robber, he was taken
to Constantinople by that most renowned warrior Belisarius, Master of the Soldiery of the East, Ex-Consul
Ordinary and Patrician. Here he afforded a great spectacle to the people in the Circus. His repentance, when
he beheld himself cast down from his royal state, came
too late. He died as a mere subject and in retirement,
though he had formerly been unwilling to submit to pri-
172 vate life. Thus after a century Africa, which in the
division of the earth's surface is regarded as the third
part of the world, was delivered from the yoke of the
Vandals and brought back to the liberty of the Roman
Empire. The country which the hand of the heathen had
long ago cut off from the body of the Roman Empire,
by reason of the cowardice of emperors and the treachery
of generals, was now restored by a wise prince and a
faithful leader and to-day is happily flourishing. And
though, even after this, it had to deplore the misery of
civil war and the treachery of the Moors, yet the triumph
of the Emperor Justinian, vouchsafed him · by God,
brought to a peaceful conclusion what he had begun. But
why need we speak of what the subject does not require?
Let us return to our theme.

173   Now Valia, king of the Goths, and his army fought so
fiercely against the Vandals that he would have pursued
them even into Africa, had not such a misfortune recalled
him as befell Alaric when he was setting out for Africa.
So when he had won great fame in Spain, he returned
after a bloodless victory to Tolosa, turning over to the
Roman Empire, as he had promised, a number of provinces which he had rid of his foes. A long time after this
174 he was seized by sickness and departed this life. Just at
that time Beremud, the son of Thorismud, whom we have
mentioned above in the genealogy of the family of the
Amali, departed with his son Veteric from the Ostrogoths, who still submitted to the oppression of the Huns

KINGDOM
OF THE
VANDALS
MADE SUBJECT
TO ROME

MIGRATION
OF THE AMALI
TO THE
VISIGOTHS

THEODORID I
419-451

Consulship of
Theodosius
439

'FIRST BREACH
BETWEEN
THEODORID I
AND THE
ROMANS

in the land of Scythia, and came to the kingdom of the Visigoths. Well aware of his valor and noble birth, he believed that the kingdom would be the more readily bestowed upon him by his kinsmen, inasmuch as he was known to be the heir of many kings. And who would hesitate to choose one of the Amali, if there were an empty throne? But he was not himself eager to make known who he was, and so upon the death of Valia the Visi-, goths made Theodorid his successor. Beremud came to 175 him and, with the strength of mind for which he was noted, concealed his noble birth by prudent silence, for he knew that those of royal lineage are always distrusted by kings. So he suffered himself to remain unknown, that he might not bring the established order into confusion. King Theodorid received him and his son with special honor and made him partner in his counsels and a companion at his board; not for his noble birth, which he knew not, but for his brave spirit and strong mind, which Beremud could not conceal.

XXXIV   And what more? Valia (to repeat what we 17(have said) had but little success against the Gauls, but when he died the more fortunate and prosperous Theodorid succeeded to the throne. He was a man of the greatest moderation and notable for vigor of mind and body. In the consulship of Theodosius and Festus the Romans broke the truce and took up arms against him in Gaul, with the Huns as their auxiliaries. For a band of the Gallic Allies, led by Count Gaina, had aroused the Romans by throwing Constantinople into a panic. Now at that time the Patrician Aëtius was in command of the army. He was of the bravest Moesian stock, the son of Gaudentius and born in the city of Durostorum. He was a man fitted to endure the toils of war, born expressly to serve the Roman state; and by inflicting crushing defeats he had compelled the proud Suavi and barbarous Franks to submit to Roman sway. So then, with the Huns as 17

allies under their leader Litorius, the Roman army
moved in array against the Goths. When the battle
lines of both sides had been standing for a long time
opposite each other, both being brave and neither side the
weaker, they struck a truce and returned to their ancient
alliance. And after the treaty had been confirmed by
both and an honest peace was established, they both
withdrew.

178 During this peace Attila was lord over all the Huns
and almost the sole earthly ruler of all the tribes of
Scythia; a man marvellous for his glorious fame among
all nations. The historian Priscus, who was sent to him
on an embassy by the younger Theodosius, says this
among other things: "Crossing mighty rivers—namely,
the Tisia and Tibisia and Dricca—we came to the place
where long ago Vidigoia, bravest of the Goths, perished
by the guile of the Sarmatians. At no great distance
from that place we arrived at the village where King
Attila was dwelling, a village, I say, like a great city,
in which we found wooden walls made of smooth-shining
boards, whose joints so counterfeited solidity that the
union of the boards could scarcely be distinguished by

179 close scrutiny. There you might see dining halls of
large extent and porticoes planned with great beauty,
while the courtyard was bounded by so vast a circuit that
its very size showed it was the royal palace." This was
the abode of Attila, the king of all the barbarian world;
and he preferred this as a dwelling to the cities he
captured.

180 XXXV Now this Attila was the son of Mundiuch,
and his brothers were Octar and Ruas who are said to
have ruled before Attila, though not over quite so many
tribes as he. After their death he succeeded to the throne
of the Huns, together with his brother Bleda. In order
that he might first be equal to the expedition he was
preparing, he sought to increase his strength by murder.

The Truce
439

Embassy to
Attila
448

CHARACTER
OF ATTILA
KING OF THE
HUNS

Attila and Bleda
joint kings
433-445

Thus he proceeded from the destruction of his own kin-
dred to the menace of all others. But though he increased   181
his power by this shameful means, yet by the balance of
justice he received the hideous consequences of his own
cruelty. Now when his brother Bleda, who ruled over

Attila sole
king
445-453

a great part of the Huns, had been slain by his treachery,
Attila united all the people under his own rule. Gathering also a host of the other tribes which he then held
under his sway, he sought to subdue the foremost nations
of the world—the Romans and the Visigoths. His army   182
is said to have numbered five hundred thousand men.
He was a man born into the world to shake the nations,
the scourge of all lands, who in some way terrified all
mankind by the dreadful rumors noised abroad concerning him. He was haughty in his walk, rolling his eyes
hither and thither, so that the power of his proud spirit
appeared in the movement of his body. He was indeed
a lover of war, yet restrained in action, mighty in counsel, gracious to suppliants and lenient to those who were
once received into his protection. He was short of stature, with a broad chest and a large head; his eyes were
small, his beard thin and sprinkled with gray; and he had
a flat nose and a swarthy complexion, showing the evi-
dences of his origin. And though his temper was such   183
that he always had great self-confidence, yet his assurance was increased by finding the sword of Mars, always
esteemed sacred among the kings of the Scythians. | The
historian Priscus says it was discovered under the following circumstances: "When a certain shepherd beheld
one heifer of his flock limping and could find no cause
for this wound, he anxiously followed the trail of blood
and at length came to a sword it had unwittingly trampled
while nibbling the grass. He dug it up and took it
straight to Attila. He rejoiced at this gift and, being
ambitious, thought he had been appointed ruler of the

whole world, and that through the sword of Mars supremacy in all wars was assured to him."

184   XXXVI   Now when Gaiseric, king of the Vandals, whom we mentioned shortly before, learned that his mind was bent on the devastation of the world, he incited Attila by many gifts to make war on the Visigoths, for he was afraid that Theodorid, king of the Visigoths, would avenge the injury done to his daughter. She had been joined in wedlock with Huneric, the son of Gaiseric, and at first was happy in this union. But afterwards he was cruel even to his own children, and because of the mere suspicion that she was attempting to poison him, he cut off her nose and mutilated her ears. He sent her back to her father in Gaul thus despoiled of her natural charms. So the wretched girl presented a pitiable aspect ever after, and the cruelty which would stir even strangers still more surely incited her father to vengeance.

185   Attila, therefore, in his efforts to bring about the wars long ago instigated by the bribe of Gaiseric, sent ambassadors into Italy to the Emperor Valentinian to sow strife between the Goths and the Romans, thinking to shatter by civil discord those whom he could not crush in battle. He declared that he was in no way violating his friendly relations with the Empire, but that he had a quarrel with Theodorid, king of the Visigoths. As he wished to be kindly received, he filled the rest of the letter with the usual flattering salutations, striving to win

86   credence for his falsehood. In like manner he despatched a message to Theodorid, king of the Visigoths, urging him to break his alliance with the Romans and reminding him of the battles to which they had recently provoked him. Beneath his great ferocity he was a subtle man, and fought with craft before he made war.

Then the Emperor Valentinian sent an embassy to the Visigoths and their king Theodorid, with this message:

87   "Bravest of nations, it is the part of prudence for us to

LEAGUE OF
THE
VISIGOTHS
AND ROMANS
AGAINST
ATTILA
451

unite against the lord of the earth who wishes to enslave
the whole world; who requires no just cause for battle,
but supposes whatever he does is right. He measures
his ambition by his might. License satisfies his pride.
Despising law and right, he shows himself an enemy to
Nature herself. And thus he, who clearly is the common
foe of each, deserves the hatred of all. Pray remember—   18$
what you surely cannot forget—that the Huns do not
overthrow nations by means of war, where there is an
equal chance, but assail them by treachery, which is a
greater cause for anxiety. To say nothing about our-
selves, can you suffer such insolence to go unpunished?
Since you are mighty in arms, give heed to your own
danger and join hands with us in common. Bear aid
also to the Empire, of which you hold a part. If you
would learn how such an alliance should be sought and
welcomed by us, look into the plans of the foe."

By these and like arguments the ambassadors of Va-   18{
lentinian prevailed upon King Theodorid. He answered
them, saying: "Romans, you have attained your desire;
you have made Attila our foe also. We will pursue
him wherever he summons us, and though he is puffed
up by his victories over divers races, yet the Goths know
how to fight this haughty foe. I call no war dangerous
save one whose cause is weak; for he fears no ill on
whom Majesty has smiled." The nobles shouted assent   19
to the reply and the multitude gladly followed. All were
fierce for battle and longed to meet the Huns, their foe.
And so a countless host was led forth by Theodorid, king

of the Visigoths, who sent home four of his sons, namely
Friderich and Eurich, Retemer and Himnerith, taking
with him only the two elder sons, Thorismud and Theodorid, as partners of his toil. O brave array, sure defense and sweet comradeship, having the aid of those who
delight to share in the same dangers!

91   On the side of the Romans stood the Patrician Aëtius,
on whom at that time the whole Empire of the West de-
pended; a man of such wisdom that he had assembled
warriors from everywhere to meet them on equal terms.
Now these were his auxiliaries: Franks, Sarmatians
Armoricians, Liticians, Burgundians, Saxons, Riparians,
Olibriones (once Roman soldiers and now the flower of
the allied forces), and some other Celtic or German tribes.
92   And so they met in the Catalaunian Plains, which are
also called Mauriacian, extending in length one hundred
leuva, as the Gauls express it, and seventy in width. Now
a Gallic *leuva* measures a distance of fifteen hundred
paces. That portion of the earth accordingly became
the threshing-floor of countless races. The two hosts
bravely joined battle. Nothing was done under cover,
93   but they contended in open fight. What just cause can
be found for the encounter of so many nations, or what
hatred inspired them all to take arms against each other?
It is proof that the human race lives for its kings, for it is
at the mad impulse of one mind a slaughter of nations
takes place, and at the whim of a haughty ruler that
which nature has taken ages to produce perishes in a
moment.
94   XXXVII But before we set forth the order of the
battle itself, it seems needful to relate what had already
happened in the course of the campaign, for it was not
only a famous struggle but one that was complicated and
confused. Well then, Sangiban, king of the Alani, smitten with fear of what might come to pass, had promised
to surrender to Attila, and to give into his keeping Aure-
95   liani, a city of Gaul wherein he then dwelt. When Theodorid and Aëtius learned of this, they cast up great earth-
works around that city before Attila's arrival and kept
watch over the suspected Sangiban, placing him with his
tribe in the midst of their auxiliaries. Then Attila, king
of the Huns, was taken aback by this event and lost confi-

THE
BEGINNING
OF THE
STRIFE

dence in his own troops, so that he feared to begin the conflict. While he was meditating on flight—a greater calamity than death itself—he decided to inquire into the future through soothsayers. So, as was their custom, they examined the entrails of cattle and certain streaks in bones that had been scraped, and foretold disaster to the Huns. Yet as a slight consolation they prophesied that the chief commander of the foe they were to meet should fall and mar by his death the rest of the victory and the triumph. Now Attila deemed the death of Aëtius a thing to be desired even at the cost of his own life, for Aëtius stood in the way of his plans. So although he was disturbed by this prophecy, yet inasmuch as he was a man who sought counsel of omens in all warfare, he began the battle with anxious heart at about the ninth hour of the day, in order that the impending darkness might come to his aid if the outcome should be disastrous.

XXXVIII   The armies met, as we have said, in the Catalaunian Plains. The battle field was a plain rising by a sharp slope to a ridge, which both armies sought to gain; for advantage of position is a great help. The Huns with their forces seized the right side, the Romans, the Visigoths and their allies the left, and then began a struggle for the yet untaken crest. Now Theodorid with the Visigoths held the right wing and Aëtius with the Romans the left. They placed in the centre Sangiban (who, as said before, was in command of the Alani), thus contriving with military caution to surround by a host of faithful troops the man in whose loyalty they had little confidence. For one who has difficulties placed in the way of his flight readily submits to the necessity of fighting. On the other side, however, the battle line of the Huns was so arranged that Attila and his bravest followers were stationed in the centre. In arranging them thus the king had chiefly his own safety in view, since by his position in the very midst of his race he

would be kept out of the way of threatening danger. The innumerable peoples of divers tribes, which he had
199 subjected to his sway, formed the wings. Amid them was conspicuous the army of the Ostrogoths under the leadership of the brothers Valamir, Thiudimer and Vidimer, nobler even than the king they served, for the might of the family of the Amali rendered them glorious. The renowned king of the Gepidae, Ardaric, was there also with a countless host, and because of his great loyalty to Attila, he shared his plans. For Attila, comparing them in his wisdom, prized him and Valamir, king of the Ostro-
200 goths, above all the other chieftains. Valamir was a good keeper of secrets, bland of speech and skilled in wiles, and Ardaric, as we have said, was famed for his loyalty and wisdom. Attila might well feel sure that they would fight against the Visigoths, their kinsmen. Now the rest of the crowd of kings (if we may call them so) and the leaders of various nations hung upon Attila's nod like slaves, and when he gave a sign even by a glance, without a murmur each stood forth in fear and trem-
201 bling, or at all events did as he was bid. Attila alone was king of all kings over all and concerned for all.

So then the struggle began for the advantage of position we have mentioned. Attila sent his men to take the summit of the mountain, but was outstripped by Thorismud and Aëtius, who in their effort to gain the top of the hill reached higher ground and through this advantage of position easily routed the Huns as they came up.
202 XXXIX Now when Attila saw his army was thrown into confusion by this event, he thought it best to encourage them by an extemporaneous address on this wise: "Here you stand, after conquering mighty nations and subduing the world. I therefore think it foolish for me to goad you with words, as though you were men who had not been proved in action. Let a new leader or an
203 untried army resort to that. It is not right for me to

ATTILA
ADDRESSES
HIS MEN

say anything common, nor ought you to listen. For what
is war but your usual custom? Or what is sweeter for a
brave man than to seek revenge with his own hand? It is
a right of nature to glut the soul with vengeance.
Let us then attack the foe eagerly; for they are ever the   204
bolder who make the attack. Despise this union of dis-
cordant races! To defend oneself by alliance is proof of
cowardice. See, even before our attack they are smitten
with terror. They seek the heights, they seize the hills
and, repenting too late, clamor for protection against
battle in the open fields. You know how slight a matter
the Roman attack is. While they are still gathering in
order and forming in one line with locked shields, they
are checked, I will not say by the first wound, but even
by the dust of battle. Then on to the fray with stout   205
hearts, as is your wont. Despise their battle line. Attack
the Alani, smite the Visigoths! Seek swift victory in
that spot where the battle rages. For when the sinews
are cut the limbs soon relax, nor can a body stand when
you have taken away the bones. Let your courage rise
and your own fury burst forth! Now show your cun-
ning, Huns, now your deeds of arms! Let the wounded
exact in return the death of his foe; let the unwounded
revel in slaughter of the enemy. No spear shall harm   206
those who are sure to live; and those who are sure to die
Fate overtakes even in peace. And finally, why should
Fortune have made the Huns victorious over so many
nations, unless it were to prepare them for the joy of
this conflict. Who was it revealed to our sires the
path through the Maeotian swamp, for so many ages a
closed secret? Who, moreover, made armed men yield
to you, when you were as yet unarmed? Even a mass of
federated nations could not endure the sight of the Huns.
I am not deceived in the issue; here is the field so many
victories have promised us. I shall hurl the first spear
at the foe. If any can stand at rest while Attila fights,

he is a dead man." Inflamed by these words, they all
dashed into battle.

207   XL   And although the situation was itself fearful, yet
the presence of their king dispelled anxiety and hesita-
tion. Hand to hand they clashed in battle, and the fight
grew fierce, confused, monstrous, unrelenting—a fight
whose like no ancient time has ever recorded. ' There such
deeds were done that a brave man who missed this marvellous spectacle could not hope to see anything so won-
208   derful all his life long. For, if we may believe our
elders, a brook flowing between low banks through the
plain was greatly increased by blood from the wounds
of the slain. It was not flooded by showers, as brooks
usually rise, but was swollen by a strange stream and
turned into a torrent by the increase of blood. Those
whose wounds drove them to slake their parching thirst
drank water mingled with gore. In their wretched plight
they were forced to drink what they thought was the
blood they had poured from their own wounds.

209   Here King Theodorid, while riding by to encourage
his army, was thrown from his horse and trampled under
foot by his own men, thus ending his days at a ripe old
age. But others say he was slain by the spear of Andag
of the host of the Ostrogoths, who were then under the
sway of Attila. ⸜ This was what the soothsayers had told
to Attila in prophecy, though he understood it of Aëtius.
210   Then the Visigoths, separating from the Alani, fell upon
the horde of the Huns and nearly slew Attila. But he
prudently took flight and straightway shut himself and
his companions within the barriers of the camp, which
he had fortified with wagons. A frail defense indeed;
yet there they sought refuge for their lives, whom but a
little while while before no walls of earth could withstand.
211   But Thorismud, the son of King Theodorid, who with
Aëtius had seized the hill and repulsed the enemy from
the higher ground, came unwittingly to the wagons of

the enemy in the darkness of night, thinking he had reached his own lines. As he was fighting bravely, some-one wounded him in the head and dragged him from his horse. Then he was rescued by the watchful care of his followers and withdrew from the fierce conflict. Aëtius 212 also became separated from his men in the confusion of night and wandered about in the midst of the enemy. Fearing disaster had happened, he went about in search of the Goths. At last he reached the camp of his allies and passed the remainder of the night in the protection of their shields.

At dawn on the following day, when the Romans saw the fields were piled high with bodies and that the Huns did not venture forth, they thought the victory was theirs, but knew that Attila would not flee from the battle unless overwhelmed by a great disaster. Yet he did nothing cowardly, like one that is overcome, but with clash of arms sounded the trumpets and threatened an attack. He was like a lion pierced by hunting spears, who paces to and fro before the mouth of his den and dares not spring, but ceases not to terrify the neighborhood by his roaring. Even so this warlike king at bay terrified his conquerors. Therefore the Goths and 21? Romans assembled and considered what to do with the vanquished Attila. They determined to wear him out by a siege, because he had no supply of provisions and was hindered from approaching by a shower of arrows from the bowmen placed within the confines of the Roman camp. But it was said that the king remained supremely brave even in this extremity and had heaped up a funeral pyre of horse saddles, so that if the enemy should attack him, he was determined to cast himself into the flames, that none might have the joy of wounding him and that the lord of so many races might not fall into the hands of his foes.

XLI Now during these delays in the siege, the Visi- 21.

goths sought their king and the king's sons their father,
wondering at his absence when success had been attained.
When, after a long search, they found him where the
dead lay thickest, as happens with brave men, they honored him with songs and bore him away in the sight of
the enemy. You might have seen bands of Goths shouting with dissonant cries and paying honor to the dead
while the battle still raged. Tears were shed, but such
as they were accustomed to devote to brave men. It was
death indeed, but the Huns are witness that it was a
glorious one. It was a death whereby one might well
suppose the pride of the enemy would be lowered, when
they beheld the body of so great a king borne forth with
15 fitting honors. And so the Goths, still continuing the
rites due to Theodorid, bore forth the royal majesty with
sounding arms, and valiant Thorismud, as befitted a son,
honored the glorious spirit of his dear father by following his remains.

RESULTS
OF
THE BATTLE

When this was done, Thorismud was eager to take
vengeance for his father's death on the remaining Huns,
being moved to this both by the pain of bereavement and
the impulse of that valor for which he was noted. Yet
he consulted with the Patrician Aëtius (for he was an
older man and of more mature wisdom) with regard to
16 what he ought to do next. But Aëtius feared that if the
Huns were totally destroyed by the Goths, the Roman
Empire would be overwhelmed, and urgently advised him
to return to his own dominions to take up the rule which
his father had left. Otherwise his brothers might seize
their father's possessions and obtain the power over the
Visigoths. In this case Thorismud would have to fight
fiercely and, what is worse, disastrously with his own
countrymen. Thorismud accepted the advice without
perceiving its double meaning, but followed it with an
eye toward his own advantage. So he left the Huns and
17 returned to Gaul. Thus while human frailty rushes into

suspicion, it often loses an opportunity of doing great things.

In this most famous war of the bravest tribes, one hundred and sixty-five thousand are said to have been slain on both sides, leaving out of account fifteen thousand of the Gepidae and Franks, who met each other the night before the general engagement and fell by wounds mutually received, the Franks fighting for the Romans and the Gepidae for the Huns.

Now when Attila learned of the retreat of the Goths, he thought it a ruse of the enemy—for so men are wont to believe when the unexpected happens—and remained for some time in his camp. But when a long silence followed the absence of the foe, the spirit of the mighty king was aroused to the thought of victory and the anticipation of pleasure, and his mind turned to the old oracles of his destiny.

THORISMUD
451-453

Thorismud, however, after the death of his father on the Catalaunian Plains where he had fought, advanced in royal state and entered Tolosa. Here although the throng of his brothers and brave companions were still rejoicing over the victory he yet began to rule so mildly that no one strove with him for the succession to the kingdom.

XLII   But Attila took occasion from the withdrawal of the Visigoths, observing what he had often desired—

THE SIEGE
AND FALL
OF AQUILEIA
452

that his enemies were divided. At length feeling secure, he moved forward his array to attack the Romans. As his first move he besieged the city of Aquileia, the metropolis of Venetia, which is situated on a point or tongue of land by the Adriatic Sea. On the eastern side its walls are washed by the river Natissa, flowing from Mount Piccis. The siege was long and fierce, but of no avail, since the bravest soldiers of the Romans withstood him from within. At last his army was discontented and eager to withdraw . Attila chanced to be walking around the walls, considering whether to break camp or delay

longer, and noticed that the white birds, namely, the storks, who build their nests in the gables of houses, were bearing their young from the city and, contrary to their
221 custom, were carrying them out into the country. Being a shrewd observer of events, he understood this and said to his soldiers: "You see the birds foresee the future. They are leaving the city sure to perish and are forsaking strongholds doomed to fall by reason of imminent peril. Do not think this a meaningless or uncertain sign; fear, arising from the things they foresee, has changed their custom." Why say more? He inflamed the hearts of his soldiers to attack Aquileia again. Constructing battering rams and bringing to bear all manner of engines of war, they quickly forced their way into the city, laid it waste, divided the spoil and so cruelly devastated it as
222 scarcely to leave a trace to be seen. Then growing bolder and still thirsting for Roman blood, the Huns raged madly through the remaining cities of the Veneti. They also laid waste Mediolanum, the metropolis of Liguria, once an imperial city, and gave over Ticinum to a like fate. Then they destroyed the neighboring country in their frenzy and demolished almost the whole of Italy.

Attila's mind had been bent on going to Rome. But his followers, as the historian Priscus relates, took him away, not out of regard for the city to which they were hostile, but because they remembered the case of Alaric, the former king of the Visigoths. They distrusted the good fortune of their own king, inasmuch as Alaric did not live long after the sack of Rome, but straightway
223 departed this life. Therefore while Attila's spirit was wavering in doubt between going and not going, and he still lingered to ponder the matter, an embassy came to him from Rome to seek peace. Pope Leo himself came to meet him in the Ambuleian district of the Veneti at the well-travelled ford of the river Mincius. Then Attila quickly put aside his usual fury, turned back on the way

POPE LEO
INTERVENES
TO SAVE
ROME
452

he had advanced from beyond the Danube and departed with the promise of peace. But above all he declared and avowed with threats that he would bring worse things upon Italy, unless they sent him Honoria, the sister of the Emperor Valentinian and daughter of Augusta Placidia, with her due share of the royal wealth. For it was said 224 that Honoria, although bound to chastity for the honor of the imperial court and kept in constraint by command of her brother, had secretly despatched a eunuch to summon Attila that she might have his protection against her brother's power; a shameful thing, indeed, to get license for her passion at the cost of the public weal.

XLIII So Attila returned to his own country, seem- 225 ing to regret the peace and to be vexed at the cessation of

war. For he sent ambassadors to Marcian, Emperor of the East, threatening to devastate the provinces, because that which had been promised him by Theodosius, a former emperor, was in no wise performed, and saying that he would show himself more cruel to his foes than ever. But as he was shrewd and crafty, he threatened in one direction and moved his army in another; for in the midst of these preparations he turned his face towards the Visigoths who had yet to feel his vengeance. But here 226 he had not the same success as against the Romans. Hastening back by a different way than before, he decided to reduce to his sway that part of the Alani which was settled across the river Loire, in order that by attacking them, and thus changing the aspect of the war, he might become a more terrible menace to the Visigoths. Accordingly he started from the provinces of Dacia and Pannonia, where the Huns were then dwelling with various subject peoples, and moved his array against the Alani. But Thorismud, king of the Visigoths, with like 227 quickness of thought perceived Attila's trick. By forced marches he came to the Alani before him, and was well prepared to check the advance of Attila when he came

after him. They joined battle in almost the same way as
before at the Catalaunian Plains, and Thorismud dashed
his hopes of victory, for he routed him and drove him
from the land without a triumph, compelling him to flee
to his own country. Thus while Attila, the famous leader
and lord of many victories, sought to blot out the fame
of his destroyer and in this way to annul what he had
suffered at the hands of the Visigoths, he met a second
228 defeat and retreated ingloriously. Now after the bands
of the Huns had been repulsed by the Alani, without any
hurt to his own men, Thorismud departed for Tolosa.
There he established a settled peace for his people and in
the third year of his reign fell sick. While letting blood
from a vein, he was betrayed to his death by Ascalc, a
client, who told his foes that his weapons were out of
reach. Yet grasping a foot-stool in the one hand he had
free, he became the avenger of his own blood by slaying
several of those that were lying in wait for him.
229   XLIV After his death, his brother Theodorid succeeded to the kingdom of the Visigoths and soon found
that Riciarius his kinsman, the king of the Suavi, was
hostile to him. For Riciarius, presuming on his relationship to Theodorid, believed that he might seize almost the
whole of Spain, thinking the disturbed beginning of
Theodorid's reign made the time opportune for this trick.
230 The Suavi formerly occupied as their country Galicia and
Lusitania, which extend on the right side of Spain along
the shore of Ocean. To the east is Austrogonia, to the
west, on a promontory, is the sacred Monument of the
Roman general Scipio, to the north Ocean, and to the
south Lusitania and the Tagus river, which mingles
golden grains in its sands and thus carries wealth in its
worthless mud. So then Riciarius, king of the Suavi, set
231 forth and strove to seize the whole of Spain. Theodorid,
his kinsman, a man of moderation, sent ambassadors to
him and told him quietly that he must not only withdraw

THE REIGN
OF KING
THEODORID II
453-466

from the territories that were not his own, but furthermore that he should not presume to make such an attempt,
as he was becoming hated .for his ambition. But with
arrogant spirit he replied: "If you murmur here and
find fault with my coming, I shall come to Tolosa where
you dwell. Resist me there, if you can." When he heard
this, Theodorid was angry and, making a compact with
all the other tribes, moved his array against the Suavi.
He had as his close allies Gundiuch and Hilperic, kings

Battle near
the Ulbius
456

of the Burgundians. They came to battle near the river   23²
Ulbius, which flows between Asturica and Hiberia, and
in the engagement Theodorid with the Visigoths, who
fought for the right, came off victorious, overthrowing
the entire tribe of the Suavi and almost exterminating
them. Their king Riciarius fled from the dread foe and
embarked upon a ship. But he was beaten back by another foe, the adverse wind of the Tyrrhenian Sea, and
so fell into the hands of the Visigoths. Thus though
he changed from sea to land, the wretched man did not
avert his death.

When Theodorid had become the victor, he spared the   23.
conquered and did not suffer the rage of conflict to con-
tinue, but placed over the Suavi whom he had conquered
one of his own retainers, named Agrivulf. But Agrivulf
soon treacherously changed his mind, through the per-
suasion of the Suavi, and failed to fulfil his duty. For
he was quite puffed up with tyrannical pride, believing
he had obtained the province as a reward for the valor
by which he and his lord had recently subjugated it. Now
he was a man born of the stock of the Varni, far below
the nobility of Gothic blood, and so was neither zealous
for liberty nor faithful toward his patron. As soon as   23.
Theodorid heard of this, he despatched a force to cast him
out from the kingdom he had usurped. They came
quickly and conquered him in the first battle, inflicting a
punishment befitting his deeds. For he was captured,

taken from his friends and beheaded. Thus at last he was made aware of the wrath of the master he thought might be despised because he was kind. Now when the Suavi beheld the death of their leader, they sent priests of their country to Theodorid as suppliants. He received them with the reverence due their office and not only granted the Suavi exemption from punishment, but was moved by compassion and allowed them to choose a ruler of their own race for themselves. The Suavi did so, taking Rimismund as their prince. When this was done and peace was everywhere assured. Theodorid died in the thirteenth year of his reign.

235   XLV   His brother Eurich succeeded him with such eager haste that he fell under dark suspicion. Now while these and various other matters were happening among the people of the Visigoths, the Emperor Valentinian was slain by the treachery of Maximus, and Maximus himself, like a tyrant, usurped the rule. Gaiseric, king of the Vandals, heard of this and came from Africa to Italy with ships of war, entered Rome and laid it waste. Maximus fled and was slain by a certain Ursus, a Roman

236   soldier. After him Majorian undertook the government of the Western Empire at the bidding of Marcian, Emperor of the East. But he too ruled but a short time. For when he had moved his forces against the Alani who were harassing Gaul, he was killed at Dertona near the river named Ira. Séverus succeeded him and died at Rome in the third year of his reign. When the Emperor Leo, who had succeeded Marcian in the Eastern Empire, learned of this, he chose as emperor his Patrician Anthemius and sent him to Rome. Upon his arrival he sent against the Alani his son-in-law Ricimer, who was an excellent man and almost the only one in Italy at that time fit to command the army. In the very first engagement he conquered and destroyed the host of the Alani, together with their king, Beorg.

KING EURICH
466-485

THE WESTERN EMPIRE FROM THE DEATH OF VALENTINIAN III TO ROMULUS AUGUSTULUS

Maximus 455

GAISERIC SACKS ROME 455

Majorian
457-461

Livius Severus
461-465

Leo I
457-474

Anthemius
467-472

Now Eurich, king of the Visigoths, perceived the fre-   23
quent change of Roman Emperors and strove to hold
Gaul by his own right. The Emperor Anthemius heard
of it and asked the Brittones for aid. Their King
Riotimus came with twelve thousand men into the state
of the Bituriges by the way of Ocean, and was received
as he disembarked from his ships. Eurich, king of the   23
Visigoths, came against them with an innumerable army,
and after a long fight he routed Riotimus, king of the
Brittones, before the Romans could join him. So when
he had lost a great part of his army, he fled with all the
men he could gather together, and came to the Burgundians, a neighboring tribe then allied to the Romans. But
Eurich, king of the Visigoths, seized the Gallic city of
Arverna; for the Emperor Anthemius was now dead.
Engaged in fierce war with his son-in-law Ricimer, he   23

Olybrius
472

had worn out Rome and was himself finally slain by his
son-in-law and yielded the rule to Olybrius.

At that time Aspar, first of the Patricians and a famous
man of the Gothic race was wounded by the swords of
the eunuchs in his palace at Constantinople and died.
With him were slain his sons Ardabures and Patriciolus,
the one long a Patrician, and the other styled a Caesar
and son-in-law of the Emperor Leo. Now Olybrius died
barely eight months after he had entered upon his reign,

Glycerius
473

and Glycerius was made Caesar at Ravenna, rather by
usurpation than by election. Hardly had a year been

Nepos
474

ended when Nepos, the son of the sister of Marcellinus,
once a Patrician, deposed him from his office and ordained him bishop at the Port of Rome.

When Eurich, as we have already said, beheld these   24
great and various changes, he seized the city of Arverna,
where the Roman general Ecdicius was at that time in
command. He was a senator of most renowned family
and the son of Avitus, a recent emperor who had usurped
the reign for a few days—for Avitus held the rule for a

few days before Olybrius, and then withdrew of his own
accord to Placentia, where he was ordained bishop. His
son Ecdicius strove for a long time with the Visigoths,
but had not the power to prevail. So he left the country
and (what was more important) the city of Arverna to
241 the enemy and betook himself to safer regions. When
the Emperor Nepos heard of this, he ordered Ecdicius
to leave Gaul and come to him, appointing Orestes in his
stead as Master of the Soldiery. This Orestes thereupon received the army, set out from Rome against the
enemy and came to Ravenna. Here he tarried while he
made his son Romulus Augustulus emperor. When
Nepos learned of this, he fled to Dalmatia and died there,
deprived of his throne, in the very place where Glycerius,
who was formerly emperor, held at that time the bishopric
of Salona.

Romulus Augustulus 476

242   XLVI Now when Augustulus had been appointed
Emperor by his father Orestes in Ravenna, it was not
long before Odoacer, king of the Torcilingi, invaded
Italy, as leader of the Sciri, the Heruli and allies of
various races. He put Orestes to death, drove his son
Augustulus from the throne and condemned him to the
punishment of exile in the Castle of Lucullus in Campania.

THE RULE OF ODOACER 476-493

243   Thus the Western Empire of the Roman race, which
Octavianus Augustus, the first of the Augusti, began to
govern in the seven hundred and ninth year from the
founding of the city, perished with this Augustulus in the
five hundred and twenty-second year from the beginning
of the rule of his predecessors and those before them,
and from this time onward kings of the Goths held Rome
and Italy. Meanwhile Odoacer, king of nations, subdued
all Italy and then at the very outset of his reign slew
Count Bracila at Ravenna that he might inspire a fear
of himself among the Romans. He strengthened his
kingdom and held it for almost thirteen years, even until

Death of Bracila 477

the appearance of Theodoric, of whom we shall speak
hereafter.

XLVII   But first let us return to that order from **244**
which we have digressed and tell how Eurich, king of the
Visigoths, beheld the tottering of the Roman Empire and
reduced Arelate and Massilia to his own sway. Gaiseric,
king of the Vandals, enticed him by gifts to do these
things, to the end that he himself might forestall the plots
which Leo and Zeno had contrived against him. Therefore he stirred the Ostrogoths to lay waste the Eastern
Empire and the Visigoths the Western, so that while his
foes were battling in both empires, he might himself
reign peacefully in Africa. Eurich perceived this with
gladness and, as he already held all of Spain and Gaul
by his own right, proceeded to subdue the Burgundians
also. In the nineteenth year of his reign he was deprived
of his life at Arelate, where he then dwelt. He was suc- **245**
ceeded by his own son Alaric, the ninth in succession
from the famous Alaric the Great to receive the kingdom
of the Visigoths. For even as it happened to the line of
the Augusti, as we have stated above, so too it appears in
the line of the Alarici, that kingdoms often come to an
end in kings who bear the same name as those at the
beginning. Meanwhile let us leave this subject, and
weave together the whole story of the origin of the Goths,
as we promised.

Leo II
473-474

Zeno
474-491

Eurich killed
485

ALARIC II
LAST KING
OF THE
VISIGOTHS
485-507

The Divided Goths: Ostrogoths

XLVIII   Since I have followed the stories of my **246**
ancestors and retold to the best of my ability the tale of
the period when both tribes, Ostrogoths and Visigoths,
were united, and then clearly treated of the Visigoths
apart from the Ostrogoths, I must now return to those
ancient Scythian abodes and set forth in like manner the
ancestry and deeds of the Ostrogoths. It appears that at

THE
OSTROGOTHS
AND THEIR
SUBJECTION
TO THE HUNS

the death of their king, Hermanaric, they were made a   Death of
Hermanaric
375 or 376
separate people by the departure of the Visigoths, and
remained in their country subject to the sway of the
Huns; yet Vinitharius of the Amali retained the insignia
47   of his rule. He rivalled the valor of his grandfather
Vultuulf, although he had not the good fortune of Hermanaric. But disliking to remain under the rule of the
Huns, he withdrew a little from them and strove to show
his courage by moving his forces against the country of
the Antes. When he attacked them, he was beaten in the
first encounter. Thereafter he did valiantly and, as a
terrible example, crucified their king, named Boz, together
with his sons and seventy nobles, and left their bodies
hanging there to double the fear of those who had sur-
48   rendered. When he had ruled with such license for
barely a year, Balamber, king of the Huns, would no
longer endure it, but sent for Gesimund, son of Hunimund the Great. Now Gesimund, together with a great
part of the Goths, remained under the rule of the Huns,
being mindful of his oath of fidelity. Balamber renewed
his alliance with him and led his army up against Vinitharius. After a long contest, Vinitharius prevailed in
the first and in the second conflict, nor can any say how
49   great slaughter he made of the army of the Huns. But
in the third battle, when they met each other unexpectedly
at the river named Erac, Balamber shot an arrow and
wounded Vinitharius in the head, so that he died. Then
Balamber took to himself in marriage Vadamerca, the
grand-daughter of Vinitharius, and finally ruled all the
people of the Goths as his peaceful subjects, but in such
a way that one ruler of their own number always held the
power over the Gothic race, though subject to the Huns.
50   And later, after the death of Vinitharius, Hunimund   KING
HUNIMUND
ruled them, the son of Hermanaric, a mighty king of
yore; a man fierce in war and of famous personal beauty,
who afterwards fought successfully against the race of

KING
THORISMUD
KILLED
404

the Suavi. And when he died, his son Thorismud succeeded him, in the very bloom of youth. In the second
year of his rule he moved an army against the Gepidae
and won a great victory over them, but is said to have
been killed by falling from his horse. When he was dead, 251
the Ostrogoths mourned for him so deeply that for forty
years no other king succeeded in his place, and during all
this time they had ever on their lips the tale of his memory. Now as time went on, Valamir grew to man's
estate. He was the son of Thorismud's cousin Vandalarius. For his son Beremud, as we have said before, at
last grew to despise the race of the Ostrogoths because of
the overlordship of the Huns, and so had followed the
tribe of the Visigoths to the western country, and it was
from him Veteric was descended. Veteric also had a son
Eutharic, who married Amalasuentha, the daughter of
Theodoric, thus uniting again the stock of the Amali
which had divided long ago. Eutharic begat Athalaric
and Mathesuentha. But since Athalaric died in the
years of his boyhood, Mathesuentha was taken to Constantinople by her second husband, namely Germanus, a
nephew of the Emperor Justinian, and bore a posthumous
son, whom she named Germanus.

But that the order we have taken for our history may 25:
run its due course, we must return to the stock of Vandalarius, which put forth three branches. This Vandalarius,
the great grand-nephew of Hermanaric and cousin of the
aforesaid Thorismud, vaunted himself among the race of
the Amali because he had begotten three sons, Valamir
Thiudimer and Vidimer. Of these Valamir ascended the
KING
VALAMIR
445?
throne after his parents, though the Huns as yet held the
power over the Goths in general as among other nations.
It was pleasant to behold the concord of these three broth- 25
ers; for the admirable Thiudimer served as a soldier for
the empire of his brother Valamir, and Valamir bade
honors be given him, while Vidimer was eager to serve

them both. Thus regarding one another with common
affection, not one was wholly deprived of the kingdom
which two of them held in mutual peace. Yet, as has
often been said, they ruled in such a way that they re-
spected the dominion of Attila, king of the Huns. Indeed
they could not have refused to fight against their kinsmen
the Visigoths, and they must even have committed parri-
cide at their lord's command. There was no way whereby
any Scythian tribe could have been wrested from the
power of the Huns, save by the death of Attila—an
event the Romans and all other nations desired. Now his
death was as base as his life was marvellous.

54   XLIX Shortly before he died, as the historian Priscus
relates, he took in marriage a very beautiful girl named
Ildico, after countless other wives, as was the custom of
his race. He had given himself up to excessive joy at
his wedding, and as he lay on his back, heavy with wine
and sleep, a rush of superfluous blood, which would ordinarily have flowed from his nose, streamed in deadly
course down his throat and killed him, since it was hindered in the usual passages. Thus did drunkenness put a
disgraceful end to a king renowned in war. On the following day, when a great part of the morning was spent,
the royal attendants suspected some ill and, after a great
uproar, broke in the doors. There they found the death
of Attila accomplished by an effusion of blood, without
any wound, and the girl with downcast face weeping
55   beneath her veil. Then, as is the custom of that race,
they plucked out the hair of their heads and made their
faces hideous with deep wounds, that the renowned warrior might be mourned, not by effeminate wailings and
tears, but by the blood of men. Moreover a wondrous
thing took place in connecton with Attila's death. For
in a dream some god stood at the side of Marcian, Emperor of the East, while he was disquieted about his
fierce foe, and showed him the bow of Attila broken in

DEATH
OF ATTILA
453

that same night, as if to intimate that the race of Huns
owed much to that weapon. This account the historian
Priscus says he accepts upon truthful evidence. For so
terrible was Attila thought to be to great empires that
the gods announced his death to rulers as a special boon.

We shall not omit to say a few words about the many   25
ways in which his shade was honored by his race. His
body was placed in the midst of a plain and lay in state
in a silken tent as a sight for men's admiration. The best
horsemen of the entire tribe of the Huns rode around in
circles, after the manner of circus games, in the place
to which he had been brought and told of his deeds in a
funeral dirge in the following manner: "The chief of the   25
Huns, King Attila, born of his sire Mundiuch, lord of
bravest tribes, sole possessor of the Scythian and German
realms—powers unknown before—captured cities and
terrified both empires of the Roman world and, appeased
by their prayers, took annual tribute to save the rest from
plunder. And when he had accomplished all this by the
favor of fortune, he fell not by wound of the foe, nor
by treachery of friends, but in the midst of his nation at
peace, happy in his joy and without sense of pain. Who
can rate this as death, when none believes it calls for
vengeance?" When they had mourned him with such   25
lamentations, a *strava,* as they call it, was celebrated over
his tomb with great revelling. They gave way in turn to
the extremes of feeling and displayed funereal grief alter-
nating with joy. Then in the secrecy of night they buried
his body in the earth. They bound his coffins, the first
with gold, the second with silver and the third with the
strength of iron, showing by such means that these three
things suited the mightiest of kings; iron because he
subdued the nations, gold and silver because he received
the honors of both empires. They also added the arms
of foemen won in the fight, trappings of rare worth,
sparkling with various gems, and ornaments of all sorts

whereby princely state is maintained. And that so great riches might be kept from human curiosity, they slew those appointed to the work—a dreadful pay for their labor; and thus sudden death was the lot of those who buried him as well as of him who was buried.

259 L After they had fulfilled these rites, a contest for the highest place arose among Attila's successors—for the minds of young men are wont to be inflamed by ambition for power—and in their rash eagerness to rule they all alike destroyed his empire. Thus kingdoms are often weighed down by a superfluity rather than by a lack of successors. For the sons of Attila, who through the license of his lust formed almost a people of themselves, were clamoring that the nations should be divided among them equally and that warlike kings with their peoples should be apportioned to them by lot like a family estate.

DISSOLUTION OF THE KINGDOM OF THE HUNS 454

260 When Ardaric, king of the Gepidae, learned this, he became enraged because so many nations were being treated like slaves of the basest condition, and was the first to rise against the sons of Attila. Good fortune attended him, and he effaced the disgrace of servitude that rested upon him. For by his revolt he freed not only his own tribe, but all the others who were equally oppressed; since all readily strive for that which is sought for the general advantage. They took up arms against the destruction that menaced all and joined battle with the

261 Huns in Pannonia, near a river called Nedao. There an encounter took place between the various nations Attila had held under his sway. Kingdoms with their peoples were divided, and out of one body were made many members · not responding to a common impulse. Being deprived of their head, they madly strove against each other. They never found their equals ranged against them without harming each other by wounds mutually given. And so the bravest nations tore themselves to pieces. For then, I think, must have occurred a most

Battle of Nedao 454

remarkable spectacle, where one might see the Goths fighting with pikes, the Gepidae raging with the sword, the Rugi breaking off the spears in their own wounds, the Suavi fighting on foot, the Huns with bows, the Alani drawing up a battle-line of heavy-armed and the Heruli of light-armed warriors.

Finally, after many bitter conflicts, victory fell unex-   262 pectedly to the Gepidae. For the sword and conspiracy of Ardaric destroyed almost thirty thousand men, Huns as well as those of the other nations who brought them aid. In this battle fell Ellac, the elder son of Attila, whom his father is said to have loved so much more than all the rest that he preferred him to any child or even to all the children of his kingdom. But fortune was not in accord with his father's wish. For after slaying many of the foe, it appears that he met his death so bravely that if his father had lived, he would have rejoiced at his glorious end. When Ellac was slain, his remaining   263 brothers were put to flight near the shore of the Sea of Pontus, where we have said the Goths first settled. Thus did the Huns give way, a race to which men thought the whole world must yield. So baneful a thing is division, that they who used to inspire terror when their strength was united, were overthrown separately. The cause of Ardaric, king of the Gepidae, was fortunate for the various nations who were unwillingly subject to the rule of the Huns, for it raised their long downcast spirits to the glad hope of freedom. Many sent ambassadors to the Roman territory, where they were most graciously received by Marcian, who was then emperor, and took the abodes allotted them to dwell in. But the Gepidae by their   26. own might won for themselves the territory of the Huns and ruled as victors over the extent of all Dacia, demanding of the Roman Empire nothing more than peace and an annual gift as a pledge of their friendly alliance. This the Emperor freely granted at the time, and to this day that race receives its customary gifts from the Roman Emperor.

Now when the Goths saw the Gepidae defending for themselves the territory of the Huns, and the people of the Huns dwelling again in their ancient abodes, they preferred to ask for lands from the Roman Empire, rather than invade the lands of others with danger to themselves. So they received Pannonia, which stretches in a long plain, being bounded on the east by Upper Moesia, on the south by Dalmatia, on the west by Noricum and on the north by the Danube. This land is adorned with many cities, the first of which is Sirmium 5 and the last Vindobona. But the Sauromatae, whom we call Sarmatians, and the Cemandri and certain of the Huns dwelt in Castra Martis, a city given them in the region of Illyricum. Of this race was Blivila, Duke of Pentapolis, and his brother Froila and also Bessa, a Patrician in our time. The Sciri, moreover, and the Sadagarii and certain of the Alani with their leader, Candac by name, received Scythia Minor and Lower Moesia. Paria, 5 the father of my father Alanoviiamuth (that is to say, my grandfather), was secretary to this Candac as long as he lived. To his sister's son Gunthigis, also called Baza, the Master of the Soldiery, who was the son of Andag the son of Andela, who was descended from the stock of the Amali, I also, Jordanes, although an un-   JORDANES
learned man before my conversion, was secretary. The Rugi, however, and some other races asked that they might inhabit Bizye and Arcadiopolis. Hernac, the younger son of Attila, with his followers, chose a home in the most distant part of Lesser Scythia. Emnetzur and Ultzindur, kinsmen of his, won Oescus and Utus and Almus in Dacia on the bank of the Danube, and many of the Huns, then swarming everywhere, betook themselves into Romania, and from them the Sacromontisi and the Fossatisii of this day are said to be descended.

Bishop Ulfilas
about 311-381

THE
LESSER
GOTHS

THE
OSTROGOTHS
IN PANNONIA

BIRTH
OF
THEODORIC
THE GREAT
454

LI   There were other Goths also, called the Lesser, 2
a great people whose priest and primate was Vulfila, who
is said to have taught them to write. And to-day they
are in Moesia, inhabiting the Nicopolitan region as far
as the base of Mount Haemus. They are a numerous
people, but poor and unwarlike, rich in nothing save
flocks of various kinds and pasture-lands for cattle and
forests for wood. Their country is not fruitful in wheat
and other sorts of grain. Some of them do not know
that vineyards exist elsewhere, and they buy their wine
from neighboring countries. But most of them drink
milk.

LII   Let us now return to the tribe with which we 2
started, namely the Ostrogoths, who were dwelling in
Pannonia under their king Valamir and his brothers Thiudimer and Vidimer. Although their territories were
separate, yet their plans were one. For Valamir dwelt
between the rivers Scarniunga and Aqua Nigra, Thiudimer near Lake Pelso and Vidimer between them both.
Now it happened that the sons of Attila, regarding the
Goths as deserters from their rule, came against them as
though they were seeking fugitive slaves, and attacked
Valamir alone, when his brothers knew nothing of it. He 2
sustained their attack, though he had but few supporters,
and after harassing them a long time, so utterly overwhelmed them that scarcely any portion of the enemy
remained. The remnant turned in flight and sought
the parts of Scythia which border on the stream of the
river Danaper, which the Huns call in their own tongue
the Var. Thereupon he sent a messenger of good tidings
to his brother Thiudimer, and on the very day the messenger arrived he found even greater joy in the house of
Thiudimer. For on that day his son Theodoric was born,
of a concubine Erelieva indeed, and yet a child of good
hope.

Now after no great time King Valamir and his brothers Thiudimer and Vidimer sent an embassy to the Emperor Marcian, because the usual gifts which they received like a New Year's present from the Emperor, to preserve the compact of peace, were slow in arriving. And they found that Theodoric, son of Triarius, a man of Gothic blood also, but born of another stock, not of the Amali, was in great favor, together with his followers. He was allied in friendship with the Romans and obtained an annual bounty, while they themselves were merely held in disdain. Thereat they were aroused to frenzy and took up arms. They roved through almost the whole of Illyricum and laid it waste in their search for spoil. Then the Emperor quickly changed his mind and returned to his former state of friendship. He sent an embassy to give them the past gifts, as well as those now due, and furthermore promised to give these gifts in future without any dispute. From the Goths the Romans received as a hostage of peace Theodoric, the young child of Thiudimer, whom we have mentioned above. He had now attained the age of seven years and was entering upon his eighth. While his father hesitated about giving him up, his uncle Valamir besought him to do it, hoping that peace between the Romans and the Goths might thus be assured. Therefore Theodoric was given as a hostage by the Goths and brought to the city of Constantinople to the Emperor Leo and, being a goodly child, deservedly gained the imperial favor.

HIS YOUTH SPENT AT CONSTANTINOPLE BEGINNING 461

LIII   Now after firm peace was established between Goths and Romans, the Goths found that the possessions they had received from the Emperor were not sufficient for them. Furthermore, they were eager to display their wonted valor, and so began to plunder the neighboring races round about them, first attacking the Sadagis who held the interior of Pannonia. When Dintzic, king of the Huns, a son of Attila, learned this, he gathered to him

THE GOTHS OVERWHELM THE REMNANT OF THE HUNS

the few who still seemed to have remained under his
sway, namely, the Ultzinzures, the Angisciri, the Bittugures and the Bardores. Coming to Bassiana, a city of
Pannonia, he beleaguered it and began to plunder its territory. Then the Goths at once abandoned the expedition
they had planned against the Sadagis, turned upon the
Huns and drove them so ingloriously from their own
land that those who remained have been in dread of the
arms of the Goths from that time down to the present
day.

CONQUEST
OF THE
SUAVI
When the tribe of the Huns was at last subdued by the
Goths, Hunimund, chief of the Suavi, who was crossing
over to plunder Dalmatia, carried off some cattle of the
Goths which were straying over the plains; for Dalmatia
was near Suavia and not far distant from the territory
of Pannonia, especially that part where the Goths were
then staying. So then, as Hunimund was returning
with the Suavi to his own country, after he had devastated Dalmatia, Thiudimer the brother of Valamir,
king of the Goths, kept watch on their line of march.
Not that he grieved so much over the loss of his cattle,
but he feared that if the Suavi obtained this plunder with
impunity, they would proceed to greater license. So in
the dead of night, while they were asleep, he made an
unexpected attack upon them, near Lake Pelso. Here he
so completely crushed them that he took captive and sent
into slavery under the Goths even Hunimund, their king,
and all of his army who had escaped the sword. Yet
as he was a great lover of mercy, he granted pardon
after taking vengeance and became reconciled to the
Suavi. He adopted as his son the same man whom he
had taken captive, and sent him back with his followers
into Suavia. But Hunimund was unmindful of his
adopted father's kindness. After some time he brought
forth a plot he had contrived and aroused the tribe of the
Sciri, who then dwelt above the Danube and abode peace-

Plot of
Hunimund
about 470

ably with the Goths. So the Sciri broke off their alliance with them, took up arms, joined themselves to Hunimund and went out to attack the race of the Goths. Thus war came upon the Goths who were expecting no evil, because they relied upon both of their neighbors as friends. Constrained by necessity they took up arms and avenged 276 themselves and their injuries by recourse to battle. In this battle, as King Valamir rode on his horse before the line to encourage his men, the horse was wounded and fell, overthrowing its rider. Valamir was quickly pierced by his enemies' spears and slain. Thereupon the Goths proceeded to exact vengeance for the death of their king, as well as for the injury done them by the rebels. They fought in such wise that there remained of all the race of ' the Sciri only a few who bore the name, and they with disgrace. Thus were all destroyed.

277   LIV. The kings [of the Suavi], Hunimund and Alaric, fearing the destruction that had come upon the Sciri, next made war upon the Goths, relying upon the aid of the Sarmatians, who had come to them as auxiliaries with their kings Beuca and Babai. They summoned the last remnants of the Sciri, with Edica and Hunuulf, their chieftains, thinking they would fight the more desperately to avenge themselves. They had on their side the Gepidae also, as well as no small reënforcements from the race of the Rugi and from others gathered here and there. Thus they brought together a great host at 278 the river Bolia in Pannonia and encamped there. Now when Valamir was dead, the Goths fled to Thiudimer, his brother. Although he had long ruled along with his brothers, yet he took the insignia of his increased authority and summoned his younger brother Vidimer and shared with him the cares of war, resorting to arms under compulsion. A battle was fought and the party of the Goths was found to be so much the stronger that the plain was drenched in the blood of their fallen foes and

SUCCESS OF
THE GOTHS
UNDER
THIUDIMER
ABOUT 470

looked like a crimson sea. Weapons and corpses, piled
up like hills, covered the plain for more than ten miles.
When the Goths saw this, they rejoiced with joy unspeak-   27
able, because by this great slaughter of their foes they
had avenged the blood of Valamir their king and the
injury done themselves. But those of the innumerable
and motley throng of the foe who were able to escape,
though they got away, nevertheless came to their own
land with difficulty and without glory.

THIUDIMER
AGAIN WARS
WITH THE
SUAVI

LV   After a certain time, when the wintry cold was   28
at hand, the river Danube was frozen over as usual. For
a river like this freezes so hard that it will support like
a solid rock an army of foot-soldiers and wagons and
sledges and whatsoever vehicles there may be—nor is
there need of skiffs and boats. So when Thiudimer, king
of the Goths, saw that it was frozen, he led his army
across the Danube and appeared unexpectedly to the Suavi
from the rear. Now this country of the Suavi has on the
east the Baiovari, on the west the Franks, on the south the
Burgundians and on the north the Thuringians. With   28
the Suavi there were present the Alamanni, then their
confederates, who also ruled the Alpine heights, whence
several streams flow into the Danube, pouring in with a
great rushing sound. Into a place thus fortified King
Thiudimer led his army in the winter-time and conquered,
plundered and almost subdued the race of the Suavi as
well as the Alamanni, who were mutually banded together. Thence he returned as victor to his own home in
Pannonia and joyfully received his son Theodoric, once

Theodoric

THIUDIMER
SENT BACK
TO HIS OWN
PEOPLE
472

given as hostage to Constantinople and now sent back by
the Emperor Leo with great gifts. Now Theodoric had   2
reached man's estate, for he was eighteen years of age
and his boyhood was ended. So he summoned certain of
his father's adherents and took to himself from the people
his friends and retainers—almost six thousand men.
With these he crossed the Danube, without his father's

knowledge, and marched against Babai, king of the Sarmatians, who had just won a victory over Camundus, a general of the Romans, and was ruling with insolent pride. Theodoric came upon him and slew him, and taking as booty his slaves and treasure, returned victorious to his father. Next he invaded the city of Singidunum, which the Sarmatians themselves had seized, and did not return it to the Romans, but reduced it to his own sway.

Capture of Belgrade

83   LVI   Then as the spoil taken from one and another of the neighboring tribes diminished, the Goths began to lack food. and clothing, and peace became distasteful to men for whom war had long furnished the necessaries of life. So all the Goths approached their king Thiudimer and, with great outcry, begged him to lead forth his army in whatsoever direction he might wish. He summoned his brother and, after casting lots, bade him go into the country of Italy, where at this time Glycerius ruled as emperor, saying that he himself as the mightier would go to the east against a mightier empire.

VIDIMER THE YOUNGER GOES TO. GAUL 473

84   And so it happened. Thereupon Vidimer entered the land of Italy, but soon paid the last debt of fate and departed from earthly affairs, leaving his son and namesake Vidimer to succeed him. The·Emperor Glycerius bestowed gifts upon Vidimer and persuaded him to go from Italy to Gaul, which was then harrassed on all sides by various races, saying that their own kinsmen, the Visigoths, there ruled a neighboring kingdom. And what more? Vidimer accepted the gifts and, obeying the command of the Emperor Glycerius, pressed on to Gaul. Joining with his kinsmen the Visigoths, they again formed one body, as they had been long ago. Thus they held Gaul and Spain by their own right and so defended them that no other race won the mastery there.

THIUDIMER IN MACEDONIA

85   But Thiudimer, the elder brother, crossed the river Savus with his men, threatening the Sarmatians and their

soldiers with war if any should resist him. From fear of this they kept quiet; moreover they were powerless in the face of so great a host. Thiudimer, seeing prosperity everywhere awaiting him, invaded Naissus, the first city of Illyricum. He was joined by his son Theodoric and the Counts Astat and Invilia, and sent them to Ulpiana by way of Castrum Herculis. Upon their arrival the town surrendered, as did Stobi later; and several places of Illyricum, inaccessible to them at first, were thus made easy of approach. For they first plundered and then ruled by right of war Heraclea and Larissa, cities of Thessaly. But Thiudimer the king, perceiving his own good fortune and that of his son, was not content with this alone, but set forth from the city of Naissus, leaving only a few men behind as a guard. He himself advanced to Thessalonica, where Hilarianus the Patrician, appointed by the Emperor, was stationed with his army. When Hilarianus beheld Thessalonica surrounded by an entrenchment and saw that he could not resist attack, he sent an embassy to Thiudimer the king and by the offer of gifts turned him aside from destroying the city. Then the Roman general entered upon a truce with the Goths and of his own accord handed over to them those places they inhabited, namely Cyrrhus, Pella, Europus, Methone, Pydna, Beroea, and another which is called Dium. So the Goths and their king laid aside their arms, consented to peace and became quiet. Soon after these events, King Thiudimer was seized with a mortal illness in the city of Cyrrhus. He called the Goths to himself, appointed Theodoric his son as heir of his kingdom and presently departed this life.

LVII   When the Emperor Zeno heard that Theodoric had been appointed king over his own people, he received the news with pleasure and invited him to come and visit him in the city, sending an escort of honor. Receiving Theodoric with all due respect, he placed him among the

Zeno
474-491

Theodoric the
Great
475-526

princes of his palace. After some time Zeno increased his dignity by adopting him as his son-at-arms and gave him a triumph in the city at his expense. Theodoric was made Consul Ordinary also, which is well known to be the supreme good and highest honor in the world. Nor was this all, for Zeno set up before the royal palace an equestrian statue to the glory of this great man.

THEODORIC
HONORED
BY ZENO
478

290   Now while Theodoric was in alliance by treaty with the Empire of Zeno and was himself enjoying every comfort in the city, he heard that his tribe, dwelling as we have said in Illyricum, was not altogether satisfied or content. So he chose rather to seek a living by his own exertions, after the manner customary to his race, rather than to enjoy the advantages of the Roman Empire in luxurious ease while his tribe lived apart. After pondering these matters, he said to the Emperor: "Though I lack nothing in serving your Empire, yet if Your Piety deem it worthy, be pleased to hear the desire of my

HE SEEKS TO
OBTAIN THE
WESTERN EMPIRE
FOR HIS
PEOPLE

291   heart." And when as usual he had been granted permis- to speak freely, he said: "The western country, long ago governed by the rule of your ancestors and prede- cessors, and that city which was the head and mistress of the world—wherefore is it now shaken by the tyranny of the Torcilingi and the Rugi? Send me there with my race. Thus if you but say the word, you may be freed from the burden of expense here, and, if by the Lord's help I shall conquer, the fame of Your Piety shall be glorious there. For it is better that I, your servant and your son, should rule that kingdom, receiving it as a gift from you if I conquer, than that one whom you do not recognize should oppress your Senate with his tyran- nical yoke and a part of the republic with slavery. For if I prevail, I shall retain it as your grant and gift; if I am conquered, Your Piety will lose nothing—nay, as I have

292   said, it will save the expense I now entail." Although the Emperor was grieved that he should go, yet when he

heard this he granted what Theodoric asked, for he was unwilling to cause him sorrow. He sent him forth enriched by great gifts and commended to his charge the Senate and the Roman People.

THEODORIC
SETS OUT FOR
ITALY
488

Therefore Theodoric departed from the royal city and returned to his own people. In company with the whole tribe of the Goths, who gave him their unanimous consent, he set out for Hesperia. He went in straight march through Sirmium to the places bordering on Pannonia and, advancing into the territory of Venetia as far as the bridge of the Sontius, encamped there. When he 293 had halted there for some time to rest the bodies of his men and pack-animals, Odoacer sent an armed force against him, which he met on the plains of Verona and destroyed with great slaughter. Then he broke camp and advanced through Italy with greater boldness. Crossing the river Po, he pitched camp near the royal city of Ravenna, about the third milestone from the city in the place called Pineta. When Odoacer saw this, he fortified himself within the city. He frequently harassed the army of the Goths at night, sallying forth stealthily with his men, and this not once or twice, but often; and thus he struggled for almost three whole years. But he 29.

HE CONQUERS
ODOACER
AND PUTS
HIM TO DEATH
493

labored in vain, for all Italy at last called Theodoric its lord and the Empire obeyed his nod. But Odoacer, with his few adherents and the Romans who were present, suffered daily from war and famine in Ravenna. Since he accomplished nothing, he sent an embassy and begged for mercy. Theodoric first granted it and afterwards deprived him of his life.   29

THEODORIC
FOUNDS THE
OSTROGOTHIC
KINGDOM IN
ITALY
493

It was in the third year after his entrance into Italy, as we have said, that Theodoric, by advice of the Emperor Zeno, laid aside the garb of a private citizen and the dress of his race and assumed a costume with a royal mantle, as he had now become the ruler over both Goths and Romans. He sent an embassy to Lodoin, king of the

Franks, and asked for his daughter Audefleda in mar-
296 riage. Lodoin freely and gladly gave her, and also his
sons Celdebert and Heldebert and Thiudebert, believing
that by this alliance a league would be formed and that
they would be associated with the race of the Goths. But
that union was of no avail for peace and harmony, for
they fought fiercely with each other again and again for
the lands of the Goths; but never did the Goths yield to
the Franks while Theodoric lived.

297   LVIII Now before he had a child from Audefleda, OF THE INCREASE
Theodoric had children of a concubine, daughters begot-   OF HIS POWER
ten in Moesia, one named Thiudigoto and another Ostro-
gotho. Soon after he came to Italy, he gave them in marriage to neighboring kings, one to Alaric, king of the
Visigoths, and the other to Sigismund, king of the Bur-   Amalaric
298 gundians. Now Alaric begat Amalaric. While his grand-   507-531
father Theodoric cared for and protected him—for he
had lost both parents in the years of childhood—he
found that Eutharic, the son of Veteric, grandchild of
Beremud and of Thorismud, and a descendant of the race
of the Amali, was living in Spain, a young man strong in
wisdom and valor and health of body. Theodoric sent
for him and gave him his daughter Amalasuentha in
299 marriage. And that he might extend his family as much
as possible, he sent his sister Amalafrida (the mother of
Theodahad, who was afterwards king) to Africa as wife
of Thrasamund, king of the Vandals, and her daughter
Amalaberga ,who was his own niece, he united with Her-
minefred, king of the Thuringians.
300   Now he sent his Count Pitza, chosen from among the
chief men of his kingdom, to hold the city of Sirmium.
He got possession of it by driving out its king Thrasaric,
son of Thraustila, and keeping his mother captive. Thence
he came with two thousand infantry and five hundred
horsemen to aid Mundo against Sabinian, Master of the
Soldiery of Illyricum, who at that time had made ready to

fight with Mundo near the city named Margoplanum, which lies between the Danube and Margus rivers, and destroyed the Army of Illyricum. For this Mundo, who 301 traced his descent from the Attilani of old, had fled from the tribe of the Gepidae and was roaming beyond the Danube in waste places where no man tilled the soil. He had gathered around him many outlaws and ruffians and robbers from all sides and had seized a tower called Herta, situated on the bank of the Danube. There he plundered his neighbors in wild license and made himself king over his vagabonds. Now Pitza came upon him when he was nearly reduced to desperation and was already thinking of surrender. So he rescued him from the hands of Sabinian and made him a grateful subject of his king Theodoric.

Theodoric won an equally great victory over the 302 Franks through his Count Ibba in Gaul, when more than thirty thousand Franks were slain in battle. Moreover, after the death of his son-in-law Alaric, Theodoric appointed Thiudis, his armor-bearer, guardian of his grandson Amalaric in Spain. But Amalaric was ensnared by the plots of the Franks in early youth and lost at once his kingdom and his life. Then his guardian Thiudis, advancing from the same kingdom, assailed the Franks and delivered the Spaniards from their disgraceful treachery. So long as he lived he kept the Visigoths united. . After 303 him Thiudigisclus obtained the kingdom and, ruling but a short time, met his death at the hands of his own followers. He was succeeded by Agil, who holds the kingdom to the present day. Athanagild has rebelled against him and is even now provoking the might of the Roman Empire. So Liberius the Patrician is on the way with an army to oppose him. Now there was not a tribe in the west that did not serve Theodoric while he lived, either in friendship or by conquest.

LIX   When he had reached old age and knew that he 304

Thiudis
531-548

Thiudigisclus
548-549

Agil
549-554

Athanagild
554-567

THEODORIC
THE GREAT DIES
526

should soon depart this life, he called together the Gothic
counts and chieftains of his race and appointed Athalaric
as king. He was a boy scarce ten years old, the son of
his daughter Amalasuentha, and he had lost his father
Eutharic. As though uttering his last will and testament,
Theodoric adjured and commanded them to honor their
king, to love the Senate and Roman People and to make
sure of the peace and good will of the Emperor of the
East, as next after God.

305   They kept this command fully so long as Athalaric
their king and his mother lived, and ruled in peace for
almost eight years. But as the Franks put no confidence
in the rule of a child and furthermore held him in contempt, and were also plotting war, he gave back to them
those parts of Gaul which his father and grandfather had
seized. He possessed all the rest in peace and quiet.
Therefore when Athalaric was approaching the age of
manhood, he entrusted to the Emperor of the East both
his own youth and his mother's widowhood. But in a
short time the ill-fated boy was carried off by an untimely

306   death and departed from earthly affairs. His mother
feared she might be despised by the Goths on account of
the weakness of her sex. So after much thought she decided, for the sake of relationship, to summon her cousin
Theodahad from Tuscany, where he led a retired life at
home, and thus she established him on the throne. But
he was unmindful of their kinship and, after a little time,
had her taken from the palace at Ravenna to an island
of the Bulsinian lake where he kept her in exile. After
spending a very few days there in sorrow, she was
strangled in the bath by his hirelings.

307   LX   When Justinian, the Emperor of the East, heard
this, he was aroused as if he had suffered personal injury
in the death of his wards. Now at that time he had won
a triumph over the Vandals in Africa, through his most
faithful Patrician Belisarius. Without delay he sent his

KING
ATHALARIC
526-534

AMALASUENTHA

Theodahad
534-536

534

Justinian
527-565
JUSTINIAN SENDS
BELISARIUS TO
AVENGE THE
DEATH OF HIS
WARDS
534

army under this leader against the Goths at the very time
when his arms were yet dripping with the blood of the
Vandals. This sagacious general believed he could not   308
overcome the Gothic nation, unless he should first seize
Sicily, their nursing-mother. Acordingly he did so. As
soon as he entered Trinacria, the Goths, who were besieg-
ing the town of Syracuse, found that they were not succeeding and surrendered of their own accord to Belisarius, with their leader Sinderith. When the Roman general reached Sicily, Theodahad sought out Evermud, his
son-in-law, and sent him with an army to guard the strait
which lies between Campania and Sicily and sweeps from
a bend of the Tyrrhenian Sea into the vast tide of the
Adriatic. When Evermud arrived, he pitched his camp   309
by the town of Rhegium. He soon saw that his side was
the weaker. Coming over with a few close and faithful
followers to the side of the victor and willingly casting
himself at the feet of Belisarius, he decided to serve the
rulers of the Roman Empire. When the army of the
Goths perceived this, they distrusted Theodahad and
clamored for his expulsion from the kingdom and for the
appointment as king of their leader Vitiges, who had been
his armor bearer. This was done; and presently Vitiges   310
was raised to the office of king on the Barbarian Plains.
He entered Rome and sent on to Ravenna the men most
faithful to him to demand the death of Theodahad. They
came and executed his command. After King Theodahad
was slain, a messenger came from the king—for he was
already king in the Barbarian Plains—to proclaim Vitiges
to the people.

Meanwhile the Roman army crossed the strait and   311
marched toward Campania. They took Naples and
pressed on to Rome. Now a few days before they arrived, King Vitiges had set forth from Rome, arrived at
Ravenna and married Mathesuentha, the daughter of

Amalasuentha and grand-daughter of Theodoric, the former king. While he was celebrating his new marriage and holding court at Ravenna, the imperial army advanced from Rome and attacked the strongholds in both parts of Tuscany. When Vitiges learned of this through messengers, he sent a force under Hunila, a leader of the Goths, to Perusia which was beleaguered by them. While they were endeavoring by a long siege to dislodge Count Magnus, who was holding the place with a small force, the Roman army came upon them, and they themselves were driven away and utterly exterminated. When Vitiges heard the news, he raged like a lion and assembled all the host of the Goths. He advanced from Ravenna and harassed the walls of Rome with a long siege. But after fourteen months his courage was broken and he raised the siege of the city of Rome and prepared to overwhelm Ariminum. Here he was baffled in like manner and put to flight; and so he retreated to Ravenna. When besieged there, he quickly and willingly surrendered himself to the victorious side, together with his wife Mathesuentha and the royal treasure.

And thus a famous kingdom and most valiant race, which had long held sway, was at last overcome in almost its two thousand and thirtieth year by that conqueror of many nations, the Emperor Justinian, through his most faithful consul Belisarius. He gave Vitiges the title of Patrician and took him to Constantinople, where he dwelt for more than two years, bound by ties of affection to the Emperor, and then departed this life. But his consort Mathesuentha was bestowed by the Emperor upon the Patrician Germanus, his nephew. And of them was born a son (also called Germanus) after the death of his father Germanus. This union of the race of the Anicii with the stock of the Amali gives hopeful promise, under the Lord's favor, to both peoples.

312

313

314

THE OSTROGOTHS OVERCOME BY BELISARIUS

Siege of Rome 537-538

Surrender of Vitiges 540

Death of Vitiges 542

Mathesuentha marries Germanus 542

Conclusion

And now we have recited the origin of the Goths, the   315
noble line of the Amali and the deeds of brave men. This
glorious race yielded to a more glorious prince and surrendered to a more valiant leader, whose fame shall be
silenced by no ages or cycles of years; for the victorious
and triumphant Emperor Justinian and his consul Belisarius shall be named and known as Vandalicus, Afri-
canus and Geticus.

Thou who readest this, know that I have followed the   316
writings of my ancestors, and have culled a few flowers
from their broad meadows to weave a chaplet for him
who cares to know these things. Let no one believe that
to the advantage of the race of which I have spoken—
though indeed I trace my own descent from it—I have
added aught besides what I have read or learned by
inquiry. Even thus I have not included all that is written
or told about them, nor spoken so much to their praise as
to the glory of him who conquered them.

COMMENTARY

Preface 1. as a certain writer says: this refers to the statement of Rufinus (about 345-410), in the preface to his version of Origen's commentary on the epistle to the Romans. Jordanes has not merely borrowed a phrase, as his words seem to indicate; he has taken over the entire introduction of Rufinus almost word for word, as Sybel first pointed out (Schmidt: Zeitschrift für Geschichtswissenschaft, vii, 288). **brother Castalius:** this form of address (compare *frater Vigili* in the introduction to his *Romana*) together with such pious expressions as *orans pro me, frater carissime. Dominus tecum. Amen.* (§ 3), *si dominus donaverit* (§ 9), *iubante domino* (§ 75), etc., naturally accord with the belief that Jordanes was a monk or an ecclesiastic. See also Introduction (p. 5). **abbreviation of the Chronicles:** namely, the *Romana*. Jordanes was engaged in writing his *Romana*, more fully entitled *De summa temporum vel origine actibusque gentis Romanorum*, but laid it aside to write the History of the Goths (*Getica*) which he published first (551 A.D.). See his preface to the *Romana* (§ 4): *aliud volumen de origine actusque Getice gentis, quam iam dudum communi amico Castalio ededissem.* **Senator:** not a title, but part of the name of Flavius Magnus Aurelius Cassiodor(i)us Senator (about 487—about 583), whose History of the Goths in twelve books is known to us only in the abridgment of Jordanes. Cassiodorus himself mentions the work in the preface to his *Variae*, where his friends are represented as saying to him: *duodecim libris Gothorum historiam defloratis prosperitatibus condidisti.*

I 4. Orosius: almost an exact quotation from Orosius I, 2, 1: *maiores nostri orbem totius terrae Oceani limbo circumsaeptum triquadrum statuere eiusque tres partes Asiam, Europam et Africam vocaverunt.*

6. Hippodes: see Julius Honorius p. 691. Gron.: *insulae orientales Oceani quae sunt Hippopodes insula, Iannessi insula, Solis perusta insula, Taprobane insula, Silefantine insula, Teron insula.* **Taprobane:** the island of Ceylon. **ten . . . cities:** see Orosius I, 2, 16: *insula Taprobane, quae habet decem civitates.* On the punctuation of this sentence in the Latin, see A. Bachmann, Zu Iordanis, in Neues Archiv 23, 175 (1898).

7. Strait of Gades: the strait of Gibraltar. **Fortunate:** the storied islands of the western Ocean, the abodes of the Blessed (μακάρων νῆσοι), are perhaps to be identified with the

143

Canary Islands. **Galicia:** *Gallicia* or *Callaecia* is the modern Galicia in N. W. Spain. **Lusitania:** approximately corresponding to Portugal. **Temple of Hercules:** this was on an island in the neighborhood of the town of Onoba (now called Huelva) in the province of Baetica. See Strabo 3, 5, 5, p. 170: εἰς νῆσον Ἡρακλέους ἱερὰν κειμένην κατὰ πόλιν Ὀνοβαν τῆς Ἰβηρίας. **Scipio's Monument:** we are to understand by this the *monumentum Caeponis in ipso mari scopulo magis quam insulae impositum* (Mela, 3, 1, 5; Strabo 3, 1, 9, p. 140), near the mouth of the *Baetis* (now the Guadalquivir). Its mention here in connection with Galicia and Lusitania is perhaps due to a confusion with the *promunturium sacrum* (Cape St. Vincent).

8. **Baleares:** the Balearic Islands. **Mevania:** Isle of Man? see Orosius 1, 2, 82: *huic* (Ireland) *etiam Mevania insula proxima est.* **Orcades:** the Orkneys. Orosius 1, 2, 78: *a tergo* (Britain) *... Orcadas insulas habet, quarum viginti desertae sunt, tredecim coluntur.*

9. **Thule:** Mainland, the largest of the Shetland Islands; or, according to others, Iceland. **Mantuan bard:** Vergil, Georgics 1, 30: *tibi serviat ultima Thyle.* **Scandza:** or *Scandia,* the Scandinavian peninsula.

II 10. **Livy tells:** see Tacitus, Agricola 10: *formam totius Britanniae Livius veterum, Fabius Rusticus recentium eloquentissimi auctores oblongae scutulae vel bipenni adsimilavere ... hanc oram novissimi maris tunc primum Romana classis circumvecta insulam esse Britanniam affirmavit.* **Caesar:** see Tacitus, Agricola 13: *primus omnium Romanorum divus Iulius cum exercitu Britanniam ingressus.*

11. **face Gaul and Germany:** Mela 3, 6, 50: (Britain) *inter septentrionem occidentemque proiecta grandi angulo Rheni ostia prospicit; dein obliqua retro latera abstrahit, altero Galliam altero Germaniam spectans; tum rursus perpetuo margine directi litoris ab tergore abducta iterum se in diversos angulos cuneat triquetra.* See also Tacitus, Agricola 10: *immensum ... spatium procurrentium extremo iam litore terrarum velut in cuneum tenuatur.* **stadia:** Dio epit. 76, 12: καὶ αὐτῆς (Britain) τὸ μὲν μῆκος στάδιοι ἑπτακισχίλιοι καὶ ἑκατὸν τριάκοντα δύο εἰσί, τοῦ δὲ δὴ πλάτους τὸ μὲν πλεῖστον δέκα καὶ τριακόσιοι καὶ δισχίλιοι, τὸ δὲ ἐλάχιστον τριακόσιοι.

12. **the sea:** see Tacitus, Agricola 10: *mare pigrum et grave remigantibus perhibent ne ventis quidem perinde attolli, credo, quod rariores terrae montesque, causa ac materia tempestatum, et profunda moles continui maris tardius impellitur ... unum addiderim nusquam latius dominari mare.* **Strabo ... relates:** Strabo 4, 5, 2, p. 200, Cas.: ἐν δὲ ταῖς αἰθρίαις ὀμίχλη κατέχει πολὺν χρόνον, ὥστε δι' ἡμέρας ὅλης ἐπὶ τρεῖς μόνον ἢ τέτταρας ὥρας τὰς περὶ τὴν μεσημβρίαν ὁρᾶσθαι τὸν ἥλιον.

13. **Cornelius . . . says**: see Tacitus, Agricola 12: *nox clara et extrema Britanniae parte brevis, ut finem atque initium lucis exiguo discrimine internoscas.* **more productive . . . pearls**: Mela 3, 6, 50. 51; *fecunda, verum iis quae pecora quam homines benignius alant. fert nemora saltusque ac praegrandia flumina alternis motibus modo in pelagus modo retro fluentia et quaedam gemmas margaritasque generantia.* **Caledonia**: the Highlands in the northern part of Scotland. With this passage compare Tacitus, Agricola 11: *rutilae Caledoniam habitantium comae, magni artus Germanicam originem adseverant. Silurum colorati vultus, torti plerumque crines et posita contra Hispania Iberos veteres traiecisse easque sedes occupasse fidem faciunt.* Also Tacitus, Histories 2,32: *Germanos . . . fluxis corporibus.*

14. **alike wild**: Mela 3, 6, 51: *fert populos regesque populorum, sed sunt inculti omnes.* **Dio . . . assures us**: Dio epit. 76, 12: δύο δὲ γένη τῶν Βρεττανῶν μέγιστά εἰσι, Καληδόνιοι καὶ Μαιᾶται. καὶ ἐς αὐτὰ καὶ τὰ τῶν ἄλλων προσρήματα ὡς εἰπεῖν συγκεχώρηκεν. **woods are their home**: so Strabo 4, 5, 2, p. 200: πόλεις δ᾽ αὐτῶν εἰσιν οἱ δρυμοὶ περιφράξαντες γὰρ δένδρεσι καταβεβλημένοις εὐρυχωρῆ κύκλον ἐνταῦθα καὶ αὐτοὶ καλυβοποιοῦνται καὶ τὰ βοσκήματα κατασταθμεύουσιν οὐ πρὸς πολὺν χρόνον. They paint their bodies: Mela, 3, 2, 51.52: *incertum ob decorem an quid aliud vitro corpora infecti. causas tamen bellorum et bella contrahunt ac se frequenter invicem infestant, maxime imperitandi cupidine studioque ea prolatandi quae possident. dimicant non equitatu modo aut pedite, verum et bigis et curribus Gallice armati: covinnos vocant: quorum falcatis axibus utuntur.* See Claudianus de laud. Stilich. 2, 247: *Britannia . . . ferro picta genas;* in Rufin. 1, 313: *membraque qui ferro gaudet pinxisse Gelonus.*

III. 16. **above**: see I 9. **Ptolemaeus . . . made mention**: Ptolemaeus 2, 11, 33: Ἀπ᾽ ἀνατολῶν δὲ τῆς Χερσονήσου τέσσαρες αἱ καλούμεναι Σκανδίαι, τρεῖς μὲν μικραί, . . . 34: μία δὲ μεγίστη καὶ ἀνατολικωτάτη κατὰ τὰς ἐκβολὰς Οὐιστούλα ποταμοῦ . . . 35: καλεῖται δὲ ἰδίως καὶ αὐτὴ Σκανδία. **Mela . . . makes mention**: Mela, 3, 3, 31: *super Albim Codanus ingens sinus magnis parvisque insulis refertus est.* The Codan Gulf appears to be the Kattegat. Mommsen is mistaken in saying (p. 58, note 2) *de Scandia auctor tacet.* In Mela 3, 6, 54, we read (as restored by Muellenhoff): *in illo sinu quem Codanum diximus eximia Scandinavia.* See Berliner Philologische Wochenschrift 14 (1894), 1389.

17. **Sarmatian Mountains**: the Carpathian range. **Vagus**: Muellenhoff (Weltkarte, p. 31) believes that this is the same stream called by the anonymous Geographer of Ravenna, 4, 11, the *Bangis,* and argues that as the Northmen called every stream that emptied into the Ocean *vâgs flôd, vâgs flôi?, vâgs straumr,* or something of the sort, the general term here is to be used as a proper name.

19. Ptolemaeus mentions: Ptolemaeus 2, 11, 35: καὶ κατέχου-
σιν αὐτῆς τὰ μὲν δυτικὰ (1) Χαιδεινοί, τὰ δ' ἀνατολικὰ (2) Φαυόναι καὶ (3) Φιραῖσοι
[τὰ δὲ ἀρκτικὰ (4) Φίννοι], τὰ δὲ μεσημβρινὰ (5) Γοῦτοι καὶ (6) Δαυκίωνες, τὰ δὲ
μέσα (7) Λευῶνοι.   **Adogit:** Muellenhoff thinks this name has been
corrupted and we are to understand by it the *Alogii* or *Halogii*
or *Hâleygir*, the inhabitants of *Hâlogalandi*, the most northern
region of Norway, now known as Nordland, and extending beyond the Arctic Circle.

21. Screrefennae: according to Muellenhoff, this form of the
name is used incorrectly by Jordanes for *Scretefennae, Screthe-
fennae, Scrithefenni* or *Scridifinni*.   Under this name he here in-
cludes all men of Finnish race.   See Procopius b. Goth., 2, 15:
Σκριθίφινοι . . . οὔτε . . . αὐτοὶ γῆν γεωργοῦσιν οὔτε τι αὐτοῖς αἱ γυναῖκες
ἐργάζονται, ἀλλὰ ἄνδρες ἀεὶ ξὺν ταῖς γυναιξὶ τὴν θήραν μόνην ἐπιτηδεύον-
ται.   θηρίων τε γὰρ καὶ ἄλλων ζῴων μέγα τι χρῆμα αἵ τε ὗλαι αὐτοῖς
φέρουσι, μεγάλαι ὑπερφυῶς οὖσαι, καὶ τὰ ὄρη, ἃ ταύτῃ ἀνέχει. καὶ κρέασι
μὲν θηρίων ἀεὶ τῶν ἁλισκομένων σιτίζονται, τὰ δέρματα δὲ ἀμφιέννυνται
Paulus hist. Lang., 1. 5: *Scritofini . . . crudis agrestium animan-
tium carnibus vescuntur, de quorum etiam hirtis pellibus sibi indu-
menta peraptant.*   **Suehans:** see Zeuss: Die Deutschen und die
Nachbarstämme (1837), p. 514.   **Thuringians . . . horses:** see
Cassiodorus var. 4, 1: *Herminafrido regi Thoringorum Theodoricus
rex . . . indicamus nos venientibus legatis vestris . . . more gentium suscepisse . . . equos argenteo colore vestitos.*   **sapphire
colored:** σαπφείρινος = like *lapis lazuli;* sables.

22. Theustes . . . Ranii (24): these twenty-seven tribes are
vaguely conceived as dwelling in a receding series of northern
regions.

24. Roduulf: Mommsen thinks he is to be identified with that
King Ῥοδοῦλφος of the Heruli mentioned by Procopius (b. Goth.,
2, 14), who was forced by his tribe to make war on the Lombards in the third year of the emperor Anastasius (the year
493), and was slain in battle.   This same man may well have
come to Theodoric at the time when he was in Moesia, namely
before 489, and asked his protection.   That he despised his own
kingdom is probably an exaggeration of the Gothic historians.

IV 25. Berig: the period of this earliest King of the Goths
is thought by Muellenhoff to be not earlier than the first century
of our era.   Relying on Pliny (N. H., 37, 2 and 4, 14), Hodgkin
argues (Italy and her invaders, 1892, I. I, 34), that the Goths were
settled on the Baltic at least as early as 330 B.C., and possibly
as early as the sixth century B.C.   **Gothiscandza:** somewhere
near the southeastern corner of the Baltic, probably not far from
the modern city of Dantzig.

26. abodes of the Ulmerugi: Zeuss (p. 484) thinks that the

Rugi who inhabited the shores of the Ocean, or rather the islands in the Vistula at its mouth, were called by the Goths *Hulmarugeis*, whence *Ulmerugi*. Savagner, in the notes to his French translation of the *Getica*, identifies "the abodes of the Ulmerugi" with Pomerania and Mecklenburg. **Vandals:** we find mention of the Vandals as a people in the northern part of Germany as early as Tacitus (*Germania* 2). **Filimer:** the date of this king of the Goths is placed by Muellenhoff at about the beginning of the Scythian war in 238 A.D. Hodgkin (I. I, 40) favors 170 A.D., the time of the Marcomannic war, as the date when a part of the Goths migrated to the mouths of the Danube.

27. Scythia . . . Oium: Ulfilas, according to Muellenhoff, would have written this word *aujôm*, dative plural of *au*, a familiar Teutonic root, meaning a watered meadow. He believes that the regions of Oium were probably in Volhynia among the streams that emptied into the Dnieper.

28. Spali: a people near the Don? We should expect to hear of the Venethi rather than the Spali. Pliny (N. H., 6, 7, 22) mentions among other races the *Spalaei* who once crossed the Tanais. **sea of Pontus:** the Euxine or Black Sea. **Ablabius:** or Ablavius; see notes on the sources of Jordanes, p. 19.

29. Josephus: see notes on the sources, p. 30. **Magog:** Josephus, antiquitates Iudaicae, 1, 6, 1: Μαγώγης (the son of Japheth) δὲ τοὺς ἀπ' αὐτοῦ Μαγώγας ὀνομασθέντας ᾤκισε, Σκύθας δὲ ὑπ' αὐτῶν (the Greeks) προσαγορευομένους. Compare Isidorus Goth. laud. 66 (from Cassiodorus?): *Gothorum antiquissima origo de Magog filio Iaphet fuit, unde et Scytharum genus extitit: nam iidem Gothi Scythica probantur origine sati, unde nec longe a vocabulo discrepant: demutata enim ac detracta littera Getae quasi Scythae sunt nuncupati.* See also Etym., 9, 1, 27: *Magog a quo quidam arbitrantur Scythas et Gothos traxisse originem.* And 89: *Gothi a Magog filio Iaphet nominati putantur de similitudine ultimae syllabae, quos veteres magis Getas quam Gothos vocaverunt.*

V 30. river Ister: or Hister, the Danube; see V 31, and XXII, 114. **Morsian Swamp:** called also *Mursianus lacus* (V 35), a swamp near Mursa in Pannonia (now Eszek). **Tyra:** Tyras is the Greek name for the Dniester, not a different stream. **Danaster:** the Dniester, a river forming the boundary between Dacia and Sarmatia. **Vagosola:** not elsewhere mentioned. But considering the order in which these rivers are named, it is clearly to be identified with the Hypanis, now called the Bug, a river of European Sarmatia. **Danaper:** elsewhere called Borysthenes (see V 44), the Dnieper, which like the other two streams mentioned above, empties into the Black Sea. **Taurus range:** a ridge in the Chersonesus Taurica, now the Crimea.   **Lake Maeotis:** the Sea of Azov.   **Bosphorus:** the Cimmerian Bosphorus, the outlet of the Sea of Azov.   **Araxes:** a river of Armenia, now the Arâs.   **like a mushroom:** compare Cassiodorus var. 3, 48: *ima* (of the mountain) *graciliora sunt quam cacumina et in mollissimi fungi modo superius extenditur, cum inferiore parte tenuetur.*   **Albani:** the natives of Albania on the Caspian, now Schirwân.   **Seres:** the Chinese.

31.   **Persis:** a country between Carmania, Media and Susiana, now Fars or Farsistân.   Here the word seems to be used in a more general sense for Persia.   **Hiberia:** or Iberia, near the Caucasus, now Georgia.

32.   **Borysthenis, Olbia:** the town of Olbia, a colony from Miletus, was situated at the mouth of the river Borysthenes. The expression *Borithenide, Olbia,* indicates that Jordanes, following his literary source for this passage, took these as the names of two towns.   However it seems not unlikely that Borysthenis and Olbia are merely two names for the same place (see Strabo, 7, 3, 17).   There were several towns of Greek origin named Olbia, and Jordanes himself (*Romana,* 167) mentions another Olbia in Sardinia.   Savagner (p. 360) incorrectly indexes Olbia on the Borysthenes under "Olbia (Terra Nuova) capitale de l'île de Sardaigne."   **Callipolis:** probably in the Tauric Chersonese.   **Cherson:** on the Euxine, perhaps Eupatoria, a city of the Tauric Chersonese.   **Theodosia:** a town of the Tauric Chersonese, now Caffa or Feodosia.   **Careon:** since this is placed between Theodosia and Myrmicion (see Strabo, 7, 4, 5, p. 310), the place meant is evidently Panticapaeum (now Kertsch), in the Tauric Chersonese.   **Myrmicion:** also in the Tauric Chersonese.   **Trapezus:** a city in Pontus, now Trebizond.   **Rhipaeian mountains:** a range of mountains supposed to be in the northern part of Scythia.   **Tanais:** the river Don. See Orosius, 1, 2, 4. 5: *Riphaei montes . . . Tanaim fluvium fundunt qui . . . Maeotidas auget paludes.*

33.   **Gepidae:** see XVII 94-95   **Tisia:** the Patisus, a river of Hungary, now the Theiss.   **Flutausis:** Mommsen thinks it probable that this river of Hungary is the same as the *Aluta* mentioned by Jordanes in XII 74.

34.   **Venethi:** Muellenhoff upholds this spelling which he says is confirmed by the Gothic *Vinithôs.*

35.   **Noviodunum:** in lower Moesia, probably the modern Isaktscha.

36.   **Vidivarii:** Muellenhoff says that this name (of which *Vividarii* in XVII 96, is a corrupt form), is a hybrid derived from the islands between the mouths of the Vistula and the adjacent

swamp. These were generally known by the Germans in the middle ages as *Widland*.

37. **Bulgares:** this tribe, with the Antes and the Sclaveni, made raids into Thrace and Illyria in 549 and 550. See Jordanes *Romana*, 388, and Procopius Goth., 3, 40, p. 560 A. **two hordes:** but see Cassiodorus var. 3, 6: *pullulat ex uno genere quadrifariam decus.* **Altziagiri:** see Zeuss, p. 715 (*Cutziagiri*). **Sabiri:** see Zeuss, p. 711, 715 (*Saviri*). **Hunuguri:** Zeuss, p. 712.

38. **in our city:** probably Constantinople; see introduction, p. 11. **old wives' tales:** with the *fabulis anilibus* of the text compare the Vulgate, I. Tim., IV, 7: *aniles fabulas devita.*

39. **Zalmoxes,** or **Zalmoxis:** mentioned by Herodotus (4, 94-96) as the reputed teacher of the Getae, who gave them the doctrine of immortality which he was supposed to have learned from Pythagoras. Even Herodotus doubts whether he was a historical character: c. 96, εἴτε δὲ ἐγένετό τις Ζάλμοξις ἄνθρωπος, εἴτ' ἐστὶ δαίμων τις Γέτῃσι οὗτος ἐπιχώριος χαιρέτω! Apuleius (*De Magia*, 26), refers to Zalmoxis as an ancient Thracian magician whose incantations and other utterances are mentioned by Plato. **Zeuta:** possibly Seuthes, who according to Suidas was the father of Abaris. **Dicineus:** the Δεκαίνεος of Strabo, 7, 3, 5, p. 298; 7, 3, 11, p. 303.

40. **Dio relates:** Dio, 68, 9: ἐπεπόμφει μὲν (*Decebalus*) . . . πρέσβεις οὐκ ἔτι τῶν κωμητῶν ὥσπερ πρότερον, ἀλλὰ τῶν πιλοφόρων τοὺς ἀρίστους. But, as Mommsen remarks, Cassiodorus did not use the annals of Dio Cassius as much as the *Getica* of Dio Chrysostom, who probably gives a similar account, judging from his words in 72 (2, p. 383, Reiske): ἔνθα ἐνίοτε βλέπουσιν ἀνθρώπους τοὺς μέν τινας πίλους ἐπὶ ταῖς κεφαλαῖς ἔχοντας, ὡς νῦν τῶν Θρᾳκῶν τινες τῶν Γετῶν λεγομένων. **Pilleati:** see XI 71. **Vergil:** Aen. 3, 35: *Gradivumque patrem, Geticis qui praesidet arvis.*

42. **Balthi:** *the Bold:* see XXIX 146. **Amali:** see note on XIV, 78, on the genealogy of this family.

43. **more . . . historian than . . . poet:** Jordanes is here repeating a literary commonplace; see Martial 14, 194; Servius ad Aen. 1, 382; Isidorus orig., 8, 7, 10. **They string Armenian bows:** Lucan, Pharsal, 8, 221: *Armeniosque arcus Geticis intendite nervis.* **In earliest times:** *ante quos* in Mommsen's text seems impossible to translate with clearness of reference. So I follow the reading *antiquitus.* **Eterpamara:** Muellenhoff regards this as a very obscure word, probably not of Germanic origin. **Fritigern:** in all probability the leader of the Visigoths in the time of Emperor Valens. **Vidigoia:** the Gothic hero mentioned in XXXIV 178.

44. **Orosius speaks:** see Orosius, 1, 14: *Vesozes rex*

*Aegypti . . . Scythis bellum primus indixit . . . Scythae . . . Ve-
sozem territum refugere in regnum cogunt . . . c.* 15: *apud Scythas
duo regii iuvenes Plynos et Scolopythus . . . ingentem iuventutem
secum traxere . . . per insidias trucidantur. horum uxores exilio
ac viduitate permotae arma sumunt . . . Amazones dictae.*   **Vesosis**: Sesostris of Egypt, Rameses II, the Great. Tradition trans-
formed him into that military hero whom the Greeks knew as
Σέσωστρις (Herod. 2, 102-110) or Σεσόωσις (Diod. Sic., 1, 53-58),
and to whom they ascribed fabulous expeditions to Thrace and
India.

45. never solidified: see Mela, 1, 19, 115: *Tanais ex Riphaeo
monte deiectus, adeo praeceps ruit, ut, cum vicina flumina tum
Maeotis et Bosphorus tum Ponti aliqua brumali rigore durentur,
solus aestus hiememque iuxta ferens idem semper et subsimilis
incitatusque decurrat.*   **boundary of Asia and Europe**: compare
Orosius 1, 2, 4, 52.

46. as from its mother: Mela, 2, 1, 7: *Callipidas Hypanis in-
cludit: ex grandi palude oritur, quam matrem eius accolae appellant
et diu qualis natus est defluit.*   **fish**: Mela, 2, 1, 6: *Borysthenes . . .
alit laetissimi pabula magnosque pisces, quibus et optimus sapor
et nulla ossa sunt.* Solinus, 15, 1: *in quo* (Borysthenes) *pisces
egregii saporis et quibus ossa nulla sunt nec aliud quam cartilagines
tenerrimae.*   **Exampaeus**: Mela, 2, 1, 7: *tantum non longe a
mari ex parvo fonte cui Exampheo cognomen est adeo amaras aquas
accipit, ut ipse quoque iam sui dissimilis et non dulcis hinc defluat.
Asiaces proximus inter Callippidas Asiacasque descendit.*   **Callipidae and Hypanis**: these two towns at the mouth of the Danaper
(or Borysthenes) are not to be identified with any other towns
mentioned by Jordanes in V 32. For Callipidae, see Strabo,
12, 3, 21, p. 550.   **Achilles**: Mela, 2, 7, 98: *Leuce Borysthenis ostio
obiecta* (insula) *parva admodum et quod ibi Achilles situs est,
Achillea cognomine.*

VI 47. Tanausis: the reign of this contemporary of Vesosis
(Sesostris) is assigned by Gutschmid to 1323-1290 B.C. See
chronological chart p. 38.   **Phasis**: a river of Colchis, now
the Rioni, emptying into the Black Sea.   **conquered . . . all
Asia**: Asia Minor, of course. Iustinus, 1, 1, 6: *fuere . . .Vezosis
Aegypti et Scythiae rex Tanaus, quorum alter in Pontum, alter
usque Aegyptum excessit.* 2, 3, 8: *primus Scythis bellum indixit
Vezosis rex Aegyptius . . . Scythae . . . legatis respondent . . .
non expectaturos Scythas dum ad se veniatur . . . nec dicta res
morata . . . rex . . . in fugam vertitur . . . Scythas ab Aegypto
paludes prohibuere. inde reversi Asiam perdomitam vectigalem
fecere.*   **Sornus**: as there is no mention of Sornus in Justin's
narrative, this statement may have been taken from Pompeius
Trogus directly, either by Jordanes or his source.

48. **Pompeius Trogus says:** see the epitome of Trogus in Iustinus, 2, 1, 3: *cum ipsi (Scythae) Parthos Bactrianosque, feminae autem eorum Amazonum regna condiderint.* Compare Arrianus Parth. (in Photius cod. 58): Πάρθους δέ φησιν ἐπὶ Σεσώστριδος τοῦ Αἰγυπτίων βασιλέως καὶ Ἰανδύσου (Trogus read Ταναύσου) τοῦ Σκυθῶν ἀπὸ τῆς σφῶν χώρας Σκυθίας εἰς τὴν νῦν μετοικῆσαι. See discussion of sources, p. 30. **Parthi:** Iustinus, 41, 1, 1.2: *Parthi . . . Scytharum exules fuere. hoc etiam ipsorum vocabulo manifestatur, nam Scythico sermone exules Parthi dicuntur.*

VII. 49. **Lampeto and Marpesia:** Iustinus, 2, 4, 12-14: *duae his (Amazonibus) reginae fuere Marpesia et Lampeto, quae in duas partes agmine diviso . . . vicibus gerebant bella, soli terminos alternis defendentes . . . itaque maiore parte Europae subacta Asiae quoque nonnullas civitates occupavere.* Compare Oros., 1, 15.

50. **Vergil:** Aen., 6, 471:*quam si dura silex aut stet Marpesia cautes.* But Vergil is referring to the mountain in the island of Paros, where the marble quarries were. Servius on Aen. 6, 471. **Caspian Gates:** the Sirdar pass. **Lazi:** a truce with Persia concluded in 545 was broken in 549 by the Romans who gave assistance to their former dependents, the Lazi (inhabitants of ancient Colchis), in their war with Persia. For the Lazic war see Bury, History of the Later Roman Empire I 441.

51. **Halys:** a large river of Asia Minor flowing into the Black Sea, now called the Kyzyl-irmák. **Gangra:** a city of Paphlagonia, afterwards called Germanicopolis, now Kiankari. **they built a . . . temple for Diana:** this tradition of a shrine to Artemis built by the Amazons is found in many classical writers. From the excavations of Mr. David Hogarth, who thoroughly explored the site in 1904-1905, it appears that no less than five temples of Artemis were successively erected on the spot where the ruins are still found to-day. The fourth, or last but one, is that mentioned by Herodotus (1, 92), toward which Croesus is said to have contributed columns. It was in building in the year 550 B.C. The last and greatest, which ranked as one of the seven wonders of the world, was begun about 350 B.C., and it was this which was sacked in the year 262 A.D. by the Goths, as mentioned by Jordanes in XX 107. (See The Archaic Artemisia, David Hogarth, London, 1908.) With this passage compare Iustinus, 2, 4, 14.15 *(Amazones) maiore parte Europae subacta Asiae quoque nonnullas civitates occupavere: ibi Epheso multisque aliis urbibus conditis.* Compare Orosius, 1, 15.

52. **a hundred years:** see Orosius, 1, 16: *mulieres patria profugae Europam atque Asiam . . . intraverunt pervagatae sunt deleverunt: centum paene annis . . . tenuerunt . . . (Gothorum) feminae maiorem terrarum partem immensis caedibus deleverunt.* **came back:**

Iustinus, 2, 4, 14.15: *partem exercitus cum ingenti praeda domum dimittunt.* Compare Orosius, 1, 15. **have . . . mentioned: see VII 50.   Caucasus mountains:** see Solinus 38, 10: *mons Taurus ab Indico primum mari surgit . . . § 12: . . . nominatus . . .ubi in excelsissimam consurgit sublimitatem Caucasus . . . § 13: quantus meridiem videt, sole inaestuat; quidquid septemtrioni oppositum est. vento tunditur et pruina.*   **53. Vasianensian region:** some part of Armenia is meant, perhaps the Βασιλισηνή of Ptolomaeus 5, 13, 13.   **Red Sea:** the Persian Gulf.   **54. the Araxes:** see note on V 30.   **the Cyrus:** now the Kur, a river emptying into the Araxes.   **the Cambyses,** the Jora, a little river of Albania which empties into the Cyrus. **cut by this river:** the Ister or Danube cuts through the mountain ranges at the Iron Gates.   Mommsen regards *Histri* in the text as incorrect geographically, though supported by all the manuscripts.   He thinks the *Danaper,* and not the *Ister,* is the river here meant.   At any rate, Jordanes does not say so.   **in Scythia is named Taurus also:** that is, in the Tauric Chersonese, or Crimea; see note on V 30.   **55. Caspian Gates:** see note on VII 50.   **Armenian . . . Cilician:** see Solinus 38, 13: *ubi dehiscit hiulcis iugis, facit portas, quarum primae sunt Armeniae, tum Caspiae, post Ciliciae.*   **Imaus:** the Himâlaya range.   **Paropamisus:** a mountain chain of central Asia, now the Hindûkûsch.   **Choatras:** mountains of Assyria and Media.   **Niphates:** part of the Taurus range in Armenia, the modern Ala-dagh.   Compare also Solinus 38, 12: *pro gentium ac linguarum varietate plurifariam nominatus apud Indos Iamus, mox Propanisus. Choatras apud Parthos, post Niphates, inde Taurus atque ubi in excelsissimam consurgit sublimitatem Caucasus. interea etiam a populis appellationem trahit.*

VIII 56. destroying the life: Iustinus 2, 4, 9. 10. 11. *ne genus interiret, concubitus finitimorum ineunt. si qui mares nascerentur, interficiebant: virgines in eundem ipsis morem . . . armis equis venationibus exercebant.* Compare Orosius 1, 15.

57. Hercules: Iustinus, 2, 4, 21-24: *Hercules ad litus Amazonum adplicuit, . . . multae . . . caesae captaeque, in his Melanippe ab Hercule, Hippolyte a Theseo . . . Theseus obtenta in praemium captiva eandem in matrimonium adsumpsit et ex ea genuit Hippolytum.* Compare Orosius 1, 15.   **Penthesilea:** Orosius 1, 15: *post Orithyiam Penthesilea regno potita est cuius Troiano bello clarissima inter viros documenta virtutis accepimus.* Compare Iustinus 2, 4, 31.   **the time of Alexander the Great:** Iustinus 2, 4, 32: *interfecta deinde Penthesilea . . . paucae quae in regno remanserant . . . usque ad tempora Alexander magni duraverunt.*

IX 58. we have proved in a previous passage: Jordanes says
nothing of this in a previous passage in the *Getica*, though in
V 40 he uses the words *Gothi* and *Gaetae* interchangeably.
testimony of Orosius Paulus: see Orosius 1, 16: *modo autem
Getae illi, qui et nunc Gothi.* **Telefus:** see Dictys 2, 4: (*Telephus*) *Hercule genitus procerus corpore ac pollens viribus divinis
patriis virtutibus propriam gloriam aequiparaverat.* c. 3: *Teuthranius Teuthrante et Auge genitus frater Telephi uterinus.* c. 5:
Astyochen enim Priami iunctam sibi (Telepho) matrimonio.
Quintus of Smyrna (6, 135) agrees with Jordanes in saying that
Astyoche was the sister, not the daughter, of Priam.

59. Moesia: see Dictys 2, 1: *Telephus . . . tum Moesiae imperator erat.* **Histria:** a country on the eastern shore of the
Adriatic Sea, afterwards included in the tenth region of Augustus. Compare Orosius 1, 1, 55: *Moesia ab oriente habet ostia
fluminis Danuvii, ab euro Thraciam, a meridie Macedoniam, ab
Africo Dalmatiam, ab occasu Histriam, a circio Pannoniam, a
septentrione Danuvium.*

60. Thesander: or Thersander. See Dictys 2, 2; *in ea pugna
Thessandrus . . . congressus cum Telepho ictusque ab eo cadit . . .*
c. 3: *Teuthranius . . . frater Telephi uterinus . . . telo eius
(Ajax) occubuit. eius casu Telephus . . . perculsus . . . fugatis
quos adversum ierat cum obstinate Vlixem inter vineas . . . insequeretur, praepeditus trunci vitis ruit . . . Achilles . . . telum iaculatus
femur sinistrum regi transfigit.* c. 10: *Telephus . . . cum nullo
remedio mederi posset.* Also Eustathius Schol. Iliad. 1, 59:
ὁ δὲ Τήλεφος . . . πέπονθε μὲν τραῦμα δεινὸν ὑπὸ Ἀχιλλέως, ἀμπέλου ἕλικι
συμποδισθέντος αὐτῷ τοῦ ἵππου . . . καὶ πεσόντος εἰς γῆν. **Eurypylus:** see
Dictys 2. 5: *Astyochen . . . Priami iunctam sibi (Telephus) matrimonio, ex qua Eurypylus genitus.* **he was killed:** see Dictys
4, 14: *nuntius Priamo supervenit Eurypylum Telephi ex Moesia adventare, quem rex . . . oblatione desponsae Cassandrae confirmaverat.* In c. 17, 18 Dictys tells how Eurypylus was slain by
Neoptolemus and his bones sent back to his father.

X 61. almost exactly six hundred and thirty years: see
chronological chart p. 39. According to Gutschmid, Jordanes
had in mind the year of the accession of Cyrus, even though he
relates the events of the last year of his reign. In this way we
get a period of six hundred and thirty-one years, 1190-559 B.C.
Pompeius Trogus relates: see Iustinus 1, 8: *Cyrus subacta
Asia . . . Scythis bellum infert. erat eo tempore regina Scytharum
Tomyris, quae . . . cum prohibere eos transitu Oaxis fluminis
posset, transire permisit . . . itaque Cyrus traiectis copiis . . .
castra metatus est . . . Cyrus . . . omnes . . . Scythas cum reginae filio interfecit . . . (Tomyris) compositis in montibus insidiis*

ducenta milia Persarum cum ipso rege trucidavit. Compare Orosius
2, 7. **as I have said:** in the last sentence above, "Tomyris,
queen of the Getae." Observe that Mommsen's comment *non
dixit antea* is cancelled in his table of *corrigenda.*
   62. Lesser Scythia: a district of Moesia, bordering on the
Black Sea, now Dobrudja. **Tomi:** famous as the place of
Ovid's banishment, now Köstendjé in Bulgaria.
   63. Antyrus: see Orosius 2,8: *Darius . . . Antyro regi Scytharum hac vel maxime causa bellum intulit, quod filiae eius petitas sibi
nuptias non obtinuisset . . . cum septingentis milibus armatorum
Scythiam ingressus . . . metuens, ne sibi reditus interrupto ponte
Histri fluminis negaretur, amissis LXXX milibus bellatorum tre-
pidus refugit.* The corrupt form of the name Antyrus (the
Ἰδάνθυρσος of Herodotus 4, 76) shows that Jordanes drew upon
Orosius rather than upon the very similar account given by
Iustinus 2, 5, 8-10. **Chalcedon:** or Calchedon, now Kadiköi, a
town in Bithynia on the Sea of Marmora, directly opposite Constantinople. **Byzantium:** the ancient city upon whose site
Constantinople was afterwards built. **Tapae:** not definitely
located, but apparently near the Danube. The place is mentioned by Dio Cassius 67. 10 and 68.8.
   64. Xerxes: see Orosius 2,9: *Xerxes septingenta milia armatorum de regno et trecenta milia de auxiliis, rostratas etiam naves
mille ducentas, onerarias autem tria milia numero habuisse narra-
tur.* See also Iustinus 2, 10, 18-20.
   65. Medopa, the daughter of King Gudila: Satyrus in Athe-
naeus 13, 15 p.557 d speaks of Κοθήλας ὁ τῶν Θρᾳκῶν βασιλεύς. For
Medopa see Stephanus on the word Γετία: ἔστι καὶ θηλυκῶς Γέτις ·
οὕτως γὰρ ἐκαλεῖτο ἡ γυνὴ τοῦ Φιλίππου τοῦ Ἀμύντου. Satyrus in Athe-
naeus 13, 5 p. 557 d calls her Μήδα. **Odessus:** a city of lower
Moesia on the Black Sea, now Varna.
   66. Sitalces . . . Perdiccas: according to Thucydides (2, 98),
in the year 429 B.C. Sitalces, King of the Odrysae concluding an
alliance with the Athenians, undertook an expedition against
King Perdiccas II of Macedon and sent against him an army
of 150,000 men. Thucydides also mentions the Getae (2. 96):
ἀνίστησεν . . . τοὺς ὑπερβάντι Αἷμον Γέτας καὶ ὅσα ἄλλα μέρη ἐντὸς τοῦ
Ἴστρου ποταμοῦ πρὸς θάλασσαν μᾶλλον τὴν τοῦ Εὐξείνου πόντου κατῴκητο · εἰσὶ
δ᾽ οἱ Γέται καὶ οἱ ταύτῃ ὅμοροί τε τοῖς Σκύθαις καὶ ὁμόσκενοι πάντες ἱπποτοξόται.
Mommsen believes that this information was also found in Dio
Chrysostom's *Getica* and that Cassiodorus took it from this
source. But Jordanes, following Cassiodorus, confuses Perdiccas II, against whom Sitalces made war in 429 B.C., with the
other Perdiccas, the general and successor of Alexander the
Great a century later, and regarding him as in a way the ruler

of Athens, inverts the part played by the Athenians in that war.
Alexander: Orosius 3, 20: *Alexander apud Babyloniam cum . . . ministri insidiis venenum potasset, interiit.*
XI 67. Buruista: see Strabo 7, 3, 5 p. 298; 7, 3, 11 p. 303; 16, 2, 39 p. 762. Hodgkin (I. I 96) says Buruista is perhaps the same as Boerebislas, a king of Dacia in the time of Augustus. **Sulla**: with Sulla's dictatorship (82-79 B.C.) we have the first definite reference in the *Getica* to historical Roman times. **the Franks now possess**: Chlodwig (Clovis) had defeated the Alamanni in 496. [Bury (I 284) gives the date as 492.]
68. islands . . . beyond our world: so the Romans regarded Britain. **unable to prevail against the Goths**: see Orosius 1, 16: *Caesar . . . declinavit* (the Getae).
69. belagines: Muellenhoff argues from the chronicles of Isidorus that the Goths had no written laws before the reign of Eurich (466-485), and thinks that Jordanes or Cassiodorus has given the Goths credit for a thing told by Dio of the Getae. **twelve signs**: of the Zodiac. With this whole passage (XI 69-70) compare what Athalaric writes to Cassiodorus, var. 9, 24: (King Theodoric) *cum esset publica cura vacuatus, sententias prudentum a tuis fabulis exigebat . . . stellarum cursus, maris sinus, fontium miracula rimator acutissimus inquirebat, ut rerum naturis diligentius perscrutatis quidam purpuratus videretur esse philosophus.*
72. Capillati: see Cassiodorus var. 4, 49: *universis provincialibus et capillatis, defensoribus et curialibus Suavia consistentibus Theodericus rex.*
73. Comosicus . . . Coryllus: these Gothic kings do not seem to be mentioned elsewhere in ancient literature. But Gutschmid (*Prosopographia imperii Romani* p. 473, 1244) conjectures that Coryllus should be Scoryllus, citing Frontinus Stratogematon 1, 10, 4: *Scorylo dux Dacorum.*
XII 73. ancient Dacia: Dacia was the name applied originally to the region which lies between the Danube, the Theiss, the Carpathians and the Pruth, extending over part of modern Hungary, Wallachia and Moldavia, with Transylvania as its central district. The Dacians under Decebalus were defeated by Trajan in 102 and 107, in campaigns still commemorated at Rome by Trajan's column, and their country became a Roman province. (On the limits of the Roman province of Dacia, see Hodgkin in the English Historical Review II, 100-103.) Aurelian (270-275) finally abandoned it, settling its inhabitants in a new province which he likewise named Dacia. This new Dacia was created from parts of Moesia Superior and Inferior (Hist. Aug., Vita Aureliani 39), and consisted of the eastern half of Servia and the western end of Bulgaria. It was eventually divided into *Dacia Ripensis*, with

156 JORDANES: ORIGIN AND DEEDS OF THE GOTHS

its Capital at Ratiaria on the Danube, and *Dacia Mediterranea*
with its capital at Serdica, modern Sofia (the capital of Bulgaria). After the disruption of Attila's empire in 454 Dacia,
namely that part of Hungary which lies east and north of the
Danube, fell to the lot of the Gepidae under Ardaric.

74. **Boutae:** not mentioned elsewhere. Possibly a corruption
of *Pons* (Augusti). See Jung, Römer und Romanen in den
Donauländern (Innsbruck 1887) p. 118 n. 2. **Roxolani:** a
people dwelling between the rivers Don and Dnieper. **Iazyges:** a Sarmatian people on the Danube. **Sarmatians:** a great
Slavic people dwelling from the Vistula to the Don, in the
modern Poland and Russia. **Basternae:** they dwelt in the
lands along the upper reaches of the Vistula north of the Carpathian mountains. **Aluta:** a river of Hungary, now the Alt.
The Roxolani here mentioned by Jordanes are the *Rhoxolani,
Sarmatica gens* of Tacitus, Histories 1, 79.

75. **Alamanni:** German tribes who formed a confederation
on the upper Rhine and Danube, and from whom the nation
got its name. Compare the French *Allemagne*. **sixty streams:**
see Ammianus 22, 8, 44: *Danuvius . . . sexaginta navigabiles paene
recipiens fluvios*. **Bessi:** a savage race in Thrace, near the
Haemus mountains, and in the vicinity of the river Hebrus.
Bury (II 15) states that the Bessi or Satri, in the region of
Rhodope, remained longest a corporate nation in the presence
of Roman influences. In the fourth century they were converted
to Christianity, and a hundred years later still held the church
service in their own tongue. **except the Nile:** Mela 2, 1, 8:
*Hister . . . ingens iam et eorum qui in nostrum mare decidunt
tantum Nilo minor:* and see Sallust, in Gellius 10, 7, 1.

XIII 76. Oppius Sabinus . . . governor . . . after Agrippa:
Fonteius Agrippa was governor of Moesia in 69-70 (Tacitus, Histories 3, 46 and Josephus Bell. Iud. 7, 4, 3), and lost his life
resisting an attack of the Sarmatae. Oppius Sabinus (about 85
or 86) did not succeed him directly, as Jordanes seems to imply,
for there were at least four governors in between. (See Stout,
The Governors of Moesia, Princton, 1911, p. 21, n. 51). Sabinus
was consul in 84, probably went to Moesia as governor the following year, and was killed in 85 or 86. **Dorpaneus:** the Diur-
paneus of Orosius 7, 10, 4. From Petrus Patricius fr. 4 (4, 185
Muell.) it is clear that he is to be identified with Decebalus,
the famous Dacian leader.

77. **Domitian hastened:** upon the death of Sabinus Domitian
set out in person for the Danube, but gave Cornelius Fuscus, his
praefectus praetorio, charge of the war. See Suetonius
Domitian 6.

78. **slew Fuscus**: see Eutropius 7, 23, 4. **Ansis**: merely another and more heroic name of the *Amali*, the royal stock of the Goths. Jacob Grimm observes that this is the same word as the Aesir of the Northmen. **genealogy**: see the chart on page 41. Compare also with this chapter XLVIII 246 onward and LVIII 297 onward.

XIV 81. **its proper place**: this is done in XL 315.

82. **we have said**: in V 38 and 42.

XV 83. **As already said**: in V 38. **Alexander**: he reigned from 222-235 A.D. **Symmachus relates**: see Literary Sources p. 32, and compare Iulii Capitolini Maximini duo, 1: *Maximinus . . . de vico Threiciae . . . barbaro . . . patre et matre genitus, quorum alter e Gothia, alter ex Alanis genitus esse perhibetur: et patri quidem nomen Micca, matri Hababa fuisse dicitur*. Also c 4: *amatus est . . . unice a Getis quasi eorum civis*. And see *Romana* 281. **Alani**: a very warlike nomadic Scythian nation, ranging from the Caucasus to the Tanais and north of the Caspian. After 406 Alans seems to have dwelt on the Loire. (Bury I. 167, note 1.)

84. **military games**: vita Maximini 2: *et in prima quidem pueritia fuit pastor . . . natali Getae filii minoris, Severus militares dabat ludos propositis praemiis argenteis . . . hic adulescens et semibarbarus et vix adhuc Latinae linguae, prope Thraecica imperatorem publice petiit, ut sibi daret licentiam contendendi cum his, qui iam non mediocri loco militarent.*

85. **eight feet**: vita 2: *magnitudinem corporis Severus miratus* c. 6: *erat magnitudine tanta, ut octo pedes digito videretur egressus.* Compare vita Maximini iun. c. 2. **camp followers**: vita 2: *primum eum cum lixis composuit . . . ne disciplinam militarem corrumperet.* **threw sixteen**: vita 2: *tunc Maximinus sedecim lixas uno sudore devicit sedecim acceptis praemiis . . . iussusque militare.* **cavalry**: vita 2: *prima stipendia equestria huic fuere.* On the third day: vita 3: *tertia forte die cum processisset Severus ad campum, in turba exultantem more barbarico Maximinum vidit iussitque statim tribuno, ut eum coerceret ac Romanam disciplinam imbueret. tunc ille ubi de se intellexit imperatorem locutum . . ad pedes imperatoris equitantis accessit. tum . . . Severus . . . equum admisit multis circumitionibus et cum . . . imperator laborasset neque ille a currendo per multa spatia desisset.*

86. **my little Thracian**: vita 3: *'quid vis, Thracisce? num quid delectat luctari post cursum?' tum 'quantum libet,' inquit, 'imperator.' post hoc ex equo Severus descendit et recentissimos quosque ac fortissimos milites ei comparari iussit. tum ille more solito septem fortissimos uno sudore vicit solusque omnium a Severo post argentea praemia torque aureo donatus est iussusque inter stipatores corporis semper in aula consistere.*

87.   he was an officer: vita 4: *diu sub Antonino Caracalla ordines duxit, centuriatus et ceteras militares dignitates saepe tractavit.* when Macrinus became emperor: vita 4: *sub Macrino, quod eum, qui imperatoris sui filium occiderat, vehementer odisset, a militia desiit.* c. 5: *Maximinus . . . tribunus.*
88.   Heliogabalus: or Elagabalus; vita 4: *occiso Macrino . . . ubi Heliogabalum quasi Antonini filium imperatorem comperit, . . . ad eum venit.* Alexander the son of Mamaea: vita 5: *quem Alexander miro cum gaudio . . . suscepit.* Mogontiacum: Mayence or Mainz.   Aquileia: see Orosius 7, 18: (Alexander) *militari tumultu apud Moguntiacum interfectus est.* c. 19: *. . . Maximinus . . . nulla senatus voluntate imperator ab exercitu . . . creatus persecutionem in Christianos . . . exercuit. sed . . . tertio quam regnabat anno a Pupieno Aquileiae interfectus.* Aquileia is a town in Triest, at the northern end of the Adriatic, still called Aquileia. For the story of its siege and capture by Attila, see XLII 219 onward.

XVI 89.   Marcomanni: a Germanic people, a portion of the tribe of the Suevi, who after their defeat by Drusus moved from the Rhine and Main to the country of the Boii (Bohemia). Quadi: a Germanic people in the modern Moravia.   one thousandth year: so Hieronymus on the year of Abraham 2262, the second of Philip's reign: *regnantibus Philippis millesimus annus Romanae urbis expletus est.*   received annual gifts: Rome was willing to pay the Goths and other barbarian tribes subsidies called *stipendia,* and given as pay; but the receiver might easily come to regard them as given for tribute.
90.   the senator Decius: he reigned as emperor from 249-251. Ostrogotha: see genealogical chart, p. 41, and XVII 98-100.
91.   Taifali: neighbors of the Goths, once settled near the Danube in Dacia. Zeuss p. 433.   Astringi: better Asdingi; see XXII 113 and Zeuss 461. Probably neighbors of the Taifali. Carpi: a people on the Danube in Dacia, Zeuss p. 697. They were subdued by Diocletian and Galerius in 295 and transported to Pannonia. (Bury I 32.)   Galerius . . . conquered them: see Orosius 7, 25, 12: *per eosdem duces* (Diocletian and Galerius) *strenue adversus Carpos Basternasque pugnatum est.* Peucini: the inhabitants of Peuce, a pine-covered island (*peuce,* πεύκη = pine-tree), the delta of the Danube.   Argaith: see Scriptores Historiae Augustae XX Gordiani tres 31, 1: *Imperavit Gordianus annis sex atque dum haec agerentur Argunt Scytharum rex finitimorum regna vastabat.* Muellenhoff regards Argaith as the correct form.   Guntheric: see The Cambridge Mediaeval History, I. 203.
92.   Marcianople: in Lower Moesia, near the Euxine; the

great city built by Trajan on the north slope of the Balkans, now represented by Pravadi, near Schumla. (Hodgkin I. I. 50).

93. Potamus: the river Panysus? The anonymous Geographer of Ravenna (4, 6 p. 185) follows Jordanes: *per quam Marcianopolim medio transit fluvius qui dicitur Potamia.* **his sister:** Marciana, Ammianus 27, 4, 12: *Mysia, ubi Marcianopolis est a sorore Traiani principis ita cognominata.*

XVII 94. in the beginning: see IV 25. **three ships:** this is the first and only mention Jordanes makes of the number of the ships.

95. gepanta: Muellenhoff rejects this derivation of the name *Gepidae.*

96. Spesis: otherwise unknown. Holder (*Iordanis, De Origine Actibusque Getarum,* Freiburg 1882) would read *dum spes is provincia.* **Vividarii:** see note on Vidivarii, V 36. **Gepedoios:** Muellenhoff points out that here is the nominative plural of the same word met before in IV 27, *Oium,* that is, *the Meadows,* the native name for Scythia. He calls attention also to the German *au* or *aue* which has the same meaning. Gepedoios thus means *the Gepid Meadows.*

97. Fastida: apparently unknown outside this account. Jordanes mentions also as kings of the Gepidae Ardaric (XXXVIII 199), Thraustila, and Thrasaric (LVIII 300). **Burgundians:** a northern tribe who dwelt between the Oder and the Vistula.

99. Galtis: Mommsen suggests for this town the Transylvanian Galt on the river Aluta. It is not mentioned elsewhere. (Hodgkin I. I 51.)

XVIII 101. Cniva: Gutschmid identifies him with Ovida, the grandfather of King Geberich (mentioned by Jordanes in XXII 113) and Cannaba or Cannabaudes, the leader of the Goths in the reign of Aurelian (*vita Aurel. 22*). See also The Cambridge Mediaeval History, I. 203. **Euscia:** Euscia or *Novae* is the modern Novo-grad on the Danube, about thirty-four miles above Rustchuk. (Hodgkin I. I 52.) **Gallus:** C. Vibius Trebonianus Gallus, governor of Moesia Inferior in 251 and Emperor from 251-253. See XIX 104. Stout (The Governors of Moesia, p. 248) regards the title *dux limitis* (XVIII 102) as as anachronism. **Nicopolis:** apparently Nikup on the Jantra, the ancient *Iatrus,* a tributary of the Danube. **the regions of Haemus:** the Balkans. **Philippopolis:** in modern times the capital of Eastern Roumelia.

102. Beroa: Augusta Traiana, a city about eighty-seven miles northwest of Hadrianople, now Eski-Zaghra. **Oescus:** a city on the Danube, near the mouth of a river of the same name.

103. took Philippopolis: it is interesting to compare with this chapter the account given by Ammianus 31, 5, 15: *duobus navium milibus perrupto Bosporo et litoribus Propontidis Scythicarum gentium catervae transgressae ediderunt quidem acerbas terra marique strages, sed amissa suorum parte maxima reverterunt, ceciderunt dimicando cum barbaris impratores Decii pater et filius . . . Anchialos capta et tempore eodem Nicopolis, quam indicium victoriae contra Dacos Traianus condidit imperator. post clades acceptas inlatasque multas et saevas excisa est Philippopolis centum hominum milibus, nisi fingunt annales, intra moenia iugulatis.*   **allied himself to Priscus**: then governor of Macedonia (*Lucio Prisco qui Macedonas praesidatu regebat,* Aurelius Victor de Caes. 29) and a brother of the late Emperor Philip. This appears to be the first attempt on the part of the Goths to create an anti-emperor. (Hodgkin I. I 53.)   **the son of Decius**: see Cassiodorus chr. ad. a. 252: *Decius cum filio suo in Abritio Thraciae loco a Gothis occiditur.* He substitutes these words for the following sentence of Prosper: *Decius cum filio in Abritto, quae est civitas Mysiae, occiditur.*   **Abrittus**: otherwise called *Forum Thembronii* or *Terebronii,* but its site is unknown. It was probably somewhere in the marshy ground near the mouth of the Danube (Hodgkin I. I 56).   **cut off . . . and slain**: Hodgkin remarks (I. I. 56) that this is one of three great disasters that foretold the final overthrow of Rome. The other two were the defeat of Varus in A.D. 9 and the Battle of Hadrianople, A.D. 378. (See XXVI 138.)

      XIX 104. **plague**: see Hieronymus on the year of Abraham 2269: *pestilens morbus multas totius orbis provincias occupavit maximeque Alexandriam et Aegyptum, ut scribit Dionysius et Cypriani de mortalitate testis est liber.*   **nine years ago**: in 542. On the date, see introduction, p. 13. For an account of this plague see Bury I. 399-403.   **Dionysius**: Bishop of Alexandria 248-265; see Eusebius, hist. eccl. 7, 22.   **Cyprian**: Thascius Caecilius Cyprianus (d. 258), Bishop of Carthage, who was martyred in the persecution started by Decius.

      106. **universal . . . favor**: see Orosius 7, 21, 6: *hac sola pernicie* (the plague) *insignes Gallus et Volusianus.*

      107. **Respa, Veduc and Thuruar**: otherwise unknown.   **as we said before**: in VII 51.   **Cornelius Avitus**: not the Emperor Avitus. The Emperor, who reigned 455-456 A.D. [see XLV 240], was named Marcus Maecilius Avitus.   **the royal city**: Constantinople.

      XX 108. **Troy and Ilium**: Jordanes oddly takes these as the names of two distinct cities and speaks of them as "recovering a little" (in A.D. 259 ±) from the Trojan War! **Thrace**: it will be noticed that Jordanes names the places attacked by the Goths in a different order than Ammianus in the passage cited above (note on XVIII 103).

109. **Anchiali:** the authors cited in Stephanus and Suidas (s.v.'Αγχιάλη), say it was not this city in Moesia but *Anchiale* in Cilicia that was founded by Sardanapalus.

XXI 110. to aid the Romans: after the disastrous campaign of 296 in which Galerius (the "Caesar Maximian" of Jordanes) was humbled on the ill-omened field of Carrhae, a considerable number of Gothic auxiliaries was taken into the Roman forces, and the Imperial armies again marched against Narses of Persia. This time, whether mainly "by their aid," as Jordanes says, or not, the Romans were victorious (297). [Gibbon I. 370. Bury's ed. of 1896.]   **Narseus:** or Narses.   **Sapor the Great:** this was the Persian king who captured the Emperor Valerian in 260 and kept him prisoner until his death in 265.   **Achilles:** or Achilleus (292-296); he arose as a usurper in Alexandria. **Maximianus Herculius:** this is the Emperor Maximian, the colleague of Diocletian.   **Quinquegentiani:** a confederation of five Moorish nations invaded the peaceful provinces of Africa in 296, 297. With this last section compare Orosius 7, 25: *rebellante . . . Achilleo in Aegypto cum et Africam Quinquegentiani infestarent, Narseus etiam rex Persarum Orientem bello premeret . . . Maximianus Augustus Quinquegentianos in Africa domuit, porro autem Diocletianus Achilleum . . . apud Alexandriam cepit et interfecit . . . Galerius Maximianus . . . per Illyricum et Moesiam undique copias contraxit . . . Narseum magnis consiliis viribusque superavit . . . castra eius invasit, uxores sorores liberosque cepit, immensam vim gazae Persicae diripuit.*

111. **Licinius:** he had been elevated to the rank of Augustus by the Emperor Galerius in 307, apparently without passing through the intermediate rank of Caesar. The first quarrel between Constantine and Licinius—then respectively masters of the West and the East—occurred in 314. The second civil war, in 323, was brought to a close by the imprisonment and death of Licinus. By this victory the Roman world was again united under the authority of one emperor.

112. **the famous city:** the part Jordanes supposes the Goths to have played in the founding of Constantinople is not very clear, even to our author himself.   **Ariaric and Aoric:** Constantine, intervening in some quarrel between the Goths and Sarmatians, took part with the latter, and the son of Ariaric was among the hostages given by the Goths upon their defeat. See Anonymous Valesianus 31: (Constantine) *adversum Gothos bellum suscepit et implorantibus Sarmatis auxilium tulit: ita per Constantinum Caesarem c prope milia fame et frigore extincta sunt:*

162   JORDANES: ORIGIN AND DEEDS OF THE GOTHS

tunc et obsides accepit, inter quos et Ariarici regis filium.   Gebe-rich: or Geberic (Hodgkin I. I 76). The reign of Geberich, ac-cording to Gutschmid, is to be dated 318-350.

XXII 113. Visimar: a Vandal king over the Sarmatians? See Gibbon II 217.   **Asdingi:** see note on XIV 91 under *Astringi.*   **Dexippus** (in fr. 24, 3 p. 685 Muell.) tells of the victory of Aurelian over the Vandals and of their return to the countries beyond the Danube after peace was made.   **Marisia:** see Strabo 7, 3, 13 p. 305; ῥεῖ δὲ δι' αὐτῶν Μάρισος ποταμὸς εἰς τὸν Δανούιον **Miliare, Gilpil:** not mentioned elsewhere.   **Grisia:** a river of Hungary. See Constantinus Porphyrogen. *de adm. imp.* 40: ῥεῖ. τέταρτος ὁ κρίσος, and Zeuss p. 447.

114. Hermunduli, or Hermunduri: a Germanic people on the Elbe, neighbors of the Chatti.

115. Pannonia: the expulsion of the Vandals (or Sarma-tians? Gibbon II. 219) and their reception by Constantine into Pannonia occurred in the year 334.   **A long time afterward:** see Orosius 7, 38: *Stilico . . . gentes . . . Alanorum Sueborum Vanda-lorum . . . Burgundionum . . . ripas Rheni quatere et pulsare Gal-lias voluit.*

XXIII 116. Hermanaric: or Hermanric, the Ostrogoth. The date is about 351-376 according to Gutschmid. Most of these thirteen northern tribes, which Jordanes says were conquered by this second Alexander, cannot now be identified with any certainty.

117. Heruli: see *Etymologicum magnum* p. 332 Gaisford: ἀπὸ τῶν ἐκεῖσε ἐλῶν Ἕλουροι κέκληνται.   Δέξιππος ἐν δωδεκάτῳ χρονικῶν. Also Stephanus of Byzantium s.v.: Ἕλουροι Σκυθικὸν ἔθνος, περὶ ὧν Δέξιππος ἐν χρονικῶν ιβ'.   **Alaric:** this chief of the Heruli must not be confused with Alaric, King of the Suavi, mentioned in LIV 277 or with the kings of the Visigoths named Alaric.   **hele:** ἕλη.

119. Venethi: or Veneti; but nee note on V 34; Wends. They dwelt in the region that is now Poland.   **we started to say:** in V 34.   **Antes, Sclaveni:** the Heruli lived in the swampy regions near the Sea of Azov; the parent stock of the Veneti (Wends) scattered in various directions, the Sclaveni going to the upper waters of the Dniester and Vistula, the Antes along the Euxine from the Dniester to the Dnieper. (Hodgkin I. I 77.)

120. Aesti: a Germanic people near the Baltic; see Tacitus, Germania 45.

XXIV 121. Orosius relates: *gens Hunnorum diu inacessis se-clusa montibus, repentina rabie percita exarsit in Gothos eosque passim conturbatos ab antiquis sedibus expulit* (7, 33, 10).   **Filimer:** see IV 26.

123. Priscus: the passage is apparently untraceable. But see Zeuss p. 708, and compare next note. **126. swept across the great swamp:** it is interesting to compare with this passage the account given by Procopius, bell. Goth. 4, 5: οὗτοι (the Huns, then called Cimmerians) μὲν ἅπαντες τῇδε ᾤκηντο, κοινὰ μὲν τὰ ἐπιτηδεύματα ξύμπαντα ἔχοντες, οὐκ ἐπιμιγνύμενοι δὲ ἀνθρώποις, δι δὴ τῆς τε λίμνης (Maeotis) καὶ τῆς ἐνθένδε ἐκροῆς ἐς τὰ ἐπὶ θάτερα ἵδρυντο· ἐπεὶ οὔτε διέβαινον ποτε τὰ ὕδατα ταῦτα οὔτε διαβατὰ εἶναι ὑπώπτευον ... προϊόντος δὲ τοῦ χρόνου φασίν, εἴπερ ὁ λόγος ὑγιής ἐστι, τῶν μὲν Κιμμερίων νεανίας τινὰς ἐν κυνηγεσίῳ διατριβὴν ἔχειν, ἔλαφον δὲ μίαν πρὸς αὐτῶν φεύγουσαν ἐς τὰ ὕδατα ἐσπηδῆσαι ταῦτα. τούς τε νεανίας ... τῇ ἐλάφῳ ἐπισπέσθαι ταύτῃ, μηχανῇ τε αὐτῆς μεθίεσθαι οὐδεμιᾷ, ἕως ξὺν αὐτῇ ἐς τὴν ἀντιπέρας ἀκτὴν ἵκοντο. καὶ τὸ μὲν διωκόμενον ὅ τι ποτ' ἦν εὐθὺς ἀφανισθῆναι ... τοὺς δὲ νεανίας τοῦ μὲν κυνηγησίου ἀποτυχεῖν, μάχης δὲ ἀφορμὴν καὶ λείας εὑρέσθαι. ἐς ἤθη γὰρ τὰ πάτρια ὅτι τάχιστα ἐπανήκοντες ἔκδηλα πᾶσι Κιμμερίοις πεποίηνται ὅτι δὴ ταύτῃ βατὰ σφίσι τὰ ὕδατα εἴη ἀνελόμενοι οὖν αὐτίκα τὰ ὅπλα πανδημεί τε διαβάντες ἐγένοντο μελλήσει οὐδεμιᾷ ἐν τῇ ἀντιπέρας ἠπείρῳ. See also the similar account given by Agathias 5, 11, p. 300 Bonn and Cedrenus 1, p. 547 Bonn. Mommsen points out that this passage is based on Priscus, as is evident not only from the agreement between Procopius and Jordanes, but furthermore from XXXIX 206, which is undoubtedly taken from Priscus and agrees with this account. **Alpidzuri, Alcildzuri, Itimari, Tuncarsi and Boisci:** these are mentioned in Priscus (Teubner text *Historici Graeci Minores* ed. Dindorf, p. 276); see Zeuss p. 708. **unlike ... in civilization:** Ammianus 31, 2, 21: *Halani ... sunt ... Hunis ... per omnia suppares, verum victu mitiores et cultu.*

128. cruelty of wild beasts: so also Ammianus 31, 2, 1: *Hunorum gens ... omnem modum feritatis excedit.* 2: *ubi quoniam ab ipsis nascendi primitiis infantum ferro sulcantur altius genae, ut pilorum vigor tempestivus emergens conrugatis cicatricibus hebetetur, senescunt imberbes absque ulla venustate . . , compactis omnes firmisque membris et opimis cervicibus prodigiosae formae, sed pandi ut bipedes existimes bestias . . . 6: equis prope adfixi . . . 9: procul missilibus telis . . . con[fligunt].*

129. this active race: see Ammianus 31, 2, 12: *hoc expeditum indomitumque hominum genus* (the Huns) *. . . per rapinas finitimorum grassatum.* And c. 3, 1: *Huni . . . Ermenrichi . . . pagos repentino impetu perruperunt.* Note that many of the actual words used by Ammianus recur in the account given by Jordanes. **Rosomoni:** not otherwise known. Muellenhoff regards the name as unhistoric. But see Schönfeld: Wörterbuch der altgermanischen Personen und Völkernamen, p. 194. **Sunilda ... Sarus and Ammius:** this tale "is peculiar to Jordanes, and is probably part of some old Gothic Saga." (Hodgkin I. I 246.)

130.   Balamber: the earliest king of the Huns of whom there is
mention in Jordanes.   See also XLVIII 248, 249.   **the
Huns . . . prevail:** the death of Hermanaric and the overthrow
of the Ostrogothic Empire by the Huns had probably taken
place by 375. According to Ammianus 31, 3 Hermanaric committed suicide: *magnorum discriminum metum voluntaria morte
sedavit.*   As Hodgkin says (I. I 247), the inclination of the
German critics is to spread the *Hunneneinfall* over five years:
372, attack upon the Alani; 374-375, overthrow of the Ostrogoths; 375-376, defeats of Athanaric.
    XXV 131.   Romania: or Roman-land, a late name for the
Roman Empire as contrasted with *Gothia.* Jordanes uses the
term several times: see *Romana* 247, 275, 313; *Getica* L 266.
they would submit: compare Ammianus 31, 4, 1: (the Goths)
*ripas occupavere Danuvii missisque oratoribus ad Valentem suscipi
se humili prece poscebant, et quiete victuros se pollicentes et daturos,
si res flagitasset, auxilia.*   **promised to become Christians:** Orosius (7, 33, 19) speaks of their acceptance of Christianity:
*Gothi antea per legatos supplices poposcerunt, ut illis episcopi, a
quibus regulam Christianae fidei discerent, mitterentur. Valens
imperator exitiabili pravitate doctores Arriani dogmatis misit.
Gothi primae fidei rudimentum quod accepere tenuerunt.* See also
Isidorus *hist. Goth. ad eram* 415: *Atanaricus Fridigernum Valentis
imperatoris suffragio superans huius rei gratia legatos cum muneri-
bus ad eundem imperatorem mittit et doctores propter suscipiendam
Christianae fidei regulam poscit. Valens autem a veritate fidei devius
et Arrianae haeresis perversitate detentus missis haereticis sacerdo-
tibus Gothos persuasione nefanda sui erroris dogmati adgregavit
et in tam praeclaram gentem virus pestiferum semine pernicioso
transfudit.*
    132.   intended to ask: Valens was by no means so ready and
willing to receive this barbarian horde as Jordanes assumes.
This was in fact one of the great crises of the empire, and
better statesmen than Valens might well have hesitated before
deciding so momentous a question. Eunapius (*Historici Graeci
Minores (Dindorf)* p. 237, says there were 200,000 men of fighting age besides old men, women and children who crossed the
Danube (Hodgkin I. I. 251).   **Arian perfidy:** see Hodgkin.
The Arian sect, named from Arius, differed from the general
body of the church in believing that the Son of God, though
divine, was a created being. Athanasius, in opposition to Arius,
was the champion of what came to be authoritatively adopted as
the orthodox belief regarding the Trinity by the Council of
Nicaea in 325. Ulfilas was an Arian because while his theological ideas were being formed, Arianism of one kind or

another—for there were many varieties—was orthodoxy at Constantinople, and Athanasius was denounced there as a dangerous heretic. Ulfilas professed the form of Arianism known as Homoion: "The Son is like unto the Father in such manner as the scriptures declare." This then was the form of Christianity he taught, and which the Goths, Vandals, Burgundians and Suavi accepted. This also was the creed of the Emperor Valens. In later times Theodoric the Great was himself unshaken in the Arianism which had been the faith of his forefathers, but he ruled with impartiality over a people the majority of whom were orthodox. Mommsen says (Intro. XLIII) that Jordanes did not find in the original of his *Getica* that sharp denunciation of Arianism in which he delights (see also XXVI 138), for Cassiodorus, though orthodox himself, was mindful of the Arian convictions of his masters. Ebert (Geschichte der christlichlateinischen Literatur, Leipzig 1874 p. 531 n. 2) believes that Jordanes' intense dislike of Arianism is best explained by the theory that he at first held this belief himself and was later converted to the orthodox party. See introduction p. 5.

133. crossed the Danube: this was in 376. Ammianus (31, 4, 1, quoted under 131 above) also tells of their embassy.

XXVI 134. Fritigern, Alatheus and Safrac: see Ammianus 31, 4, 8: *primus cum Alavivo suscipitur Fritigernus* c. 4, 12: *Vithericus Greuthungorum rex cum Alatheo et Safrace quorum arbitrio regebatur, . . . ut simili susciperetur humanitate obsecravit . . .* c 5, 3: *Greuthingi . . . ratibus transiere.* **Lupicinus and Maximus:** Lupicinus was Count of Thrace, and Maximus probably Duke of Moesia (Hodgkin I. I 254). **cursed lust for gold:** a reminiscence of Vergil's *auri sacra fames,* Aen. 3, 57.

135. demanded their sons: Ammianus (31, 4. 9) likewise records the inhuman conduct of these Roman commanders: *potestatibus praefuere castrensibus homines maculosi quibus Lupicinus antestabat et Maximus, alter per Thracias comes, dux alter.* c. 4, 11: *cum traducti barbari victus inopia vexarentur, turpe commercium duces invisissimi [ex]cogitarunt et quantos undique insatiabilitas colligere potuit canes pro singulis dederunt mancipiis: inter quae [et filii] ducti sunt optimatium.*

137. took arms: Ammianus (31, 5, 5) gives the following account of the banquet and its consequences: *Alavivo et Fritigerno ad convivium conrogatis Lupicinus . . . 6 dum in nepotali mensa ludicris concrepantibus diu discumbens vino marcebat et somno, . . . satellites omnes, qui praetorio honoris et tutelae causa duces praestolabantur, occidit. 7: hocque populus qui muros obsidebat dolenter accepto ad vindictam detentorum regum . . . multa minabatur et saeva. útque erat Fritigernus expediti consilii, veritus* *ne teneretur obsidis vice cum ceteris, exclamavit graviore pugnandum exitio, ni ipse ad leniendum vulgus sineretur exire cum sociis, quod arbitratum humanitatis specie ductores suos occisos in tumultum exarsit. hocque inpetrato egressi omnes exceptique cum plausu et gaudiis ascensis equis evolarunt moturi incitamenta diversorum bellorum.*   **as strangers** and **pilgrims**: compare the *ut advenae et peregrini* of Jordanes with the Vulgate *tanquam advenas et peregrinos*, I. Petr. 2, 11; *quasi advenam et peregrinum*, Levit. 25, 35; also Gen. 23, 4, Num. 9, 14, Levit. 25, 47. There seems to be a like Biblical reminiscence in *Getica* LIV 279.   **the Goths . . . began to rule**: their power was actually used only to plunder and destroy. Innocent subjects of the Empire were thus their victims. (Gibbon III 101.)

138. set out for . . . Thrace: see Ammianus 31, 11, 1: *Valens tandem excitus Antiochia . . . venit Constantinopolim.*   **Hadrianople**: Ammianus 31, 12 10: *signa . . . commoventur impedimentis et sarcinis prope Hadrianopoleos muros . . . conlocatis.*   **emperor lay hidden**: the same story is told by Victor *epit.* 46: *hic Valens cum Gothis lacrimabili bello commisso sagittis saucius in casa deportatur vilissima, ubi supervenientibus Gothis igneque supposito incendio concrematus est.* See also Hieronymus on the year of Abraham 2395; Orosius 7, 33, 15. The following account is given by Ammianus 31, 13, 12: *imperator . . . sagitta perniciose saucius ruit . . .* 14: *dicunt Valentem . . . cum candidatis et spadonibus paucis prope ad agrestem casam relatum . . . circumsessum ab hostibus, qui esset ignorantibus, dedecore captivitatis exemptum.*   **judgment of God**: thus it seemed to Orosius also (7, 33, 19): *itaque iusto iudicio dei ipsi eum vivum incenderunt, qui propter eum etiam mortui vitio erroris arsuri sunt.* See Isidorus *hist. Goth. ad eram* 416.   **their glorious victory**: Ammianus (31, 13, 19) says of this Roman disaster: *nec ulla annalibus praeter Cannensem pugnam ita ad internecionem res legitur gesta, quamquam Romani aliquotiens reflante Fortuna fallaciis lusi bellorum iniquitati cesserunt ad tempus, et certamina multa fabulosae naeniae flevere Graecorum.*

XXVII 139. his uncle: Gratian was the son of Valentinian I, and nephew of Valens.

XXVIII 142. King Athanaric: or Aithanaric. An old enemy of Fritigern, this chieftain had dwelt secure in the mountains and forests of Caucaland in Dacia until driven out by Alatheus and Safrac. (See Ammianus 27, 5, 10: *Athanaricus proximorum factione genitalibus terris expulsus.*) He then fled for refuge to Theodosius. (Hodgkin I. I 308.)

144. departed this life: see Cassiodorus on the year 382: *Athanaricus rex Gothorum Constantinopolim ibique vitam exegit.*

Also Ammianus 27, 5, 10: *ubi* (at Constantinople) . . . *Atha-*
naricus . . . fatali sorte decessit et ambitiosis exequiis ritu sepultus
est nostro. Marcellinus on the year 381: *Athanaricus rex Gothorum,*
cum quo Theodosius imp. foedus pepigerat, Constantinopolim mense
Ianuario venit eodemque mense morbo periit. Also Orosius 7, 34,
6, 7; Idatius on the year 381; Zosimus 4, 34; Socrates 5, 10.

145. **submitted to the Roman rule:** see Orosius 7, 34, 7:
universae Gothorum gentes rege defuncto adspicientes virtutem
benignitatemque Theodosii Romano sese imperio dediderunt. **Eu-**
genius: Jordanes has made a mistake here. Gratian was assassinated in the year 383 by order of Maximus the Spaniard, who
then usurped the throne. Eugenius (392-394), the rhetorician,
was elevated to imperial power by Arbogast the Frank, upon the
death of Valentinian II. He was the last enemy of Theodosius
and was slain after the battle of the Frigidus in 394.

XXIX 146. **his sons:** Arcadius and Honorius.

147. **Stilicho and Aurelian:** they held the consulship in 400.
See Prosper *ad annum* p. 400: *Stilicone et Aureliano. Gothi*
Italiam Alarico et Radagaiso ducibus ingressi. Jordanes, apparently knowing nothing of the campaigns in Greece, proceeds at
once to Alaric's invasion of Italy (Hodgkin I. II 653; see also
Bury I 67; Cambridge Mediaeval History, page 261 and 457).
river Candidianus: this stream is now called the Candiano. The
bridge is mentioned also by Cassiodorus on the year 491:
Odovacar cum Herulis egressus Ravenna nocturnis horis ad pontem
Candidiani a. d. n. rege Theoderico memorabili certamine superatur.
the royal city of Ravenna: Ravenna was the residence of the
western Roman emperors (402-476), Ostrogothic kings (to 540)
and Byzantine exarchs (to 750). See Hodgkin I. II, 851-917.

148. **Alveroí:** the Italian *Veneti* (*Romana* 180) or *Venetes*
(*Getica* 222, 223). To be distinguished from the *Venethi* mentioned in XXIII 119. **above the Ionian Sea:** Ravenna was
three miles from the Adriatic, sometimes known as *Mare Supe-*
rum, and in fact a northward extension of the *Mare Ionium*.
like an island: see Cassiodorus var. 12, 24: *Venetiae . . . ab*
austro Ravennam Padumque contingunt, ab oriente iucunditate
Ionii litoris perfruuntur, ubi alternus aestus egrediens modo claudit,
modo aperit faciem reciproca inundatione camporum: hic vobis
aliquantulum aquatilium avium more domus est, namque nunc
terrestris, modo cernitur insularis.

149. **sweeps with his oars along:** with the language of this
passage compare Vergil, Aen. 5, 162:

> *quo tantum mihi dexter abis? huc derige gressum;*
> *litus ama et laeva stringat sine palmula cautes.*

Fossa Asconis: see Agnellus *lib. eccl. Rav.* 70; also 79: *in loco qui dicitur Fossa Sconii iuxta Fluvium.*

150. Eridanus: the poetical name of the Po. See Vergil, Georgics 4, 372. **turned aside by . . . Augustus:** he had made Ravenna his naval station for the Adriatic. **Dio relates:** the passage is lost.

151. Fabius says: a writer not mentioned elsewhere. Mommsen curtly observes: *quinam fuerit nescio* (Intro. XXXIII).

XXX 152. embassy to . . . Honorius: the story of the siege of Ravenna rests on the authority of Jordanes alone. His whole account of Alaric's movements in Italy is very much confused (Hodgkin I. II. 711).

153. invasion of Gaiseric: the Vandals together with the Suavi and Alani entered Gaul in 406, and three years later they poured into Spain through the passes of the Pyrenees. In Spain there was severe warfare for many years. Gaiseric became king of the Vandals upon the death of his father Gunderic in 427.

154. Pollentia: the modern Pollenza, near Turin. The battle of Pollentia was fought on Easter Sunday, April 6, 402, and Alaric was attacked while he was attending the service of the day. Hodgkin (I. II 720), by a curious slip, places both Easter Sunday and Good Friday in the year 402 on the 6th of April. See Bury I 109; Cambridge Medieval History 265 and 460.

155. almost exterminated it: that the dubious battle of Pollentia was a Gothic victory is asserted also by Cassiodorus on the year 402: *Pollentiae Stiliconem cum exercitu Romano Gothi victum acie fugaverunt.* Prosper merely says: *Pollentiae adversus Gothos vehementer utriusque partis clade pugnatum est.* Orosius says of this battle (7, 37, 2): *taceo de infelicibus illis apud Pollentiam gestis, cum barbaro et pagano duci . . . cuius inprobitati reverentissimi dies et sanctum pascha violatum est cedentique hosti propter religionem, ut pugnaret, extortum est; . . . pugnantes vicimus, victores victi sumus.* **returned again to Liguria:** Pollentia is in Liguria. Alaric's march toward Rome took place in the year 408. See Bury I 115.

156. finally entered Rome: after his third and final siege of Rome in 410 Alaric sacked the city. The first siege occurred in 408, the second in 409. See Bury I 121; Hodgkin I. II 766 — 810; Cambridge Medieval History 270-274. **merely sacked it:** see Cassiodorus on the year 410. To Prosper's words: *Roma . . . a Gothis Halarico duce capta,* he adds: *ubi clementer usi victoria sunt.* Also var. 12, 20: *exemplum . . . in historia nostra magna intentione rettulimus. nam cum rex Alaricus urbis Romae depraedatione* *satiatus apostoli Petri vasa suis deferentibus excepisset, mox ut rei causam habita interrogatione cognovit, sacris liminibus deportari diripientium manibus imperavit, ut cupiditas, quae depraedationis ambitu admiserat scelus, devotione largissima deleret excessum.* And Orosius 7, 39, 15: *tertia die barbari quam ingressi urbem fuerant sponte discedunt facto quidem aliquantarum aedium incendio, sed ne tanto quidem, quanto septingentesimo conditionis eius anno casus effecerat.* See also Orosius 7, 39, 1 and Augustine, *De Civitate Dei* I, 1. **Bruttii:** the modern Calabria. **Adriatic Sea:** here as in LX 308 and *Romana* 151 Jordanes is referring to the Ionian Sea; he also refers to the Mediterranean as the Adriatic (see *Romana* 223: *Rodus . . . totius Atriae insularum metropolis*).

157. **sunk several of his ships:** see Orosius 7, 43, 12 (quoted below in note on XXXIII 173).

158. **Busentus:** a little river now called the Busento, which flows around Cosenza (*Consentia*), where Alaric died. **Athavulf:** or Ataulfus; he was Alaric's brother-in-law.

XXXI 159. **returned again to Rome:** a doubtful statement. What Orosius (7, 43, 3) says of Athavulf seems to disprove it: *is, ut saepe auditum atque ultimo exitu eius probatum est, satis studiose sectator pacis militare fideliter Honorio imperatori ac pro defendenda Romana republica inpendere vires Gothorum praeoptavit.* See Bury I 137; Cambridge Medieval History 274 and 399. **Placidia:** Galla Placidia was the daughter of Theodosius I and the Empress Galla, and granddaughter of Valentinian I.

160. **Forum Julii:** as Mommsen points out, Jordanes is here in error either with regard to the region or the city. In Aemilia there is a Forum Livii; a Forum Julii is found both in Venetia and in Gallia Narbonensis. But we learn from other authors (Olympiodorus fr. 24; Idatius p. 18 Ronc.) that the marriage took place at Narbonne. See Bury I 147; Cambridge Medieval History 402. **Then Athavulf set out for Gaul:** Jordanes has the order of facts reversed. It was in 412 that he left Italy, never to return. The wedding of Athavulf and Placidia took place at Narbonne in 414. (Hodgkin I. II 829, 833.)

161. **we have said before:** see XXII 115. **crossed over into Gaul:** see Isidorus Goth. laud. 68 (which Mommsen thinks is taken from Cassiodorus): *Wandalica et ipsa crebro opinata barbaries non tantum praesentia eorum* (the Goths) *exterrita quam opinione fugata est.*

162. **in Spain:** the invasion of Spain by the Vandals and the Alani occurred in 409. See note on XXX 153. Also Bury I 142; Cambridge Medieval History 274 and 304. **Geberich:** see XXII 113 and following.

163. he . . . fell: Athavulf was assassinated in 415. Two
years later his widow, Galla Placidia, married Constantius III
and bore him a son who ruled later as Valentinian III (425-455).
Euervulf: Olympiodorus frag. 26 names a certain Dubius as his
slayer; he says ἀναιρεῖ αὐτὸν (Athavulf) εἰς τῶν οἰκείων Γότθων Δούβοις
τοὔνομα ἔχθραν παλαιὰν καιροφυλακήσας. See Hodgkin I. II 834 n. 1.
Segeric: or Singeric. See Orosius 7, 43, 9: *Segericus rex a Gothis
creatus . . . a suis interfectus est.* He reigned only a week. See
Hodgkin, The Dynasty of Theodosius 175, and Bury I 149.
XXXII 164. Valia or Wallia, the founder of the Visigothic
kingdom, with its capital at Tolosa. He received a grant in
southern Gaul and was at first under Roman supremacy but
soon made himself independent. See Bury I 152, Cambridge
Medieval History 404. **Constantius**: this is Constantius III
who became emperor in 421. The meeting of Constantius and
Valia at the pass in the Pyrenees, where they made a treaty of
peace, took place in the year 416.

165. on the following terms: see Orosius 7, 43, 12: *Vallia . . .
pacem optimam cum Honorio imperatore . . . pepigit: Placidiam
imperatoris sororem . . . fratri reddidit: Romanae securitati peri-
culum suum obtulit, ut adversus ceteras gentes, quae per Hispanias
consedissent, sibi pugnaret et Romanis vinceret.* **a certain Constantine**: see Marcellinus on the year 411: *Constantinus apud
Gallias invasit imperium filiumque suum ex monacho Caesarem fecit.
ipse apud Arelatum civitatem occiditur, Constans filius apud Vien-
nam capite plectitur.* See also Orosius 7, 40, 4.7; 42, 3, 4; Bury
I 139-144. **Arelate**: Arelas or Arelate in southern Gaul, on
the eastern branch of the Rhone, is the modern Arles. **Vienne**:
the Roman *Vienna* was a city of Gallia Narbonensis on the
Rhone, the modern Vienne. **Jovinus**: see Marcellinus on the
year 412: *Iovinus et Sebastianus in Gallias tyrannidem molientes
occisi sunt.* See also Orosius 7, 42, 6; and Bury I 144 onward.

166. twelfth year of Valia's reign: this would be the year
427. But as Valia reigned only four years (415-419), "the
twelfth year of Valia's reign" mentioned by Jordanes is a
statement of no value, except as meaning "the twelfth year
after the year of Valia's accession." If the first irruption of the
Huns is dated at 375 and a few years are allowed for their
conquest of Pannonia the "almost fifty years" of Jordanes is a
fairly accurate statement. **Pannonia**: see Marcellinus on
the year 427: *Pannoniae quae per L annos ab Hunnis retinebantur,
a Romanis receptae sunt.* **Hierius and Ardabures**: consuls in
427. See Prosper and Cassiodorus, chronicle for this year:
gens Vandalorum [Cassiodorus adds *a Gothis exclusa*] *de Hispaniis
ad Africam transit.*

XXXIII 167. Boniface: he was one of the chief advisers of the Empress Placidia, the mother of Valentinian III, and held the rank of *Comes Africae.* According to Procopius (*De bello Vandalico* I, 3) it was due to a plot of Aëtius that Boniface's loyalty was suspected, and that in 427 he was declared a public enemy of Rome. It was then that he summoned the Vandals to his assistance from Spain. Hodgkin I. II 876, Bury I 156, Cambridge Medieval History 409.

168. disaster of the Romans: the sack of Rome by Gaiseric occurred in 455. See XLV 235 and note; also Bury I 235.

170. order of succession: Mommsen gives the following chronology for the Kings of the Vandals:

Gaiseric	427-477
Huneric	477-484
Gunthamund	484-496
Thrasamund	496-523
Ilderich	523-530
Gelimer	530-534

171. Justinian: Emperor of the East from 527 to 565; see LX 307 onward. **Belisarius:** this great soldier was born about 505, and received the appointment of *Magister Militum per Orientem* in 530. His conquest of the Vandals occurred in the year 534. (Hodgkin III 580.) For the Vandalic war see Bury I 385 onward. **a great spectacle:** Belisarius was rewarded for his success by the honor of a triumph, and Gelimer walked before him in the triumphal procession, together with the other Vandal captives. (Hodgkin III 624.) **private life:** after the celebration of the triumph, Gelimer received estates in the province of Galatia and lived there with his exiled countrymen.

172. third part of the world: see Marcellinus on the year 534: *provincia Africa, quae in divisione orbis terrarum a plerisque in parte tertia posita est, volente deo vindicata est.* See also Orosius I, 2, 83; *Codex Iustinianus* I, 27, 1 pr. and Cassiodorus var. II, 13. **the misery of civil war:** a war with the Moors followed directly upon the departure of Belisarius from Africa, and after raging for several years was brought to a successful conclusion by his lieutenant Solomon in 539 (Gibbon IV 298). See Bury I 387 onward.

173. such a misfortune: his ships were wrecked. See XXX 157, also Orosius 7, 43, 11.12: (Valia) *territus maxime iudicio dei, quia, cum magna superiore abhinc anno Gothorum manus . . . transire in Africam moliretur in XII milibus passuum Gaditani freti tempestate correpta miserabili exitu perierat, memor etiam illius acceptae sub Alarico cladis, cum in Siciliam Gothi transire* *conati in conspectu suorum miserabiliter arrepti et demersi sunt, pacem . . . cum Honorio . . . pepigit.*   a bloodless victory: a reference to the peace concluded with Honorius; see passage from Orosius cited in preceding note, also XXXII 165 and note. **Tolosa:** the capital of the Visigothic Kingdom in Gaul, now Toulouse.

174. mentioned above: see XIV 81.   **Veteric:** see XIV 81. **still submitted to . . . the Huns:** see XXIV 130.

175. Theodorid: this is Theodorid I who was slain in the Battle of the Catalaunian Plains in 451. See XL 209.   **XXXIV 176. Theodosius and Festus:** consuls in 439. **Count Gaina:** the revolt of Count Gaina, or Gainas, and the consequent outbreak of popular frenzy against the Goths in Constantinople actually occurred in 400, though Jordanes seems to assign it to the consulship of Theodosius and Festus, the year 439. Gaina was killed on the shores of the Danube by the Hun Uldis, who sent his head to Arcadius. (Hodgkin I. II 695.)   For details of the revolt of Count Gaina see Bury I 83-89, Cambridge Medieval History 262-263.   **Aetius:** the great Roman general who defeated Attila at the Battle of the Catalaunian Plains (Châlons) in 451. See XXXVI 191. **Durostorum:** the modern Silistria on the lower Danube.

177. Litorius: Jordanes probably got his information from Prosper on the year 439: *Theodosio XVII et Festo. Litorius qui secunda ab Aetio patricio potestate Hunnis auxiliantibus praeerat . . . pugnam cum Gothis imprudenter conseruit . . . tantam ipse hostibus cladem intulit, ut nisi inconsideranter proelians in captivitatem incidisset, dubitandum foret, cui potius parti victoria adscriberetur . . . pax cum Gothis facta, cum eam post ancipitis pugnae lacrimabile experimentum humilius quam umquam antea poposcissent.* See Bury I 172, Cambridge Medieval History 411.

178. Attila: he and his brother Bleda gained the rule over the Huns in 433 and Bleda was murdered twelve years later. See XXXV 180.   **an embassy:** in 448 the Emperor Theodosius II sent an embassy to Attila and the chief ambassador, Maximin, invited Priscus, the man of letters, to accompany him. From Priscus we learn much of Attila's own country and court. (Hodgkin II 60.)   The account of Priscus is well translated by Bury (I 212).   **mighty rivers:** see Priscus fr. 8 (4 p. 83 Muell.): ναυσιπόροις τε προσεβάλομεν ποταμοῖς, ὧν οἱ μέγιστοι μετὰ τὸν Ἴστρον ὅ τε Δρήκων λεγόμενος καὶ ὁ Τίγας καὶ ὁ Τιφήσας ἦν. καὶ τούτους μὲν ἐπεραιώθημεν. **Tisia:** the river Theiss. See also the Corpus. Inscr. Lat. III p. 247 for these rivers.   **Vidigoia:** see V 43. **village . . . like a great city:** see Priscus fr. 8 (p. 89 Muell.): ἔνδον δὲ τοῦ περιβόλου πλεῖστα ἐτύγχανεν οἰκήματα, τὰ μὲν ἐκ σανίδων ἐγγλύφων

καὶ ἡρμωσμένων εἰς εὐπρέπειαν, τὰ δὲ ἐκ δοκῶν . . . ἐνταῦθα τῆς Ἀττήλα ἐνδι-
αιτωμένης γαμετῆς.

179. **dining halls**: see Priscus fr. 8 (p. 91 Muell.): πρὸς δὲ τοῖς
τοίχοις τοῦ οἰκήματος πάντες ὑπῆρχον οἱ δίφροι ἐξ ἑκατέρας πλεύρας . . . βαθμοὶ
τινες ἐπὶ τὴν αὐτοῦ (Attila) ἀνῆγον εὐνὴν καλυπτομένην ὀθόναις καὶ ποικίλοις
παραπετάσμασι κόσμου χάριν.

XXXV 180. Bleda: Marcellinus says under the year 445:
Bleda rex Hunnorum Attilae fratris sui insidiis interimitur.

183. Priscus says: for the story of the sword of Mars, see
Priscus fr. 8 (p. 91 Muell.): ἔσεσθαι δὲ οὐκ εἰς μακρὰν τῆς παρούσης αὐτῷ
(Attila) δυνάμεως αὔξησιν· σημαίνειν καὶ τοῦτο τὸν θεὸν τὸ τοῦ Ἄρεος ἀνα_
φήναντα ξίφος, ὅπερ ὂν ἱερὸν καὶ παρὰ τῶν Σκυθικῶν βασιλέων τιμώμενον, οἷα δὴ
τῷ ἐφόρῳ τῶν πολέμων ἀνακείμενον, ἐν τοῖς πάλαι ἀφανισθῆναι χρόνοις, εἶτα διὰ
βοὸς εὑρεθῆναι.

XXXVI 184. mentioned shortly before: in XXXIII 170.
incited . . . to . . . war: see Priscus fr. 15 (p. 98 Muell.): ἔχειν
αὐτῷ (Attila) ἐδόκει καλῶς . . . ἐς τὴν ἑσπέραν στρατεύεσθαι τῆς μάχης αὐτῷ
μὴ μόνον πρὸς Ἰταλιώτας, ἀλλὰ καὶ πρὸς Γότθους καὶ Φράγγους ἐσομένης, πρὸς
μὲν Ἰταλιώτας ὥστε τὴν Ὀνωρίαν μετὰ τῶν χρημάτων λαβεῖν, πρὸς δὲ Γότθους
χάριν Γιζερίχῳ κατατιθέμενον. See Bury I 175, Cambridge Medieval
History 364 and 415. **Huneric**: see note on XXXIII 170.

185. sent ambassadors into Italy: this was in the year 451.

188. give heed: W. Fröhner (Philologus, supplbd. 5, 55 [1889]
would read *fovete*, not *favete*.

190. Friderich . . . Eurich, Retemer . . . Himnerith: of
these four sons, Eurich alone became king. He reigned from
466 to 485. **Thorismud and Theodorid**: Thorismud succeeded
his father as king of the Visigoths, reigning from 451-453, and
his brother Theodorid succeeded him, as Theodorid II, reigning
from 453-466.

192. Catalaunian Plains: the site of this great battle is
usually placed at Châlons-sur-Marne, but von Wietersheim and
Hodgkin believe it was fought near Méry-sur-Seine; see Hodgkin II 143-145; also Bury I 177 and Cambridge Medieval
History 416 note 2. The description of the battle, as well as
the general account of Attila is believed by Mommsen (Introduction XXXVI) to have been taken over solidly from Priscus.
Hodgkin (II 125, note) regards Cassiodorus as a more probable
source, because of the strong Gothic coloring.

XXXVII 194. Sangiban: see Prosper Tiro on the year 440:
*deserta Valentinae urbis rura Alanis, quibus Sambida praeerat,
partienda traduntur*. **Aureliani**: the present Orleans. Gregory
of Tours (2, 7) gives a different version of this siege.

XXXVIII 199. Valamir, Thiudimer and Vidimer: see also
XLVIII 252 and following. **the king they served**: the Ostro-

goths, it will be remembered, at this time submitted to the overlordship of the Huns.   **Ardaric:** see L 260, 262, 263. Also *Romana* 331 and Bury, I 261 note 2.

200.   keeper of secrets: Cassiodorus says (var. 11, 1): *Vnalamer . . . enituit fide.*   **we had said:** in XXXVIII 199.   **in fear and trembling:** compare with the *cum timore et tremore* of Jordanes the Vulgate Phil. II 12: *cum metu et tremore.*

XXXIX 206.   the Maeotian swamp: see XXIV 123.

XL 209.   Andag: the father of Baza, to whom Jordanes was *notarius.* See note on L 266.   **in prophecy:** see XXXVII 196.

210.   nearly slew Attila: see Cassiodorus on the year 451: *Romani Aetio duce Gothic auxiliaribus contra Attilam in campo Catalaunico pugnaverunt, qui virtute Gothorum superatus abscessit.* Prosper neither mentions the place nor gives the Goths credit for the victory.

XLI 216.   his brothers: it will be remembered that Theodorid I had sent home four of his sons before the battle; see XXXVI 190.

218.   the old oracles: such as the good omen of the sword of Mars, XXV 183.

XLII 219.   Aquileia: see XV 88.   The river Natissa or Natiso (Ammianus 21, 12, 8) is the modern Natisone; Mount Piccis is not mentioned elsewhere.

221.   forced their way: Prosper has nothing about this.   Cassiodorus says on the year 452: *Attila . . . Aquileiam magna vi dimicans introivit.*   The refugees from the cities sacked and burned by Attila fled to the lagoons at the mouths of the Piave and the Brenta, occupying the islands which later became the site of the city of Venice.   See Bury I 179, 180.

222.   Mediolanum: Milan.   **Ticinum:** on the Ticinus river; the modern Pavia.   **Priscus relates:** the passage is not preserved.

223.   Pope Leo: Pope from 440-461.   Prosper (on the year 452) says of this embassy: *suscepit . . . negotium . . . papa Leo . . . ita summi sacerdotis praesentia rex gavisus est, ut et bello abstineri praeciperet et ultra Danuvium promissa pace discederet.*   See Bury I 179, Hodgkin II 156-161.   **Ambuleian district:** this region is not elsewhere mentioned.   The Mincius is a tributary of the Po in Cisalpine Gaul, now called the Mincio.   **Honoria:** the daughter of Galla Placidia and Constantius III, whom Galla Placidia married upon the death of her first husband Athavulf.   See also the account given by Priscus fr. 16 (p. 99 Muell.): ὁ Ἀττήλας . . . τῶν ἀμφ' αὐτὸν ἄνδρας ἐς τὴν Ἰταλίαν ἔπεμπεν ὥστε τὴν Ὀνωρίαν ἐκδιδόναι. εἶναι γὰρ αὐτῷ ἡρμοσμένην πρὸς γάμον, τεκμήριον ποιούμενος τὸν παρ' αὐτῆς πεμφθέντα δακτύλιον, ὃν καὶ ἐπιδειχθησόμενον ἐστάλκει · παραχωρεῖν δὲ αὐτῷ τὸν Βαλεντινιανὸν καὶ τοῦ ἡμίσεως τῆς βασιλείας μέρους. Attila's demand was refused. See also *Romana* 328 and Bury I 174, 175. **XLIII 225.** promised him by Theodosius: that is, Theodosius II (402-450). This refers to tribute money. See Priscus fr. 19 (p. 99 Muell.); ὁ Ἀττήλας μετὰ τὸ τὴν Ἰταλίαν ἀνδραποδίσασθαι ἐπὶ τὰ σφέτερα ἀναζεύξας τοῖς κρατοῦσι τῶν ἑῴων Ῥωμαίων πόλεμον καὶ ἀνδραποδισμὸν τῆς χώρας κατήγγελλεν, ὡς μὴ ἐκπεμφθέντος τοῦ παρὰ Θεοδοσίου τεταγμένου φόρου.

227. Catalaunian Plains: this second defeat of Attila by the Visigoths on the very site of the former battle is generally disbelieved by historians, since it is mentioned by no other author (Hodgkin II 170).

228. Ascalc: Prosper of Aquitaine, Idatius and Isidorus say Thorismud was slain by his brothers and their dependents. Nor is this inconsistent with the account given by Jordanes who speaks of those *that were lying in wait*. Ascalc probably played the part of betrayer.

XLIV 229. Riciarius: or Rechiarius, king of the Suavi in Spain from 448-456. For his death see XLIV 232. his kinsman: he had married Theodorid's sister.

230. Austrogonia: the *Autrigones* actually dwelt on the west of *Gallaecia*. See Mela 3, 1, 15; Pliny 3, 3, 27; Florus 4, 12; Orosius 6, 21; Corpus inscr. lat. II p. 394. Monument of . . . Scipio: see I 7. Tagus: now the Tajo.

231. moved his array: probably in the year 456 (Hodgkin II 388). Gundiuch: or Gundiok, a brother-in-law of Ricimer XLV 236). Hilperic: or Chilperic. See Hodgkin II 388.

232. Ulbius: according to Idatius the battle took place at a river called the Urbicus, now the Obrego, near Asturica Augusta (now Astorga) in northwestern Spain. Tyrrhenian Sea: this geographical reference is baffling, for the battle was fought at Oporto.

233. Agrivulf: he ruled over the Suavi in Spain in 456-457. See Idatius on the year 457: *Aiulfus deserens Gothos in Gallaecia residet*. Varni: or Varini; see Zeuss 132 and 360.

234. Rimismund: he ruled the Suavi from 458 onward.

XLV 235. Eurich: he too was a son of Theodorid I; see XXXVI 190. with such eager haste: a euphemistic way of saying that he assassinated his brother. Valentinian: he was murdered on the Campus Martius in 455. In the *Romana* 334 Jordanes, following Marcellinus, says that the deed was done by two dependents of Aëtius. See Bury I 182. laid it waste: compare the account of the events of this year (455) as given by Marcellinus: *Valentinianus princeps dolo Maximi patricii . . . truncatus est. idem Maximus invasit imperium tertioque tyrannidis* *suae mense membratim Romae a Romanis discerptus est. Gense- ricus rex Wandalorum . . . ex Africa Romam ingressus est eaque urbe rebus omnibus spoliata.* The Vandals are said to have been summoned from Africa by the Empress Eudoxia, widow of Valentinian III, whom Maximus had forced to marry him. (Hodgkin II 203). But see Bury I 235, Cambridge Medieval History 308. **was slain:** Maximus was murdered after a reign of about three months; see Bury I 235, Hodgkin II 205.

236. Majorian: the Emperor Majorian was killed in August 461. See Marcellinus on this year: *Maiorianus Caesar apud Dertonam iuxta fluvium qui Hira dicitur interemptus est: locum eius Severus invasit.* Compare also *Romana* 335, where Jordanes seems to have drawn on the *Getica* as a source. See Bury I 240 **Dertona:** a city in Liguria, now Tortona. For the river Ira see Corpus inscr. lat. V. p. 828. **Anthemius:** so Marcellinus on the year 467: *Leo imperator Anthemium patricium Romam misit imperatoremque constituit.* After the death of Severus there was for twenty months no emperor in the west; an interregnum which, as Hodgkin (II 440) points out, "prepared the way for the abolition of the dignity of Augustus in 476." Anthemius was the son-in-law of Marcian, Leo's predecessor in the east. See Bury I 243-244, Cambridge Medieval History 426. **Rici- mer:** Ricimer, the grandson of Valia, king of the Visigoths, was the power behind the Roman throne for the sixteen years (456-472) after Avitus [XLV 240] was deposed (Hodgkin II 399). See Bury I 234-249, Cambridge Medieval History 422. **Beorg:** Hodgkin (II 440) suggests that he may have been the successor of Sangiban (XXXVII 194). Beorg was killed in 464.

237. Brittones: see Gregory of Tours 2, 18: *Britanni de Biturica a Gothis expulsi sunt multis apud Dolensem vicum peremptis.* **Rio- timus:** supposed to be the same as the Riothamus to whom a letter of Sidonius (3. 9) is addressed.

238. Arverna: the Arverni were a people of Gaul in the region now called Auvergne. See XLV 240, and Hodgkin II 486-488.

239. Olybrius: see Marcellinus on the year 472: *viii id. Nov. Anthemius imp. Romae a Ricimere genero suo occiditur. loco eius Olybrius substitutus.* See Bury I 248, Cambridge Medieval History 428. **Aspar:** he was of the Alani, a general and ex- consul, and his power in the eastern empire was great for many years. (Hodgkin II 442.) It was mainly through his influence that Leo became emperor (457-474). Compare Marcellinus on the year 471: *Aspar primus patriciorum cum Ardabure et Patriciolo filiis, illo quidem olim patricio, hoc autem Caesare generoque Leonis principis appellato, Arrianus cum Arriana prole spadonum ensibus* *in palatio vulneratus interiit.* See *Romana* 338. **barely eight months:** Marcellinus on the year 472: *septimo mense imperii sui vita defunctus est.* **rather by usurpation:** so Marcellinus on the year 473: *Glycerius apud Ravennam plus praesumptione quam electione Caesar factus est.* Glycerius was raised to the throne by Gundobad, a Burgundian, the nephew of Ricimer (Hodgkin II 478). See Bury I 274-276. **Nepos:** Julius Nepos was elevated to the imperial dignity by the rulers of the east, who refused to recognize Glycerius as the emperor. Though proclaimed at Constantinople in 473, he did not arrive in Italy until the following year (Hodgkin II 480). **deposed him:** see Marcellinus on the year 474: *Glycerius . . . a Nepote Marcellini quondam patricii sororis filio imperio expulsus in Portu urbis Romae ex Caesare episcopus ordinatus est.* See *Romana* 338. **bishop:** the ex-emperor Glycerius was consecrated as Bishop of Salona, and sent off to Dalmatia. **Port of Rome:** the fortified harbor town known as *Portus Augusti* (that is, Nero) *et Traiani,* opposite Ostia.

240. already said: in XLV 237. **.Arverna:** see XLV 238. **Ecdicius:** see Gregory of Tours, hist. Franc. 2, 24, and Hodgkin II 494. **Avitus:** he was raised to the imperial dignity in 455 and died the following year. It was in 456 that he was deposed by Ricimer and consecrated bishop at Placentia.

241. Orestes: see Marcellinus on the year 475: *Nepote Orestes protinus effugato Augustulum filium suum in imperium collocavit.* See *Romana* 344. Orestes had been the secretary of Attila. **fled to Dalmatia:** it is a curious coincidence that these two deposed emperors should end their days in the same city.

XLVI 242. Torcilingi . . . Sciri . . . Heruli: these races dwelt in the region to the north of the middle Danube (Hodgkin II 510). **invaded Italy:** see Marcellinus on the year 476: *Odovacer rex Gothorum Romam obtinuit. Orestem Odovacer ilico trucidavit. Augustulum filium Orestis Odovacer in Lucullano Campaniae castello exilii poena damnavit.* See also *Romana* 344 and Bury I 278-281, Cambridge Medieval History 430. **Castle of Lucullus:** the *Lucullanum,* the magnificent villa built near Naples by L. Licinius Lucullus, who defeated Mithridates in 73 B.C. and died 57-56 B.C.

243. seven hundred and ninth year: that is, dating the beginning of the rule of Augustus from the assassination of Julius Caesar in 44 B.C. **five hundred and twenty-second year:** the sentence is taken over almost unchanged from Marcellinus on the year 476. The chronology may be explained as follows:

Founding of Rome.....................753 B.C.
Accession of Augustus in 709th year
    after (= 708 years)............... 45 B.C.
Romulus Augustulus in 522nd year
    after accession of Augustus (=
    521 years) ....476 A.D.

Although the total reckoning comes out correctly, the date of the assassination of Julius Caesar should, of course, be 44, not 45, B.C. See also *Romana* 345.   **slew Count Bracila:** see Marcellinus on the year 477: *Bracilam comitem Odovacer rex apud Ravennam occidit.*   **almost thirteen years:** Odoacer fled to Ravenna in 489 after the Battle of Verona; see LVII 293.

    XLVII 245.   ninth in succession: the following is a list of the Visigothic kings mentioned by Jordanes:

Alaric I	395-410
Athavulf	410-415
Segeric	415
Valia	415-419
Theodorid I	419-451
Thorismud	451-453
Theodorid II	453-466
Eurich	466-485
Alaric II	485-507
Amalaric	507-531
Thiudis	531-548
Thiudigislus	548-549
Agil	549-554
Athanagild	554-567

stated above: in XLVI 243.

    XLVIII 246.   Hermanaric: he died in 375; see XXIV 130 and note.   **Vinitharius:** see genealogical chart, p. 41.

    247.   Boz: not otherwise mentioned.

    248.   Balamber: see XXIV 130 and note.   **Gesimund:** Mommsen (*Index Personarum*, p. 143, under *Gesimundus*) points out that it is evident from two passages that a generation has fallen out in one branch of the family tree of the Amali as given in XIV 79.   For in XLVIII 252 Vandalarius the son of Vinitharius and Thorismud the son of Hunimund are called cousins, which requires the same number of generations between each of them and their common ancestors, and furthermore Gesimund, who is here (XLVIII 248) called the son of Hunimund the Great, is not found in the genealogical list, though the other Amali with whom he is mentioned are all named there. Furthermore (though Mommsen does not attach much importance to this argument), by the addition of one generation Eutharic and Amalasuentha are made to be of the same generation. Mommsen believes that Gesimund has fallen out, not between Hunimund and Thorismud, but between Hermanaric and Hunimund. For both Jordanes (XLVIII 250) and Cassiodorus himself (var. 11, 1) speak of Hunimund's beauty, so we must admit that he began to rule when a young man. And yet, if Hermanaric died at the age of 110, it is scarcely likely that he left a youthful son as his successor. Furthermore what Jordanes says in XLVIII 248—that when the Huns expelled Vinitharius from his kingdom they summoned Gesimund, the son of Hunimund the Great, and (XLVIII 250) that this Hunimund ruled the Goths upon the defeat and death of Vinitharius—is scarcely credible.

Mommsen therefore argues that in XIV 81 the author should have written: *Hermanaricus genuit [Gesimundum; Gesimundus autem genuit] Hunimundum.* And likewise, since the words in parentheses had fallen out, instead of *Gesimundo Hermanarici filio* in XLVIII 248 there was substituted *Gesimundo Hunimundi magni filio* and in the XLVIII 250 instead of *Hunimundus filius Gesimundi* was substituted *Hunimundus filius Hermanarici.*

Hodgkin (III 9) believes that Gesimund was probably an elder brother of Thorismud. Erhardt (Göttingische gelehrte Anzeigen 1886, 1-2, page 677) is of the opinion that the contradictions found in *Getica* 246-252 clearly indicate that the genealogical table as given in 79 has been cleverly restored—probably by Cassiodorus—and is not to be relied upon. Accordingly he considers Mommsen's attempt to reconcile Jordanes' various statements with each other as equally untrustworthy. See the genealogical chart on p. 41.

249. Erac: possibly the river Phasis in Colchis; see VI 47.

250. personal beauty: Cassiodorus 11, 1: *enituit . . . Vnimundus forma.* bloom of youth: Cassiodorus 11, 1: *enituit . . . Thorismut castitate.*

251. for forty years: Köpke (Die Anfänge des Königthums bei den Gothen, p. 141) seeks to explain this legendary forty years of mourning by a notice preserved in a letter of Cassiodorus (var. 8, 9). He assumes that we must interpolate a reign, namely that of a Gensemund who, as Cassiodorus says: "though only adopted as a son-in-arms, joined himself with such devotion to the Amal race that he rendered service of anxious fidelity to its heirs, although he himself was besought to wear the crown." (Hodgkin's translation.) But Hodgkin points out that the point of this story seems rather to be that Gesimund *refused*

the crown. Hodgkin's explanation seems rather more probable:
that the Goths did for a time hesitate to fill the place of their
beloved king, and the Huns, who were their overlords, so pro-
longed this period that it was a generation before they succeeded in restoring the Amal line to the throne. (Hodgkin III
8.)   we have said before: in XXXIII 174.   Amalasuentha: or
Amalasuntha, the daughter of Theodoric and Audefleda. See
also LIX 304 onward.   divided long ago: that is, when Beremud went to the Visigoths; see XXXIII 174.   second
husband: Mathesuentha's first husband was Vitiges, the armor-
bearer of Theodahad (LX 309).

252.   stock of Vandalarius: with the sections of this chapter
compare also XIV 79 onward and LVIII 297 onward.

253.   Thiudimer served: so Cassiodorus 11, 1: *enituit . . .
Vnalamer fide, Theudimer pietate.*

XLIX 254.   Priscus relates: the passage is not preserved.

257.   took annual tribute: see Priscus fr. 3 (p. 90 Muell.):
οὐδενὶ τῶν πώποτε τῆς Σκυθικῆς ἢ καὶ ἑτέρας ἀρξάντων γῆς τοσαῦτα ἐν ὀλίγῳ
καταπεπρᾶχθαι, ὥστε καὶ τῶν ἐν τῇ ὠκεανῷ νήσων ἄρχειν καὶ πρὸς πάσῃ τῇ
Σκυθικῇ καὶ Ῥωμαίους ἔχειν ἐς φόρου ἀπαγωγήν.

L 260.   Ardaric: see also XXXVIII 199 and *Romana* 331.
Nedao: or Netad: this stream was probably in the part of
Hungary west of the Danube. (Hodgkin II 192.)   By this
victory in 454 the Ostrogoths were at last freed from the yoke
of the Huns after almost eighty years of subjection to them.
See Bury I 261.

261.   the Suavi fighting on foot: W. Fröhner (Philologus supplbd. 5, 55 [1889] would read *lapide* for *pede,* referring to the use
of the sling.

263.   Marcian: he reigned from 450-457.

264.   Sirmium . . . Vindobona: Sirmium corresponds to a
town of Hungary called Mitrovitz; Vindobona is the modern
Vienna.

265.   Castra Martis: Castra Martis or *Castramartena urbs,* as
it here called, was a city of Dacia Ripensis.   Duke of Pentapolis: in Libya; see Procopius *bell. Vand.* 2, 21.   Froila and
Bessa: of Blivila, mentioned above, and Froila, we know no
more than Jordanes states. Procopius (*bell. Goth.* i, 16) says
of Bessa (or Bessas): οὗτος Γότθος μὲν ἦν γένος τῶν ἐκ παλαιοῦ ἐν Θρᾴκῃ
ᾠκημένων, Θευδερίχῳ τε οὐκ ἐπισπομένων, ἡνίκα ἐνθένδε ἐς Ἰταλίαν ἐπῆγε τὸν
Γότθων λεών.· From another passage (4, 11) it appears that he
was over seventy years of age in 551. The fact that Jordanes
speaks of Bessa as *Patrician in our time* helps to establish the
date of the *Getica.*   Sciri: see XLVI 242.   Sadagarii:
Zeuss p. 709.

266. **Paria . . . Candac:** this short section contains practically all that we know of Jordanes on his own statement: that he was the son of Alanoviiamuth (but see Introduction p. 3) and grandson of Paria, the notary of that Candac who led the Sciri, Sadagarii and certain of the Alani into Scythia Minor and Lower Moesia. And, if I read the Latin aright, Jordanes himself was secretary of Gunthigis, otherwise known as Baza, the son of Candac's sister and Andag, whose father Andela was of the royal family of the Amali.

```
      [Alani]            [Ostrogoths]
    ┌──────┐           Andela (Amalus)
    │      │                 │
  Candac  sister married Andag (see XL 209)
                         │
                 Gunthigis, or Baza
```

before my conversion: see introduction p. 5. **Rugi:** previously mentioned in III 24 and perhaps in IV 26 (Ulmerugi). **Bizye:** Bizye was a town of Thrace, not far from Constantinople. **Arcadiopolis:** this town, formerly called Bergula, was near Bizye. **Hernac:** Priscus calls him Ἡρνάχ see fr. 36 (p. 107 Muell.). **Emnetzur and Ultzindur:** not mentioned elsewhere. But see note on LIII 272. **Oescus and Utus and Almus:** Mommsen thinks that these are three tributaries of the Danube with three towns bearing the same names situated at their mouths. There is no other mention of Utus. **Sacromontisi and . . . Fossatisii:** not mentioned elsewhere.

LI 267. **Vulfila:** Bishop Ulfilas lived probably from 311-381. See Bessel, Ueber das Leben des Ulfilas und die Bekehrung der Gothen zum Christenthum (Göttingen, 1860). **taught them to write:** see Socrates *hist. eccl.* 4, 33: Οὐλφίλας ὁ τῶν Γότθων ἐπίσκοπος γράμματα ἐφεῦρε Γοτθικά. **Nicopolitan region:** see XVIII 101, and note on Nicopolis.

LII 268. **Scarniunga and Aqua Nigra:** these streams in Pannonia are not mentioned elsewhere, and it seems impossible to identify them. **Lake Pelso:** see *corpus inscr. lat.* III p. 523. Either the Neusiedler See in the northwest corner of Hungary or the Platten See, more than a hundred miles southeast of it. (Hodgkin III 13.)

270. **like a New Year's present:** strena, not strenua as in Jordanes, is the correct form. **Theodoric, son of Triarius:** he was a kinsman of Aspar and perhaps therefore a friend of the Emperor Leo (Hodgkin III 17). In after years the two Theodorics crossed each others paths and their relations with the Emperor Zeno were intricate and ever changing. See Bury I 262 onward, Cambridge Medieval History 470 onward.

LIII 272. Sadagis: see Zeuss p. 709.   Dintzic: in Priscus
fr. 36, 38 (p. 107, 108 Muell.) he is called Δέγγιϑιχ.   Ultzinzures: in L 266 mention is made of a certain Ultzindur.   Compare Agathias 5, 11: ἅπαντες κοινῇ μὲν Σκύθαι καὶ Οὖννοι ἐπωνομάζοντο ·
ἰδίᾳ δὲ κατὰ γένη, τὸ μέν τι αὐτῶν Κοτρίγουροι, τὸ δὲ Οὐτίγουροι, ἄλλοι δὲ
Οὐλτίζουροι, αἱ ἄλλοι Βουρουγούνδιοι.   Zeuss p. 709. Angisciri: see
Zeuss p. 709.   Bittugures: Agathias 2, 13 speaks of Οὐννικὸν τὸ
ἔθνος οἱ Βίττορες.   See also Zeuss p. 709.   Bardores: see Zeuss
p. 709.   Bassiana: Mommsen (corpus inscr. lat. III) places this
city on the Raab in Hungary, about twenty miles east of Stein-
am-Anger.

273. Hunimund: to be distinguished from Hunimund the
Amal, mentioned in XIV 81.   Dalmatia was near Suavia:
Mommsen (p. 165) shows that Jordanes is in error. He con-
founds Suavia with Savia, the Roman province which borders
on Dalmatia.   Moreover the narrative of Jordanes makes it
clear that Hunimund came into Dalmatia from Germany.   For
the situation of the Suavi see LV 280 and note.   According to
Procopius (bell. Goth. 1, 12), the Suavi were neighbors of the
Thuringi and Alamanni.   See Bury I 262, note 3.

276. Valamir . . . was . . . slain: Jordanes gives a résumé
of these and the following events in the Romana 347.   Thus
were all destroyed: Hodgkin (III 22) remarks that Jordanes
dwells upon the destruction of the Sciri, perhaps to obscure the
real issue of the fight.   In addition to the loss of their king,
the Goths may have suffered a severe defeat at the hands of the
Suavi; a surmise rendered all the more probable by the events
recounted in the following sections.

LIV 277. Alaric: this Alaric, king with Hunimund of the
German Suavi, is to be distinguished from either of the two
Alarics, the Visigothic kings, and Alaric King of the Heruli
(XXIII 117).   Beuca and Babai: Beuca is not mentioned
elsewhere; Babai appears again in LV 282.   Edica and
Hunuulf: not mentioned elsewhere; but see Hodgkin II 517 n.
the river Bolia: not mentioned elsewhere.

278. a crimson sea: Jordanes is at his best in describing
battle scenes and appears to take delight in the bloody details
he recounts. Compare XL 208.

279. they rejoiced with joy unspeakable: the ineffabili exul-
tatione laetantur of Jordanes seems to be made over from
exultabitis laetitia inenarrabili in the Vulgate I Petr. 1, 8. See
note on XXVI 137 for another Vulgate reminiscence. That
both of these Biblical echoes are referable to a single book of
the New Testament is noteworthy.

LV 280. country of the Suavi: Hodgkin (III 21) thinks the diagram suggested by Jordanes:

	Thuringians	
Franks	Suavi	Bavarians
	Burgundians	

must be replaced by this:

	Franks	
Burgundians	Suavi	Bavarians
	Burgundians	

281. almost subdued: a form of statement which may mean to our author almost anything from a drawn battle to a defeat.

282. summoned . . . adherents: as Hodgkin (III 24) observes, this was a reproduction of the old Germanic *Comitatus* which Tacitus describes (Germania 13): *haec dignitas, hae vires: magno semper electorum iuvenum globo circumdari in pace decus, in bello praesidium.* **Camundus:** if a Roman general bore such a name, he was probably of barbarian origin or descent (Hodgkin III 24). **Singidunum:** now Belgrade.

LVI 283. Glycerius ruled. see XLV 239.

285. river Savus: a tributary of the Danube in Pannonia, now the Save. **Naissus:** Nisch. Bury I 262, note 5. **Astat and Invilia:** not otherwise mentioned. **Ulpiana:** its site is doubtful. Mommsen thinks it was the first stage from Castrum Herculis on the road to Scupi. See *Corpus inscr. lat.* III pp. 268. 1024. **Castrum Herculis:** a place fourteen miles from Naissus. See *Corpus inscr. lat.* III p. 268.

286. Stobi: probably now represented by the village of Czerna Gratzko near the confluence of the Czerna and Vardar (Erigon and Axius). Here the roads from Scupi, Sardica, Heraclea and Thessalonica met (Hodgkin III 28). **Heraclea and Larissa:** Heraclea is Monastir in Macedonia; Larissa is in Thessaly. **Thessalonica:** now Salonica. **Hilarianus:** *magister officiorum* and *Patricius* at Leo's court; see *Codex Iustin.* 1, 23, 6. **the emperor:** Leo II, 473-474.

287. places they inhabited: Mommsen identifies as follows the places mentioned in the text *Cerru, Pellas, Europa, Mediana, Petina, Bereu, Sium): Cyrrhus* and *Pella*, neighboring towns in *Macedonia prima;* Pella is the birthplace of Alexander the Great. *Europus* and *Methone*, in the same province. *Pydna* and *Beroea*, also towns of this province; the former famous as the scene of the defeat of Perseus (B.C. 168), the latter the Berea mentioned in Acts 17, 10. *Dium* on the Thermaic Gulf. (See map, Hodgkin III 28.)

LVII 289. Consul Ordinary: this was in 484. He was made

Patrician and Master of Soldiery in 478, for helping restore Zeno to the throne after the revolt of Basiliscus. In the *Romana* 384 we find these same things related, the writer adhering there a little more closely to the account given by Marcellinus

291. **it will save the expense:** in Orosius (7, 43) Valia, king of the Visigoths says to the Emperor Honorius: *tu cum omnibus pacem habe omniumque obsides accipe: nos nobis confligimus, nobis perimus, tibi vincimus: immortalis vero quaestus erit rei publicae tuae, si utrique pereamus.*

292. **sent him forth:** see *Anonymus Valesianus* 49: *Zeno recompensans beneficiis Theodericum quem fecit patricium et consulem, donans ei multum et mittens eum ad Italiam.* **Hesperia:** the poetic name for Italy, *the western country.* **Sontius:** now the river Isonzo. See *corpus inscr. lat.* V pp. 75. 935. Theodoric dated his reign in Italy from the battle of the Isonzo (Hodgkin III 191). The Annals of Ravenna on the year 490 say: *his consulibus ingressus est rex Theodericus in fossato pontis Sontis et fugit Odoacer rex de fossato et abiit in Beronam.* Hodgkin gives the date as 489.

293. **Odoacer:** see XLVI 242. **Pineta:** the famous pine forest near Ravenna. **harrassed . . . the Goths:** see Anonymus Valesianus 54: *hoc consule* (the year 491) *exiit Odoachar rex de Ravenna nocte cum Herulis ingressus in Pineta in fossato patricii Theoderici . . . et victus Odoachar fugit Ravenna idibus Iuliis.*

294. **begged for mercy:** see the continuator of Prosper (*Havniensis*) on the year 493: *Odoachar pacem ab Theudorico postulans accepit, qua non diu potitus est. . . Theodoricus cum pacem cum Odoachar fecisset, ingressus est Classem III k. Mart. ac deinde ingressus est Ravennam, pacis specie Odoachrem interfecit.*

295. **deprived him of his life:** the assassination of Odoacer is the darkest blot on the career of Theodoric the Great. Theodoric invited his rival to a banquet in the Palace of Lauretum and there slew him with his own hand. See Bury I 281, Hodgkin III 212, Cambridge Medieval History 440. **Lodoin:** this is Chlodwig or Clovis, king of the Franks from 481-511. **daughter Audefleda:** Gregory of Tours (*hist. Franc.* 3, 31) says she was his sister: *Theodoricus rex Italiae Chlodovechi regis sororem in matrimonio habuit.*

296. **Celdebert . . . Thiudebert:** we learn from Gregory of Tours 3, 1 that the sons of Clovis were *Theudericus, Chlodomerus Childebertus* and *Chlotocharius,* and that *Theuderic,* the eldest, had a son named *Theudebert.* So when Jordanes speaks of Celdebert, Heldebert and Thiudebert, the first two names seem to have arisen from dittography, while the third is not that of a son but of a grandson of Clovis.

LVIII 297. Thiudigoto . . . Ostrogotho: see Procopius *bell,*
Goth. I, 12: τῷ τηνικαῦτα τῶν Οὐισιγότθων ἡγουμένῳ Ἀλαρίχῳ τῷ.
νεωτέρῳ (Theodoric) Θευδεχοῦσαν τὴν αὐτοῦ θυγάτερα παρθένον ἡγγύησεν.
also *Anonymus Valesianus* 63: *uxorem habuit ante regnum, de qua
susceperat filias: unam dedit nomine Arevagni Alarico regi Visi-
gotharum in Gallia et aliam filiam suam nomine Theodegotha Sigis-
mundo filio Gundebaudi regis.* Alaric: Alaric II reigned from
485-507. See XLVII 245. He was slain in battle by Clovis.
Sigismund: king of the Burgundians from 516-523.
298. Thorismud: Eutharic was the grandson of Beremud and
great grandson of Thorismud. See genealogical table, p. 41.
Amalasuentha: the daughter of Theodoric and Audefleda. For
her later history see LIX 305-306.
299. Amalafrida: the name of her first husband is unknown.
Theodahad: king from 534-536. His unnatural cruelty is related
in LIX 306. Thrasamund: see above, XXXIII 170. He
reigned from 496-523. Amalaberga: see Procopius *bell. Goth.*
I, 12: Ἐρμενεφρίδῳ δὲ τῶν Θορίγγων ἄρχοντι Ἀμελοβέργαν τὴν Ἀμαλαφρίδης
τῆς ἀδελφῆς παῖδα.
300. Count Pitza: for the duties of the *Comes Gothorum,* see
Cassiodorus *var.* 7, 3 (Hodgkin III 253). For Pitza see Ennodius *paneg.* 12 p. 410 Sirm. (quoted in the next note below) and
Cassiodorus *var.* 5, 29. Possibly the person to whom Procopius refers (*bell. Goth.* I, 15) under the year 536: Πίτζας Γότθος ἀνήρ
Thrasaric: in Ennodius *paneg.* 12 p. 410 Sirm. we read: *Sirmien-
sium civitas olim limes Italiae fuit, in qua seniores domini excuba-
bant . . . haec postea per regentium neglectum in Gepidarum iura
concessit . . . urebant animum principis* (Theodoric) *dolosi blan-
dimenta commenti et circa alios Gepidas quorum ductor est Gun-
derit, intempestiva Traserici familiaritas . . . postquam liquido
Traserici patuere commenta, Gothorum nobilissimos Pitzia,
Herduic et pubem nullis adhuc dedicatam proeliis destinasti
ut si oblatis pactionibus adquiesceret, semel invaso locorum
potiretur arbitrio . . . fugit sponte aliena et sine impulsu
exercitus tui deseruit quod debebat. continuo Pitzia . . . non
adquisitam esse terram credidit, sed refusam.* Thraustila: see
Paulus *hist. Rom.* 15, 15: *Theodericus . . . prius quam Italiam ad-
ventaret, Trapstilam Gepidarum regem insidiis sibi molientem bello
superans extinxit.* Mundo: a Hun, aided by the Goths in 505.
In Ennodius *paneg.* 12, p. 411 sirm. after the narrative of the
capture of Sirmium by Pitza, we read: *quibus* (Pitza and his
army) *ibi ordinationem moderantibus per foederati Mundonis attrec-
tationem Graecia est professa discordiam secum Bulgares suos in
tutela deducendo . . . quid strages militum revolvam et Sabiniani
ducis abitionem turpissimam?* See Bury I 285 note. Sabinian: the

son of the general of the same name who fought with Theodoric in Macedonia twenty-six years before. **Margoplanum:** probably one of the two cities of Upper Moesia—Horrea Margi and Margus. The form Margoplanum is not elsewhere found. Hodgkin believes the battle took place at Horrea Margi in the valley of the Morava. **Margus:** a stream in Moesia, now the Morava.

301. Attilani: descendants of Attila.

302. Ibba: see *add. ad Victorem Tunnunensem* on the year 509: *Gesalicus ab Helbane Theodorici Italiae regis duce ab Hispania fugatus Africam petit.* Isidorus *hist. Goth.* 38, on the year 507: *Gesalicus . . . ab Ebbane Theoderici regis duce duodecimo a Barcilona urbe miliario commisso proelio in fugam vertitur.* This is the Ibba *vir sublimis dux* to whom Cassiodorus writes *var.* 4, 17. **Thiudis:** upon the death of Alaric II in 507, his son Amalaric succeeded to the throne and ruled the Visigoths until 531. Thiudis reigned from 531-548.

303. the present day: the year 551, when the *Getica* was written. See introduction, page 13. **Athanagild:** Isidorus, *hist. Goth. ad eram* 587, says Athanagild's insurrection occurred in the third year of King Agil's reign, that is, in 551. The *additamenta ad Victorem Tunnunensem* (p. 372 Ronc.) for the year 552 say: *Agila mortuo Athanagildus qui dudum tyrannidem adsumpserat Gothorum rex efficitur.* Mommsen (Intro. p. XV note 31) believes that Athanagild's revolt started in 550. For Athanagild and Liberius see Bury I 415. **Liberius the Patrician:** see Procopius *bell. Goth.* 3, 39 on the year 549. Compare also 3, 40 and 4, 24.

LIX 304. Athalaric: a résumé of the following sections is given in *Romana* 367 onward.

306. Theodahad: the son of Amalafrida; see LVIII 299. Also Bury I 388 onward, Hodgkin III 641 onward. **Bulsinian lake:** the lake of Bolsena, in Etruria. **by his hirelings:** see the continuator of Marcellinus on the year 534: *Theodahadus rex Gothorum Amalasuentham reginam creatricem suam de regno pulsam in insula laci Bulsiniensis occidit. cuius mortem imp. Iustinianus ut doluit sic et ultus est.*

LX 307. triumph over the Vandals: Belisarius conquered Africa in 534 and was rewarded by a magnificent triumph at Constantinople in the autumn of the same year.

308. Sicily, their nursing mother: great exports of corn were sent every year from Sicily to Rome. **Trinacria:** *the triangular land,* the poetic name for Sicily. **Sinderith:** the surrender of Syracuse in 535 is recorded by Procopius *bell. Goth.* 1, 5 and by Marcellinus, but they do not mention the name of the Gothic leader. **Evermud**: the Continuator of Marcellinus on the year 536 calls him Ebremud. Procopius says (*bell. Goth.* 1, 8): ἐκ δὲ Γότθων αὐτόμολος παρὰ Βελισάριον Ἐβριμοὺθ ξὺν παισὶ τοῖς ἑπομένοις ἦλθεν, ὁ Θευδάτου γαμβρός, ὃς τῇ ἐκείνου θυγατρὶ Θευδενάνθῃ ξυνῴκει. **Adriatic**: see note on XXX 156.

309. Rhegium: a city of Calabria on the Strait of Messina, now Reggio. Evermud's defection occurred in the year 536.

310. Barbarian Plains: probably the Pomptine marshes between Rome and Terracina. Procopius says of this region (*bell. Goth.* 1, 11): (The Goths) ἐς χωρίον ξυνελέγησαν Ῥώμης ὀγδοήκοντα καὶ διακοσίοις σταδίοις διέχον, ὅπερ Ῥωμαῖοι καλοῦσι Ῥέγετα. ἐνθένδε γὰρ ἐνστρατοπεδεύσασθαι σφίσιν ἔδοξεν ἄριστον εἶναι. πεδία γὰρ πολλὰ ἐνταῦθά ἐστιν ἱππόβατα. See also *Corpus inscr. lat.* X p. 691. **executed his command**: see the continuator of Marcellinus on the year 536: *Gothorum exercitus Theodahadum regem habens suspectum Vitigis in regnum adsciscit. qui mox in campo Barbarico regnum pervasit, expeditione soluta Romam ingreditur . . . ibique residens dirigit Ravennam, Theodahadum occidit.*

311. took Naples: Belisarius besieged this city for some time before he finally succeeded in taking it. **on to Rome**: so the city was restored to the empire after sixty years of barbarian rule. **married Mathesuentha**: see the Continuator of Marcellinus on the year 536: *Ravennamque ingressus Matesuentham neptem Theodorici sibi sociam in regno plus vi copulat quam amore.* Compare *Romana* 373. Mathesuentha, it will be remembered, was the daughter of Amalasuentha and Eutharic of Spain (LVIII 298) and sister of Athalaric (LIX 304). **Hunila**: see Procopius *bell. Goth.* 1, 16: Οὐίτιγις . . . στρατιάν τε καὶ ἄρχοντας Οὔνι. λάν τε καὶ Πίτζαν ἐπ' αὐτοὺς ἔπεμψε· οἷς Κωνσταντῖνος ὑπαντιάσας ἐν τῷ Περυσίας προαστείῳ ἐς χεῖρας ἦλθε . . . Ῥωμαῖοι . . . τοὺς πολεμίους ἐτρέψαντο. **Perusia**: Perugia.

312. a long siege: this siege of Rome began in the spring of 537 (Hodgkin IV 127). **Count Magnus**: a subordinate cavalry officer of the force under Belisarius. He was in charge of the aqueduct party at the siege of Naples (536), and in the following year he was sent to Tibur. In 540 it became his duty to blockade Ravenna. See Hodgkin IV 4, 56, 219, 327; Procopius *bell. Goth.* 2, 28. **Ariminum**: the siege of Ariminum, the modern Rimini, occurred in 538. Two years later Vitiges gave up the unequal contest and surrendered to Belisarius at Ravenna. See Hodgkin IV 334, and Bury I 393 onward.

313. two thousand and thirtieth year: from 1490 B.C. to 540 A.D. See chronological table, p. 38.

314. Germanus: the son of Justinian's brother. *fratri* in the text is evidently a mistake of the copyist for *fratrueli* (compare

XIV 81 and XLVIII 251). The death of Mathesuentha's first husband Vitiges took place in 542, and her marriage to Germanus followed soon after.   a son (also called Germanus): Germanus the Younger became a great noble of Constantinople but did not realize the hopes of Jordanes. His daughter married Theodosius, the son of Emperor Maurice (582-602). On his death the imperial power was offered to Germanus but he declined it. Later he made two attempts to gain the position he had refused; as a result of the first he was forced to become a priest and renounce his official position, and in consequence of the second (605) he and his daughter were put to death on an island in the Sea of Marmora. Thus the Amal line finally came to an end (Hodgkin IV 569).   Anicii: a very ancient Roman family of distinction, both in classical and Christian times. Cassiodorus speaks of this family (var. 10, 11) in the following terms: *Anicios paene principibus pares aetas prisca progenuit.* It is not known whether this family really had an ancestral relation to the house of Justinian. Possibly the mother of Germanus was a descendant of the Anicii.

LaVergne, TN USA
08 April 2010
178562LV00008B/52/P

9 781120 854162